Three French Dramatists

T0382160

Three French Dramatists

RACINE   MARIVAUX

MUSSET

BY

ARTHUR TILLEY, M.A.

Fellow of King's College, Cambridge

CAMBRIDGE

At the University Press

1933

CAMBRIDGE
UNIVERSITY PRESS

University Printing House, Cambridge CB2 8BS, United Kingdom

Cambridge University Press is part of the University of Cambridge.

It furthers the University's mission by disseminating knowledge in the pursuit of education, learning and research at the highest international levels of excellence.

www.cambridge.org
Information on this title: www.cambridge.org/9781316626047

© Cambridge University Press 1933

First published 1933
First paperback edition 2016

A catalogue record for this publication is available from the British Library

ISBN 978-1-316-62604-7 Paperback

CONTENTS

PREFACE

The three great dramatists who form the subject of the following pages may be said to follow one another in spiritual succession, for Marivaux has been rightly called the disciple of Racine and Musset has learnt more than one lesson from Marivaux. They have certain characteristics in common. In the first place, they are all chiefly concerned with the careful and faithful portrayal of passion and character—in other words they are psychological dramatists—and we are less interested in the outward actions of their characters than in the working of their minds and emotions. Secondly, all three have a strong dramatic sense, which is shewn partly by their instinctive feeling for movement and dramatic presentation and partly by the undivided attention they give to the working out of their drama. Racine never, Marivaux and Musset very seldom, make use of their characters as mouthpieces for their personal opinions and sentiments. Thirdly, they all possess a style which is at once individual and of great distinction and charm. And, widely different though these styles are, their appeal to us to-day is as potent as it was when they had the attraction of novelty. It is even possible that the realistic tone, whether homely or witty, of the conversation of much modern drama may not wear so well as the artistry of these bygone masters. In spite, however, of their great qualities none of the three can be said to be popular in this country. They have warm admirers, but the admiration is not widely spread. Yet their genius for psychology and their high regard for form should make them acceptable to readers of the modern novel. Indeed, modern novelists, however proficient in the Freudian psychology, might profit by a study of these careful explorers of the human heart. But to be appreciated as they deserve, they demand, especially Racine, a more than a bowing acquaintance. They must be read carefully and re-read, and few of their plays can be passed over as wholly unimportant. It is for this reason that I have made my survey of their drama as comprehensive as possible, while I have only noted such biographical details as serve to throw light on their dramatic development.

The accepted text of Racine is that of P. Mesnard in the *Grands Écrivains de France*, 8 vols. The last volume consists of a *Lexique* by Ch. Marty-Laveaux, to which is prefixed an admirable study of Racine's style by Mesnard. The fullest selection of Marivaux's *Théâtre* is the recent one edited by Xavier de Courville, 5 vols., 1929–30. It is well printed on good paper and contains 17 plays, including *Le Prince Travesti*, *L'Ile des Esclaves*, *La Dispute*, *La Colonie*, and *Les Acteurs de Bonne Foi*. All these are omitted in Nelson's edition in 2 vols. (Ed. Lutetia), which, however, contains *L'Heureux Stratagème* and *Le Préjugé vaincu*. I have read the remaining plays in one of the editions (with a separate pagination for each play) published in Marivaux's lifetime— 2 vols., Briasson, 1932; 5 vols., Prault, 1738–40; 5 vols., Duchesne, 1758 (founded on the preceding). I must also mention Jouaust's charming edition in the *Librairie des Bibliophiles* (2 vols., no date), which contains seven comedies. Musset's *Comédies et Proverbes* has been frequently reprinted; a new edition, by M. Pierre Gastinel, is announced as shortly forthcoming in *Les Textes Français*.

My chief debt is to the plays themselves, but I must mention a few books that I have found especially helpful. These are for Racine, J. Lemaître's *Jean Racine*, 1908 and M. Gonzague Truc's *Le Cas Racine*, 1921 and *Jean Racine*, 1926; for Marivaux, G. Larroumet, *Marivaux, sa vie et ses œuvres*, 1882; for Musset, L. Lafoscade, *Le Théâtre d'Alfred de Musset*, 1901, Arvède Barine, *Alfred de Musset*, 1893 (a delicate and sympathetic study), and for biographical details, L. Séché, *Documents inédits*, 2 vols., 1907 and Paul de Musset's biography, 1877. I have also consulted with advantage

Preface

M. Henry Lyonnet's *Les "Premières" de Jean Racine*, 1924, and *Les "Premières" de Alfred de Musset*, 1927. If he has also published a similar work on Marivaux, it has escaped my notice. There is, too, always something to be learnt from Faguet's *Propos de Théâtre* and Sarcey's *Quarante Ans de Théâtre*, giving as they do the direct impressions of experienced and able dramatic critics.

A. T.

CAMBRIDGE
1932

I

Racine

Lorsque vous peignez des héros, vous faites ce que vous voulez. Ce sont des portraits à plaisir, où l'on ne cherche point de ressemblance, et vous n'avez qu'à suivre les traits d'une imagination qui se donne l'essor, et qui souvent laisse le vrai pour attraper le merveilleux. Mais, lorsque vous peignez les hommes il faut peindre après nature.

Though this criticism, which Molière puts into the mouth of Dorante in *La Critique de l'École des Femmes*, is doubtless aimed principally at the great Corneille, it applies equally to his brother Thomas and to Quinault, both of whom rivalled him, if they did not surpass him, in popularity. In fact the younger Corneille's *Timocrate*, with its unprecedented run of eighty performances, was the most successful play of the seventeenth century, and Quinault's *La Mort de Cyrus*, produced in the same year 1656, did not come much behind it. During the years 1662–1666 Thomas Corneille, who was a very skilful playwright, the Scribe and Sardou of his day, as Lemaître happily calls him, produced four tragedies of the romantic type, all now forgotten, while Quinault was represented by *Astrate* (1663) and two others. Both dramatists love an intricate plot, improbable incidents, and high-flown sentiment. Their characters are either null or factitious and, like their incidents, are taken from a common conventional stock.

The great Corneille's later plays, inferior though they are to his masterpieces, are of a higher quality. They only resemble those of his rivals in their complicated plots and subordination of incident to character, but this had been his practice ever since *Héraclius* (winter of 1646–1647). His latest productions were *Sertorius* (1662), which is in parts a fine tragedy, and *Sophonisbe* (1663), both with intricate plots, and he was soon to produce another tragedy in *Othon* (1664). Sertorius and Othon are supermen, such as Corneille loved, but though they are drawn from imagination rather than from observation, they are very different from the impossible and essentially immoral heroes of Thomas Corneille and Quinault.

Such was the condition of French tragedy when Molière criticised it. A year later—on June 20, to be precise—he produced at his theatre a new tragedy by a new writer. The tragedy was entitled *La Thébaïde ou Les Frères ennemis* and the writer was Jean Racine. He was not altogether unknown. He had submitted three odes to Chapelain, the adviser of Colbert in questions of the royal patronage, and had received a gratification for each. He was now twenty-four years of age, having in his earlier years come under two influences which were deeply to affect his art—Port-Royal and Greek literature. His mother had died when he was a year old and his father, who had married again, two years later. He was then taken charge of by his paternal grandparents, but on the death of his grandfather in 1649, his grandmother, who was a devout Jansenist, retired to Port-Royal. Two years later he was sent to the college of Beauvais, where the education seems to have been on Port-Royal lines. In 1655, when he was nearly sixteen, he was admitted to Port-Royal itself. This was a great favour, for the rule was that pupils should not be received above the age of ten. Here he remained for three years, and thus it may be said that up to the age of eighteen he breathed an atmosphere of Port-Royal and Jansenism.

Soon after his admission the Little Schools were dispersed (1656) and he became almost the sole pupil of two remarkable teachers, Claude Lancelot and Jean Hamon, both of whom took a special interest in him, as one whose family had long had close relations with Port-Royal. Hamon, a saint and a mystic, was the object of his ardent veneration, and forty years later he expressed in his will a wish to be buried at Port-Royal-des-Champs at the foot of his grave. But it was Lancelot, the author of various *New Methods* for learning languages and of the *Jardin des Racines grecques*, who guided him in his study of Greek literature, and strengthened his sympathy with the Greek spirit. The careful notes that he made in his copies of many classical authors, and his extensive commentary on Pindar's *Olympics* and on the first ten books of the *Odyssey*, testify to his interest. The notes on Greek authors that have been preserved are very much more numerous than those on Latin authors. Sophocles and Plutarch come first and then the *Iliad* and Euripides. His copy of Plutarch shews that he read, pen in hand, all the *Lives*, in 1655, that is to say in his first year at Port-Royal, and the whole of the *Moral Works* in the following year.

The *Remarks on the Odyssey*, preserved in a manuscript of the Bibliothèque Nationale, which are the most striking testimony to his love and understanding of Greek literature, belong to a later period, namely April 1662, when he was living with his uncle at Uzès. They fill 126 pages and consist of a running analysis of the text accompanied by citations, illustrations from other authors, and various observations either on the subject-matter or on the beauty of the poetry. It is the work of a man who can read the text with perfect ease, but who is interested, not in technical scholarship, but in the absorbing narrative, the artistic skill of the narrator, the presentment of character, and the light thrown on Greek life and manners. His longest citations are the descriptions of the palace and the gardens of Alcinous in the seventh book. He notes with pleasure that Homer does not mind calling common objects by their proper names, as in the account of the boat that Ulysses made with Calypso's help. This, he says, can be done with more grace in Greek than in Latin or French. "The French language avoids with extreme dislike descending to details, because its ears are delicate and cannot bear that common things like an awl, a saw, or an auger should be named in a serious discourse." It is interesting to find Racine warmly approving in Homer those humble words at which Victor Hugo accused him of "looking askance" in his own poetry. He also calls attention to the simple language in which Ulysses addresses Athene, when she appears in the guise of a young girl carrying a pitcher, and he notes Homer's skill in varying his tone to suit the character either of the speaker or of the person whom he is addressing.

While Racine's Hellenism reflected so visibly the teaching of Port-Royal, it was otherwise with his Jansenism. It was not eradicated—far from it—but for many years it had little or no influence either on his manner of life or on his drama. Port-Royal was followed by a year of philosophy at the Collège d'Harcourt, a college friendly to Port-Royal, and after this he continued to reside in Paris, where Port-Royal still kept an eye on him. He was under the tutelage of his cousin Nicolas Vitart, an old pupil of Lancelot's, and now the intendant of that Duc de Luynes who had accompanied Pascal to Port-Royal and had resided with the Solitaries while his château was being rebuilt. Vitart was not an austere tutor, and the young Racine led a frivolous, though not a dissipated life. His chief friend was the Abbé Le Vasseur, a man of light verses and many loves. Another intimate was La Fontaine, whose wife was a very distant cousin. Eighteen years his senior, he was singularly ill-qualified to act as mentor. In this pleasure-loving but lettered society Racine began seriously to prepare himself for a literary career. He wrote a sonnet in praise of Mazarin and printed an ode on the marriage of Louis XIV, for which, as we have seen, on the recommendation of Chapelain he received a gratification from the king. He also wrote *Amasie*, a tragedy of which we know nothing but the title, and was introduced by his friend Le Vasseur to two actresses with a view to their good offices at their respective theatres. All this made his Jansenist relatives, especially his aunt, the Mère Agnes, who was one of the Port-Royal abbesses, tremble for his salvation. He was sent in disgrace to the Duc de Luynes's château at Chevreuse, where he read Ariosto and continued to amuse himself. But towards the end of 1661 he consented with a good grace to go and live with his uncle, the vicar-general of Uzès in Languedoc, with a view to preparing for orders and obtaining a benefice. The Church seemed to promise a better career than literature.

He spent nine months at Uzès and was considerably bored in the little provincial town, which he calls "la plus maudite ville du monde". Correspondence with his Paris friends helped him to bear his exile. His letters, of which twenty-four have come down to us, are charming specimens of epistolary art. They are written with evident care, but the style is easy and lively as well as correct. They contain little news, for there was little to give, but they throw light on his mind and character. He appears in them as a youth of much practical intelligence with a keen eye to his own prospects. He is more interested in human beings than in nature. It is an omen of his future dramatic work that he notes as a characteristic of the people of Languedoc the unmeasured violence of their passions. Indeed, as M. Truc points out in some pertinent remarks on the letters, nothing escapes his observation. "He is already a psychologist and a dramatist."

In other ways, too, he was preparing for his future career as a dramatist. He continued, as we have seen, to read Greek literature with enthusiasm and penetration; he studied Italian and Spanish; he meditated on subjects for dramas; and he wrote more odes. In August or September 1662, the search for a benefice proving unsuccessful, he gave up the idea of taking orders and returned to Paris to pursue once more a literary career. Fortune was favourable to him. Two more odes that he submitted to Chapelain brought him grants from the royal bounty. He found a patron in the Duc de Saint-Aignan, recently elected to the French Academy, and probably through him was admitted to the royal *levée*. There one morning he encountered Molière, whose acquaintance he had recently made. Thus Racine was neither quite an unknown writer nor a complete stranger when Molière accepted his tragedy of *La Thébaïde*.

The new tragedy contained one element of novelty, which was to be a permanent characteristic of Racine's drama. The plot, unlike those of the two Corneilles and Quinault, was a simple one, without any complications. His predecessor, Rotrou, had collected for his *Antigone* material from Euripides, Sophocles, Seneca, and Statius, and had tacked the story of Antigone on to that of her brothers. But Racine, intent upon simplicity and unity, confined himself to the single theme of the hatred between Eteocles and Polynices. He took something from Seneca and Rotrou, but he trusted chiefly to the *Phoenissae*, one of the plays which justifies Aristotle in calling Euripides "the most tragic of poets". Not that he followed Euripides at all closely, for there was much in him, as we know from Racine's notes on the play, that he regarded either as feeble or as unconnected with the subject. It has been noted as a sign of his interest in psychology that he regards the hatred between the twins as pre-natal, but he does not attempt to work out this idea. It may be said that he does not portray "heroes" in Eteocles and Polynices, but, if they are not superhuman, like Corneille's heroes, they are inhuman in the ferocity of their hatred, while Creon, whose character is partly of Racine's invention, is a real devil. The one person in the play who is "portrayed after nature" and who is really alive is Antigone. Love, as Racine himself suggests in his preface, is perhaps out of place in so grim and terrible a tragedy, but the scene between Antigone and Hémon (II, I) is a beautiful picture of pure and unselfish love. It is also noteworthy as the first-fruits of that knowledge of the female heart which was to be one of the glories of Racine's mature art. In this scene, too, especially in Antigone's speech beginning,

> Oui je l'avois bien cru qu'une âme si fidèle
> Trouverait dans l'absence une peine cruelle;

6

Racine

and in Hémon's answer, ending with the supremely Racinian line

Et, pour tout dire enfin, je m'éloignai de vous.

and more or less in the whole play we see Racine's style, not, indeed, at its strongest, and as yet under the influence of Corneille, but already remarkable for its transparent clarity and for that simplicity which is the crown of art. It is this alluring style, coupled with the well-balanced construction of the play, that makes it readable, in spite of the little interest that one can take in either the plot or the characters. There are two or three obvious imitations of Corneille, but, apart from these, which are unimportant, and from the style, the only trace of Corneille's influence is in Creon's habit of uttering political axioms and commonplaces.

La Thébaïde was fairly successful, as successful as could have been expected for the first play of a new writer. But Racine, of whom his son says that "he had in his youth an unmeasured passion for glory", wanted more than this. He wanted at once to please the critics and to capture the public. So he would write a play more in accordance with the fashion of the day than *La Thébaïde*. He would take as his model not only Pierre Corneille, but also Thomas Corneille and Quinault. His hero should be a superman, but he should also be a lover, and what better hero could he find than Alexander the Great? Here was a genuine superman, one who took the world as his province, a great statesman, a great general, a civiliser as well as a conqueror. He would have not only one superman but two, and the second should be Porus, the most powerful of the princes who opposed Alexander's invasion of India. And both these heroes should be in love. This was the design which Racine carried out in his next tragedy, *Alexandre le Grand*. It was produced at the Palais-Royal on December 4, 1665, and was a triumphant success. But critics complained that he had made Porus greater than Alexander, and they were right. Porus is a fine Cornelian figure, and the object of his "flame", Axiane, who with her mixture of admiration

7

and hatred for his conqueror, Alexander, is evidently modelled on Cornélie in *La Mort de Pompée*, is not unworthy of him. But Alexander seems to have stepped straight out of a novel of La Calprenède or Mlle de Scudéry. Saint-Évremond is not too severe when he says in his well-known dissertation on the play, "I recognise nothing of Alexander but the name; I cannot find his genius, his temperament, or his qualities.... He is as little of a hero in love as he is in war....He is a warrior whose glory fails to excite our ardour, a lover whose passion fails to move us to tenderness". There is even less attempt to "portray men after nature" in *Alexandre* than in *La Thébaïde*. Glory and love are the only motives of action. Glory and love stimulate Porus to fight for his country. Glory calls Alexander to conquest and slaughter; glory, the glory of magnanimity, dictates his generosity to Porus. But, as he vows to Cléofile, love is now more powerful with him than glory, and for her *beaux yeux* he will continue the war. The great captain of antiquity, with his *soupirs*, his *feux*, his *flammes*, his *beaux nœuds*, his *divins appas*, becomes a seventeenth-century Céladon.

But whatever defects we may find in the play to-day, it was a great success when it was produced, and on December 14 a private performance was commanded before the king, to whom as the lover of Mlle de La Vallière and busy with his preparations for the invasion of Flanders and La Franche Comté this drama of glory and love must have had a particular appeal. Four days later Molière's company "were surprised", as La Grange gently phrases it in his Register, to find that there was to be a performance at the Hôtel de Bourgogne to which theatre it was shortly transferred. It was an unusual and an unfriendly proceeding, and it was no excuse that Racine believed that his Cornelian tragedy would be better interpreted by Montfleury and his fellow-actors, whose declamatory style Molière had burlesqued in *L'Impromptu de Versailles*.

This was not Racine's only regrettable action at this time.

Racine

We have seen that before he went to Uzès Port-Royal viewed with alarm his incipient relations with the stage. In a tone of grave remonstrance the Mère Agnes wrote, "I have learnt with sorrow that you associate more than ever with persons whose name is an abomination to all who have the smallest grain of piety". Later, in January 1666, when *Alexandre* was still being played with triumphant success, Racine's former teacher, Pierre Nicole, in the course of a controversy with Desmarets de Saint-Sorlin, declared that the qualities of a writer of romances and plays "are not very honourable in the judgment of well-bred people, but from the point of view of the Christian religion and the precepts of the Gospel they are horrible". Rightly or wrongly, Racine considered that he was personally aimed at, and the first half of the remark, as Lemaître shrewdly notes, stung him sharply, for it wounded his pride and his vanity. Accordingly he published, without signing it, but without attempting to hide his authorship, a short and admirably written letter, which was a masterpiece of malignant and unscrupulous attack. There were two replies from Port-Royal, and Racine wrote a second letter even more biting than the first, but his friend Boileau dissuaded him from publishing it. It was found amongst his papers after his death, for with the vanity of an author he had not destroyed it.

However much thirst for success and pride in its achievement had hardened Racine's heart they did not make him less clear-sighted with regard to his art. Rather, they gave him confidence to follow in future the promptings of his genius. In his next play, *Andromaque*, he once for all abandoned the attempt to portray heroes. What was the reason for this change? Unfortunately we know too little about him during the years 1665–1666 to be able to answer this question with any certainty. We can only conjecture. It may have occurred to Racine that the success of *Alexandre* was partly due to the fact that the spectators, including Louis XIV himself, saw in its hero a likeness to the young king, that the criticisms of his character were more or less just, and that the attempt to make him at once a superman and a lover was a mistake. If this was Racine's view, it would have been confirmed by the failure of Corneille's *Agésilas* in February 1666. It bears evident traces of Quinault's influence, and, though called a tragedy, because it deals with kings and princesses, is really a *comédie héroique*. It has a very complicated plot and three pairs of lovers, who make love with dignified gallantry and in approved *précieux* language. It failed, one may conjecture, because realism, the realism of truth to nature, of portraying men as they are, was gaining ground. Nearly five years before this La Fontaine, after the production of Molière's *Les Fâcheux*, had said, "Il ne faut pas quitter la nature d'un pas". In 1665 Boileau had read to his friends, of whom Racine was then one, his *Les Héros de Roman*, in which he ridicules Quinault's *Astrate* as well as the romances of La Calprenède and Mlle de Scudéry, and in the same year he had read and doubtless shown to Racine his third Satire, in which there is further ridicule of Quinault and *Astrate*. In the following year, 1666, he published it in his first volume of *Satires*.

That Boileau had considerable influence over his friend is undoubted, and we may well believe that he not only taught him, as, according to Brassette, he claims to have done, to make "difficilement des vers faciles" but that he shepherded him towards the path of nature, and reason, and common sense. Whatever the cause, Racine's new conception of his art took effect in a tragedy which he entitled *Andromaque*. Produced in November 1667, it is hardly of less importance in the history of French drama than the *Cid*. It is remarkable that a young man, not quite twenty-eight, should have written so finished a work, of which almost the only imperfection is that its structure is almost too perfect in its symmetry. It is equally remarkable that in this his first experiment on the new lines he should have fixed the plan upon which all his tragedies, at least those written before his retirement, were to be constructed. Without cavil and without attempting to get round them, he accepted the two rules which a misunderstanding of Aristotle had imposed upon French classical drama, the rule of the unities and the rule that tragedy should deal with princes. Already in his first two plays he had realised that observance of the unities necessitated a simple plot and that the drama should open at the point when events were on the eve of a crisis. His first two tragedies on the new lines are good examples of this. In the first scene of *Andromaque* Oreste announces to Pylade that he has come to Epirus on behalf of the Greeks to take Astyanax from Pyrrhus. In *Britannicus* Agrippine declares at the very opening of the play that,

> L'impatient Néron cesse de se contraindre;
> Las de se faire aimer, il veut se faire craindre.
> Britannicus le gêne, Albine; et chaque jour
> Je sens que je deviens importune à mon tour.

In *Bérénice* the crisis is only foreshadowed in the first act, but in the second scene of the second act—the first scene is very short—it has arrived. Rome has given her decision; Bérénice must be dismissed:

> Rome, pas une loi qui ne se peut changer,
> N'admet avec son sang aucun sang étranger.

But Racine also saw that, if neither he nor his audience were to be hampered or in any way troubled by the unities, he must do away with all but the minimum of physical action, and must devote himself to the portrayal of souls with their passions, their conflicting desires, and their blind escapes from dilemmas. Further he realised that supermen are not so interesting to the majority of people as men and women with like passions as themselves; that princes and princesses, beneath their trappings and their fair outward seeming, are often ordinary folk, but that in some ages, especially in the heroic age of Greece or in the Imperial age of Rome, their passions are free to express themselves without fear of the law or public opinion. Brunetière aptly quotes from Fontenelle's parallel between Corneille and Racine two remarks which call attention to Racine's preference for ordinary characters. "Corneille's characters are true, though they are not common: Racine's characters are not true, only because they are common", and "Sometimes Corneille's characters have something false in them, as the result of being noble and singular; often Racine's characters have something ignoble (*bas*) in them as the result of being natural".

There are four principal characters in *Andromaque*— Oreste, Hermione, Pyrrhus, and Andromaque. Oreste is in love with Hermione, Hermione with Pyrrhus, and Pyrrhus with Andromaque. But Hermione rejects Oreste, Pyrrhus rejects Hermione, and Andromaque, whose heart is in the grave with Hector, rejects Pyrrhus.

With all three lovers love is a passion—consuming, remorseless, ineradicable. But they are not without hope. Hermione despairing of Pyrrhus, may turn to Oreste; Andromaque, in order to save her son, may accept Pyrrhus. As we have seen, the arrival of Oreste in Epirus precipitates the crisis and calls for immediate action. Andromaque is the mistress of the situation; either she must accept Pyrrhus in return for his promise not to give up Astyanax and so be faithless to the memory of her Hector, or she must refuse Pyrrhus and bring death to her son. Confronted with this agonising dilemma she makes a terrible resolve. She will marry Pyrrhus and then kill herself. The marriage is announced, and Hermione is filled with fury; she sends for Oreste and greets him with

Je veux savoir, Seigneur, si vous m'aimez.

. . . . . .

Vengez-moi.

. . . . . .

Courez au temple. Il faut immoler....

ORESTE.

Qui?

HERMIONE.

Pyrrhus.

But when Oreste comes to tell her that Pyrrhus has fallen, not indeed by his hands, but before the fury of his Greek soldiers, she turns on him with "Barbare, qu'as tu fait?" and overwhelms him with violent reproaches. Then she kills herself on Pyrrhus's body, and Oreste goes mad.

It is a simple and deeply poignant story and its dramatic interest is sustained throughout by the treatment of the characters. Oreste is a young man of melancholy temperament. Betrothed to Hermione in childhood, but afterwards rejected by her father in favour of Pyrrhus, he regards himself as a special mark for the malignity of the gods:

> De quelque part sur moi que je tourne les yeux,
> Je ne vois que malheurs qui condamnent les dieux.
>
> .   .   .   .   .   .
>
> Excuse un malheureux qui perd tout ce qu'il aime,
> Que tout le monde hait, et qui se hait lui-même.

When he hears of Hermione's death he cries out with superb irony:

> Grace aux dieux, mon malheur passe mon espérance!
> Oui, je te loue, ô ciel, de ta persévérance.
>
> .   .   .   .
>
> J'étais né pour servir d'exemple à ta colère,
> Pour être du malheur un modèle accompli.

In other ways, too, he proves weak. In the fine scene between him and Pylade (III, 1) he expresses his final determination to carry off Hermione with weak iteration: "Je le veux achever, oui, je le veux". He is like wax in the hands of Hermione. Her command that he should kill Pyrrhus, whom he hates as a rival but whom he respects as a man, is utterly repugnant to him—"Soyons ses ennemis, et non ses assassins"—but he gives way because he is a slave to his passion.

Hermione, like Oreste, is a victim to unrequited love, but she suffers also from a sense of the cruel indignity of her position. She has been sent to a foreign country to marry the king, but he, filled with love for another woman, cannot make up his mind whether he will keep or break his promises:

> Hermione elle-même a vu plus de cent fois
> Cet amant irrité revenir sous ses lois,
> Et de ses vœux troublés lui rapportant l'hommage
> Soupirer à ses pieds moins d'amour que de rage.

It is no wonder that the unhappy woman, tossed as she is between hope and despair, has come to hate him as well as to love him—

> Ah! je l'ai trop aimé pour ne le point haïr.

—or that with her complete lack of self-control she gives exaggerated expression to whichever feeling is paramount at the moment. She has other faults besides lack of self-control. She is vain; when Oreste is on the point of suggesting that Pyrrhus has grown tired of her, she cuts him short with

> Jugez-vous que ma vue inspire des mépris?

She is arrogant and heartless. After Oreste has announced that Pyrrhus is prepared to marry her, she exults in her triumph and she scoffs at Oreste and his unhappy love:

> N'avons-nous d'entretien que celui de ses pleurs?

When Andromaque, of whom, as might be expected, she is profoundly jealous, comes to implore her protection for Astyanax, she answers her with cruel curtness and a bitter gibe:

> S'il faut fléchir Pyrrhus, qui le peut mieux que vous?

Racine tells us in his second preface that Euripides's *Andromache* had suggested to him Hermione's jealousy and violent outbursts, but he has made her more interesting and less hateful than the Hermione of Euripides's poor and ill-constructed play, who is anxious to have Andromache put to death as Pyrrhus's slave and concubine.

Pyrrhus in the second scene of the first act receives Oreste with a quiet and haughty dignity, and shews his courage and

generosity by declaring that he will protect Hector's son
against the whole of Greece. But his generosity is far from
disinterested. He counts on it to win Andromaque's acceptance of his suit, and when she refuses he resorts to threats:

> Je n'épargnerai rien dans ma juste colère:
> Le fils me répondra des mépris de la mère.

Thus his love is thoroughly selfish and makes him incon-
siderate for others. Though he is well aware of Oreste's love
for Hermione, he cruelly sends him to tell her that he is prepared to marry her. And when he has changed his mind and
is about to marry Andromaque, he must needs go himself to
Hermione to announce it. This last act of his has been
criticised as unnatural, but it is surely only another instance
of his insensibility to the feelings of others. "Violent, mais
sincère" is Andromaque's opinion of him, and she has
planned to kill herself after the marriage in the belief that he
will protect Astyanax. But he is not sincere towards Hermione. He declares that they were plighted to one another
by their fathers without love, but that, till *par un coup funeste*
he lost his heart to Andromaque, he was prepared to carry
out the engagement. But, according to Hermione, he vowed
that he was in love with her, and he knew very well that

> Sur la foi d'une amour si saintement jurée

she was passionately in love with him.

> Je n'ai point aimé, cruel! Qu'ai-je donc fait?

is Hermione's cry at the opening of her magnificent retort.
More ruthless than Oreste and insincere into the bargain,
he is equally weak and vacillating. He endeavours to win
Andromaque; he gives her up and falls back on Hermione;
and it is not till his cruel and unchivalrous threats seem to
have proved successful with Andromaque, that he finally
breaks faith with Hermione. "Maître de tout sans de lui"
is M. Truc's just comment on him. He is very far from being
a hero, but he is true to nature.

In contrast to these playthings of passion, storm-tossed

and rudderless, Racine presents the noble figure of Andromaque. She, too, has to choose between two alternatives, and each is worse to her than death. But she faces the choice with calm self-control, a resolute will, and a selfless courage. The dilemma is a terrible one. Shall she sacrifice the mother, or the wife, for in spirit she is still the wife of the great Hector? Some critics have said that she is first and foremost the mother. But Racine had deeply impressed upon his memory the great passage in the Sixth Book of the *Iliad*, which tells of the parting of Hector from Andromache and Astyanax before he goes forth to fight, and especially the two famous lines, which have been called "the two most comprehensive lines ever breathed by love":

Ἕκτορ, ἀτὰρ σύ μοί ἐσσι πατὴρ καὶ πότνια μήτηρ
ἠδὲ κασίγνητος, σὺ δέ μοι θαλερὸς παρακοίτης.[1]

Indeed Racine makes Andromaque refer to this meeting, but, possibly in order to increase the pathos, as if it had taken place before Hector went to fight with Achilles. For him then Andromaque was before all things the wife of Hector, and in the eyes of Andromaque Pyrrhus was the son of Achilles, the slayer of Hector, and the man who in cold blood had killed Hector's father and sister. In the face of this the idea, which some critics have held, that Andromaque in order to influence Pyrrhus in favour of her son practises upon him the arts of coquetry, seems to me impossible, nor do I believe that it is supported by the passage which Racine excised from the fifth act before the production of the play. Andromaque in fact does and says nothing to make herself attractive to Pyrrhus. Hector and her grief for him are continually on her lips:

Et quel époux encor! Ah souvenir cruel!
Sa mort seule a rendu votre père immortel.
Il doit au sang d'Hector tout l'éclat de ses armes;
Et vous n'êtes tous deux connus que par mes larmes.

[1] But, Hector, thou art to me father and mother and brethren, and thou art my dear husband.

Just as she is free from personal vanity, so is she free from false pride. As soon as she learns that Pyrrhus will marry Hermione she throws herself weeping at her feet and implores her help for her son. She is sometimes bitter, both to Pyrrhus and to Hermione, but she is never declamatory. Amid the violent passions and contentions that surround her, she moves quietly and sadly, a figure of grief.

Besides the four principal characters there are four confidants; at least there are four characters who fill this position, for Pylade is Oreste's bosom friend and Phœnix is Pyrrhus's tutor, as he had been that of his father before him. Except that Pylade's self-sacrificing friendship invests him with some individuality, all four are wholly without life or interest. Their function is to enable the principal characters to reveal their thoughts and sentiments, and they do this the more effectively because they are on the side of prudence as against passion or, in the case of Andromaque, fidelity to a memory. Their advice, it need hardly be said, is never followed.

In his portrayal of these characters Racine shews an extraordinarily intimate knowledge of the human heart, especially in his treatment of Hermione, whose varying moods and passionate utterances have made her rôle an object of ambition to every French actress who aspires to make a name in tragedy. The structure of the play is worthy of the characters and is managed with consummate art. It called forth the admiration of Scribe, that master of the "well-made play". The only criticism that can be made on it is that it is a little too mechanical, that it conforms a little too closely to plan. But the manner in which the idiosyncrasies of each character are brought out and at the same time the drama is carried forward to its terrible *dénouement*, chiefly by dialogue, either between the characters and their confidants—there are only two soliloquies—or between the characters themselves, is beyond all praise. The drama opens on a quiet note, but in the last scene of the first act, when Pyrrhus, having failed to move Andromaque by his prayers, tries to intimidate her with threats, the note suddenly changes to one of anger, and from this point the conflict between the characters becomes more and more intense. The next scene, the first of the second act, is remarkable for the dramatic quality of Hermione's two great speeches—really one, for she continues her thought without heeding her confidante's interruption. The next scene is an admirable dialogue between Hermione and Oreste, in which her character is most skilfully developed and she leaves Oreste with renewed hope. It is at once dashed by Pyrrhus's announcement, "Je l'épouse" (II, 4). But in the next scene (II, 5) Pyrrhus again wavers:

> Faut-il livrer son fils? faut-il voir Hermione?

The whole of the third act is most moving and powerful. It opens with the fine scene between Oreste and Pylade, in which Oreste declares for carrying off Hermione, and this is followed by the three equally fine scenes (III, 2–4) referred to already, in which the recesses of Hermione's character are unerringly probed. And just as in a Greek tragedy her arrogance, as shewn in her cruel rebuff of Andromaque, is the signal for the sudden reversal of her fortunes ($\pi\epsilon\rho\iota\pi\acute{\epsilon}\tau\epsilon\iota\alpha$). It is brought about by a fresh meeting between Andromaque and Pyrrhus (III, 6, 7), which leads him to change his mind once more:

> Je renvoie Hermione, et je mets sur son front,
> Au lieu de ma couronne, un éternel affront;
> Je vous conduis au temple où son hymen s'apprête;
> Je vous ceins du bandeau préparé pour sa tête.

In the last scene of the act Andromaque, who is now compelled to come to a decision, announces her intention of consulting her husband in his grave, and in the next (IV, 1), having formed her heroic and terrible resolve, she bids Céphise, her confidante, watch over the motherless Astyanax. We then come back to Hermione and we have the great scene between her and Oreste, in which he weakly agrees to become the agent of her crime (IV, 3) and the equally great scene (IV, 5) between her and Pyrrhus, in which he brutally announces to her his decision and she retaliates with the magnificent "Je ne t'ai point aimé, cruel?" The fifth act opens with her superb soliloquy—one of Rachel's great triumphs—in which she sounds in turn the notes of hatred, tenderness, anger, pity, and regret. In the next scene her confidante's account of the marriage proceedings excites her beyond control, so that when Oreste arrives with his "Madame, c'en est fait" and relates to her the manner of Pyrrhus's death, she overwhelms him with a torrent of reproach, ending with

> Je renonce à la Grèce, à Sparte, à son empire,
> A toute ma famille; et c'est assez pour moi,
> Traître, qu'elle ait produit un monstre comme toi.

It may be truly said that Racine in Hermione and Oreste and Pyrrhus has ceased to portray heroes. They are not only selfish with the ordinary selfishness of lovers, but they are all ready to do violence to the objects of their love, in order to satisfy their passion or their anger. They are weak and vacillating; they lack self-control; they act from impulse and not from deliberate intention. In station they are kings and princesses, but they have the souls of ordinary folk. Andromaque, on the other hand, has no thought of self. A captive, and therefore not mistress of her fate, and faced with a terrible dilemmà, she is firm in her resolve that she will never give herself to Pyrrhus. But in spite of her heroic intention she is not a Cornelian heroine. She is neither proud nor haughty; she is impolitic in her dealings with Pyrrhus; she cannot control her tears, nor altogether her tongue. She has the weaknesses of a true woman, and for that reason she wins not only our admiration but our sympathy.

The story too, stripped of the glamour with which the genius of Racine has invested it, is an ordinary one. It might have happened in any age, in any country, in any condition of life. Leaving out Andromaque, it is the story of a young man madly in love with a girl who has been thrown over by another man, but whose passion, though now mingled with hate, is as violent as ever. His approaching marriage fills her with fury. She calls on her adorer to kill him, and when he obeys she commits suicide and he goes mad. What is this but a *crime passionnel,* such as has often been tried in the criminal courts?

The transfer of *Alexandre* to the Hôtel de Bourgogne was not the only bad turn that Racine did to Molière's company, for he robbed them of one of their actresses. Mlle Du Parc was much admired as Axiane—chiefly, it seems, for the beauty of her person and her dress—and it was probably for her *beaux yeux* rather than for her acting that Racine carried her off. She left the Palais-Royal just before Easter—the end of the theatrical year—1667 and joined the Hôtel de Bourgogne. The interest of her *liaison* with Racine lies in the fact that his passion must have formed part of that experience of the conquering power of love which, as M. Truc points out, was so necessary and so helpful to his art. We should therefore like to know more of the lady, for what we know is not very much. Marquise-Thérèse de Gorla was the daughter of an Italian *opérateur,* or vendor of quack medicines. In 1653 she married René Berthelot, called Du Parc, whose acting name of Gros-René was suggested by his rotund figure, and joined Molière's company. She had no part in either *L'École des Maris* or *L'École des Femmes,* but she played Climène, who is a *précieuse,* in *La Critique de l'École des Femmes,* Dorimène in *Le Mariage forcé,* Aglante in *La Princesse d'Élide,* Elvire in *Don Juan,* and Arsinoé (almost certainly) in *Le Misanthrope.* None of these are parts of the first importance. She had no part in *La Thébaïde,* but, as we have seen, she played Axiane, which is the principal female part, in *Alexandre.* According to Boileau, as reported by Brossette, she was not a great tragic actress, nor was she, judging from the parts assigned to her, more than competent in comedy. But her beauty and her queenly presence made her a real acquisition.

She is credited with being of a haughty and capricious temper, but on very slight evidence. There is a tradition that Molière, La Fontaine, and the two Corneilles all sighed in vain for her favours. But as regards the first two there is no evidence, and the elder Corneille's well-known verses to her seem to indicate that his homage was not serious. Besides, it is possible that she may have been faithful to her Gros-René. However, in November 1664 he died, and, when she played the part of Axiane, she was a widow with four children. We get a glimpse of her character in *L'Impromptu de Versailles*, in which she says that she does not know why Molière has given her the part of an affected woman for "no one in the world is less affected (*façonnière*) than I am". "True", replies Molière; "and it is just by representing a person so contrary to your character that you can best shew that you are a good actress." There is evident irony in this remark, for there would be no point in it if it was meant to be taken literally. We also know that Mlle Du Parc and her husband left Molière's company at Easter 1659 and rejoined it a year later, which may indicate that she was changeable and capricious. But we must not build upon this slender foundation a conjecture that Racine in his relations with her suffered from her airs or her caprice. We do know, however, that this beautiful actress had, as was natural, hosts of adorers and that Racine was very sensitive and had an irritable temper. It is therefore not a rash conjecture that he experienced in his own person the jealousy that he depicts in many of his characters, in Hermione, Roxane, and Phèdre, in Oreste and Britannicus. He had, however, one great advantage over his rivals. He could give Mlle Du Parc a leading part in his new tragedy of *Andromaque*, and, helped by her lover's careful coaching, she filled it with success. But their idyll was of short duration. A year later, on December 11, 1688, she died, and a long procession of mourners—actors, poets, painters, adorers—followed her to the grave. Among them was Racine—"à demi trépassé", says an eye-witness.

He had quite recently produced his comedy of *Les Plaideurs*, a clever and amusing piece, but which neither he nor the public seems to have valued very highly. It doubtless did not take him long to write, so that possibly during the whole of the two years that elapsed between the production of *Andromaque* and that of *Britannicus* (December 13, 1669) he was occupied with his new tragedy. "It is the tragedy", he says in his preface, "at which I have worked the hardest." Perhaps, as Lemaître suggests, he was irritated by comments that, though he might represent love scenes with success, he could not write a great historical tragedy like old Corneille. So he determined to take his next subject from Roman history, and naturally he turned to the historian whom he calls "the greatest painter of antiquity", and whose insight into character and passion was served by a dramatic instinct hardly inferior to his own. And what better characters could he have for a drama than Agrippina and Nero, two of the most spectacular criminals of the Roman empire, the mother, who had shrunk from no crime to become the wife and mother of emperors, and the son, who, having got rid of his mother by murdering her, indulged without restraint in cruelties and debaucheries that have made his name infamous for all time?

The new subject demanded a different treatment. *Andromaque* was a study of passion, or, to be more precise, of the passion of love as it affected three ordinary persons. Racine's new theme was a struggle for domination between a hardened criminal and a criminal in the making, and accordingly he subordinated the study of passion to the study of character. The subject, as he himself says, "is no less the disgrace of Agrippine than the death of Britannicus". But the two issues are closely bound together. Néron kills Britannicus, not only in order to obtain possession of Junie, but also to free himself from the control of his mother:

> Il faut que sa ruine
> Me délivre à jamais des fureurs d'Agrippine.

Racine

With the view of giving full development to the portrayal of these two characters, the tragedy is planned on broad lines. The first act is devoted to Agrippine, and Néron does not appear in it. The second act, in which Agrippine does not appear, is devoted to Néron. In the third act Agrippine's character is still further revealed and Néron's is rapidly developed. In the second scene of the fourth act they meet for the first time face to face, and they do not meet again till after the murder of Britannicus. Agrippine's character is brought out in the first act by means of conversations, first with her confidante, Albine, and then with Burrhus. It is made clear that what she values is not real power, but merely the outward show of it—the right to be present behind a screen at the deliberations of the senate and to sit on a throne beside the emperor when he receives ambassadors. To these and similar rights she clings desperately, and from a rather less vulgar motive she cannot bear to think that Néron is slipping from her authority, "Néron m'échappera, si ce frein ne l'arrête". She is jealous of Seneca and Burrhus, without realising that she has neither the knowledge nor the ability to take their place. She prides herself on her popularity with the senate and people, whereas in reality she is detested. She courts Britannicus, forgetting that she had by her wicked arts deprived him of the succession. When she reappears upon the scene in the third act, she attacks Burrhus with a storm of violent and wild threats. She, the daughter of Germanicus, will appear with the son of Claudius before the soldiers; she will confess all the crimes—banishments, assassinations, even the poisoning of Claudius—that she had committed in collusion with Burrhus and Seneca. It is the violence of a weak and beaten woman:

Ma place est occupée, et je ne suis plus rien.

Her speech to Albine in the fourth scene is a wail of despair. But she makes one more effort to bend Néron to her will. In the great speech which begins with

Approchez-vous, Néron, et prenez votre place

23

she recounts to him, in language than which nothing could be simpler or more effective, all the manœuvres by which she had raised him to the throne. With infinite skill she glides over her crimes. "Silanus...marqua de son sang ce jour infortuné"; "L'exil me délivra des plus séditieux"; and finally of Claudius's death, "Il mourut. Mille bruits en courent à ma honte". Then, when she has finished her confession, she makes a fatal mistake. She turns on Néron and reproaches him with ingratitude.

The effect of her speech on him is very different from what she had expected. But before we consider this we must go back to the second act, in which Néron makes his first appearance. We have already learned from Agrippine's lips that he has declared his enmity to Britannicus, that he is impatient of all restraint, and that he has carried off Junie in the middle of the night. His next step is to give peremptory orders—"je veux, je l'ordonne"—to Burrhus and to order Pallas, his mother's favourite and chief supporter, to leave Rome before nightfall. He then avows to Narcisse, the freedman who is his evil genius, that he is in love with, nay that he idolises, Junie. But his next words make it plain that what he calls love is really lust—and cruel lust:

> J'aimois jusqu'à ses pleurs, que je faisois couler.

Narcisse expresses surprise, but he promptly seizes the opportunity first to inflame Néron's jealousy of Britannicus, and then to urge him to take advantage of his imperial power, to divorce Octavie, and throw off the control of his mother:

> Vous verrons-nous toujours trembler sous sa tutelle?
> Vivez, régnez pour vous: c'est trop régner pour elle.

But Néron is still afraid of his mother:

> Mon génie étonné tremble devant le sien.

To get the better of Britannicus and Junie he resorts to a dastardly trick. He makes love to Junie in the fashionable language of Racine's day and declares his intention to marry her after divorcing Octavie. She refuses, because she loves Britannicus. Very well—she shall see Britannicus, but—this is the devilish design—she must make it plain that she no longer loves him, and let her bear in mind that he will be in hiding and will watch her closely:

> Madame, en le voyant, songez que je vous vois.

The interview takes place. Britannicus is deceived, but Néron is not. He has detected Junie's ardent love even in her silence and he is bent on revenge. In the third act he has done with hesitation. He makes it clear to Burrhus that Junie must be his wife, and Burrhus, left alone, exclaims:

> Enfin, Burrhus, Néron découvre son génie.
> Cette férocité que tu croyois fléchir
> De tes foibles liens est prête à s'affranchir.

Néron's next step on the path of crime is caused by his discovering Britannicus at Junie's feet. When Britannicus courageously, though rashly, faces him as his rival not only for Junie but for the empire, he orders his guards to confine them in separate apartments, and the moment afterwards bids Burrhus place his mother also under restraint. And this leads the way to the great scene in which for the first time in the play Néron and Agrippine are brought together.

As I have said above, Agrippine's speech had not the effect that she intended. Néron at once points out that her continual suspicions and complaints have made those who heard them believe that she had been all the time working in his name for herself. He would gladly, he said, have relinquished to her the power that she was clamouring for,

> Mais Rome veut un maître, et non une maîtresse.

And then he roundly accuses her of conspiring with Britannicus and Pallas to make Britannicus emperor. His speech shews not only brutal directness but also a clear-sighted vision both of the present and the future remarkable in so young a man. It was a masterly stroke to accuse his mother of treason, but Néron was encouraged to shew this bold front by her narrative. If she had gained her ends by criminal means, of which she hardly takes pains to conceal the nature, and yet had suffered from nothing but accusatory rumours, which she had without difficulty checked, what crime might not he, the actual emperor, commit with impunity? His mind is made up; Britannicus shall die. But to his mother he pretends that he will accept her terms; he will forgive Pallas and he will come to a reconciliation with Britannicus. To Burrhus he reveals his real intentions:

> J'embrasse mon rival, mais c'est pour l'étouffer.

The scenes with Burrhus (IV, 3) and Narcisse (IV, 4) represent him between his good and his evil genius. In manly tones Burrhus urges him to keep to the path of virtue, and for the moment he wavers. Then Narcisse tells him that a new poison of a most deadly nature has been prepared for Britannicus. Néron says that he has changed his mind, but Narcisse, with an insight into Néron's nature that may be called devilish, does his tempter's work. He appeals in turn to his fear—perhaps Britannicus, who will certainly hear about the order to poison him, will be bolder than his rival— to his jealousy—will Néron resign Junie to him?—to his *amour-propre*—Agrippine has openly boasted that she has re- gained her authority over him. And then he points out that he has nothing to fear from public opinion. But his speech, with its contemptuous scorn and savage irony, is so remark- able an example of the "tender" Racine's command of in- cisive language that I must give it in full:

> Et prenez-vous, Seigneur, leurs caprices pour guides?
> Avez-vous prétendu qu'ils se tairoient toujours?
> Est-ce à vous de prêter l'oreille à leurs discours?
> De vos propres désirs perdez-vous la mémoire?
> Et serez-vous le seul que vous n'oserez croire?
> Mais, Seigneur, les Romains ne vous sont pas connus:
> Non, non, dans leurs discours ils sont plus retenus.
> Tant de précaution affoiblit votre règne:
> Ils croiront, en effet, mériter qu'on les craigne.

Au joug, depuis longtemps, ils se sont façonnés;
Ils adorent la main qui les tient enchaînés.
Vous les verrez toujours ardents à vous complaire.
Leur prompte servitude a fatigué Tibère.
Moi-même, revêtu d'un pouvoir emprunté,
Que je reçus de Claude avec la liberté,
J'ai cent fois, dans le cours de ma gloire passée,
Tenté leur patience, et ne l'ai point lassée.
D'un empoisonnement vous craignez la noirceur?
Faites périr le frère, abandonnez la sœur;
Rome, sur les autels prodiguant les victimes,
Fussent-ils innocents, leur trouvera des crimes:
Vous verrez mettre au rang des jours infortunés
Ceux où jadis la sœur et le frère sont nés.

Finally, when Néron objects that he has given his promise to Burrhus, Narcisse represents to him that the death of Britannicus will be a master-stroke to free Néron from the domination of Burrhus and Seneca—those arrogant ministers, who proclaim that they are the real masters of Rome while Néron is content with the applause of the circus and the theatre. That determines Néron:

Viens, Narcisse: allons voir ce que nous devons faire.

The fifth act adds further touches to the characters of Agrippine and Néron. In a scene with Junie Agrippine expresses confidence in her victory:

Il suffit, j'ai parlé, tout a changé de face.

This belief in her regained power over her son and in his sincerity shews a credulity which betokens a weak rather than a generous woman. She is soon disillusioned, for she has no sooner spoken the words than Burrhus bursts in with the account of Britannicus's death. Néron follows, and the callous way in which he meets Agrippine's "Je connais l'assassin" is significative. The "humble and timid" boy, just beginning to feel the irksomeness of restraint, has hardened into an open and practically self-confessing criminal.

Agrippine and Néron are among the finest examples of

Racine's skill in portraying character. The treatment, inevitably, is not the same for both. Agrippine's character, which is already formed, has only to be revealed; Néron's is carefully developed. Agrippine, whose criminal past is kept in the background till she makes her guarded confession to Néron, is represented as a woman of second-rate ambition and intelligence. She clings to power, but to its semblance and not to its reality. She entirely misjudges Britannicus's disposition to her, and she is even blinder with regard to her own son. She is grossly deceived as to her popularity with the Roman people. She has no tact, and no control over her temper, to which she gives violent and ill-timed expression. In short, in spite of her imperious demeanour and regal pose, she is a weak, pretentious, and blustering woman. Like the characters of *Andromaque* she might belong to any age. It is different with Néron. It is true that in his desire to rid himself of his mother's control he is a type that is common in all ages. But the method to which he, a boy of nineteen and a novice in crime, resorted to free himself from all control, namely the murder of his stepbrother, is that of an Oriental despot. Moreover, he is no ordinary criminal. He is, as few characters are, either in real life or fiction, altogether bad. He is as Racine says a *monstre naissant*. He has not a single generous or redeeming feature. His love for Junie is a mere lustful caprice. His trick to separate her from Britannicus is incredibly mean. His attitude towards his mother is in the last degree ungrateful and hard-hearted. He is vain of his appearance, vain of his accomplishments, vain of his reputation as a virtuous ruler, and it is only his fear of exchanging this for the reputation of a tyrant that in any way shakes his resolution to assassinate Britannicus. But he is no fool. He allows, indeed, Narcisse to play upon his fears and desires, but he reads his mother like an open book. His reply to Burrhus's sententious remark,

On n'aime point, Seigneur, si l'on ne veut aimer.

might make one smile, if one could smile at Néron:

Je vous croirai, Burrhus, lorsque dans les alarmes
Il faudra soutenir la gloire de nos armes,
Ou lorsque, plus tranquille, assis dans le sénat,
Il faudra décider du destin de l'État;
Je m'en reposerai sur votre expérience.
Mais, croyez-moi, l'amour est une autre science,
Burrhus; et je ferois quelque difficulté
D'abaisser jusque-là votre sévérité.

In fact one is almost tempted to wonder whether he has not
developed too quickly, between the second and third act,
from a timid love-sick boy to a grown man who knows the
world and human nature and who will use his knowledge
unscrupulously to his own advantage. The answer is, I think,
that Racine means to portray a "monster", of whom Burrhus
in the last line of the play says prophetically,

Plût aux dieux que ce fût le dernier de ses crimes.

This was his first crime, and perhaps for that reason the
title of the play is *Britannicus*. For Britannicus, who is only
sixteen—Racine having added two years to his real age—is too
young to be the real hero of the play and is naturally over-
shadowed by Néron. Nevertheless, both he and Junie are
firmly drawn characters and make a deeper impression at
each reading of the play, and Britannicus has the impulsiveness, the generosity, the readiness to believe in good, of
youth. This comes out especially in the first scene of the fifth
act:

Je m'en fie aux transports qu'elle m'a fait paraître;
Je m'en fie à Burrhus; j'en crois même son maître:
Je crois qu'à mon exemple, impuissant à trahir,
Il hait à cœur ouvert, ou cesse de haïr.

He is not without ambition and does not forget that he is the
son of the last emperor and was at one time recognised as his
successor. He has courage and can hold his own with Néron
(III, 8). Junie has equal courage and greater calmness. In
every scene in which she appears she is admirable, alike in
the scene with Néron (II, 3), when she repels him with quiet

dignity, or in the three scenes with Britannicus (II, 6, III, 7, and v, 1), which come as welcome interludes of pathetic beauty between the criminal machinations of Néron and Narcisse.

The character of Narcisse admirably serves its purpose, but he is not so much a human being as the devil's mouth-piece. Burrhus has always found favour, from Racine's day, when he was praised by Boileau, to modern times, when critics are unanimous in their verdict. I confess that in his first scene, that with Agrippine (I, 2), I find him rather dis-appointing. He is not my idea of the blunt soldier that he claims to be. He is rather priggish at first, and his chief speech, which is fine but a little dull, is too full of details borrowed from Tacitus. But in the later acts (III, 1–3) he is much better, and in the scene with Néron to which I have referred above (IV, 3) he is really fine, especially in the great speech when he flings himself at Néron's feet.

In spite of the pains which Racine had taken with *Britannicus*, it was not a success, either with the public or with the critics until the king had pronounced in its favour. The criticisms were numerous. Some said that Racine had made Néron too cruel, others that he had made him too good. Some were scandalised that he had chosen a man as young as Britannicus for the hero. Some complained that he had taken liberties with history, and others declared that the play ought to have ended with the death of Britannicus. Racine was always irritated by criticism, and he was especially irritated on this occasion, because he knew that the criticism came from the friends of Corneille, who, resenting the success of *Andromaque*, were determined that it should not be repeated. Recognising that attack is the best form of defence, he wrote a preface charged with barbed darts, chiefly directed against Corneille. He does not mention him by name, but the allusion to several of his tragedies is unmistakable and the mention in connexion with Terence of a "vieux poète malintentionné" is clearly a hit at his veteran rival. The great poet who was the creator of French classical tragedy deserved more respectful treatment from this young man of thirty, but Racine, when he was irritated and had a pen in his hand, knew neither mercy nor reverence. The ability of the preface is undeniable, but it is especially remarkable for its succinct statement of what in Racine's opinion a tragedy should be—"a simple action, charged with little matter, as becomes an action which occupies a single day, advancing gradually to its end, and sustained by the interests, the sentiments, and the passions of the characters".

In his next tragedy Racine followed this ideal with religious strictness. "Titus Berenicem dimisit invitus invitam." These five words from Suetonius tell the whole story of *Bérénice*, which was produced on November 21, 1670. In the twenty-one remarkable pages which Lytton Strachey devotes to Racine in his *Landmarks of French Literature* he happily contrasts *Bérénice* with Shakespeare's *Antony and Cleopatra*—a tragedy with three characters, which takes place in a single room and occupies little more than the time of its actual performance, with a tragedy, which has at least forty speaking characters, of every rank and occupation, and in which the constantly shifting scene embraces three continents and the action is prolonged over several years. As he points out, the two dramas have in a sense the same subject, that is to say, the conflict between love and duty resulting from the antipathy of Rome to an Oriental queen. It may be noted that Bérénice was a direct descendant of Cleopatra, and Paulin, the confidant of Titus, actually refers to Antony's infatuation for her as a warning to his master. Antony, he says, "forgot in her arms glory and country". He lost "all for love"; Titus and Bérénice lost love, or rather the fruits of love, for duty. In making duty triumph, Racine has followed Corneille, but his manner of treating the theme is, as M. Truc says, his own. In the first place the characters are not Cornelian but have human weaknesses. Titus is afraid to tell Bérénice that she must leave Rome and imposes the task upon Antiochus, who is also in love with her, though Titus is ignorant of it.

Three French Dramatists

Antiochus cannot help revealing to Bérénice that his love for her is as strong as ever; a Cornelian hero would have kept silence. Bérénice, who believes that her love for Titus is on the point of being crowned by marriage, asks Antiochus, with unconscious cruelty, to share her happiness, and when she hears Titus's decision that she must leave Rome turns against Antiochus as the bearer of the news. On Titus coming to her in person, she overwhelms him with reproaches and leaves him with a cry for vengeance. Another sign of natural human weakness in all three characters is their irresolution. No sooner has Titus said, "Je connais mon devoir, c'est à moi de le suivre", than on the receipt of a message that Bérénice wishes to speak to him he wavers. His fine soliloquy in the fourth act is full of hesitation. In the third act Antiochus cannot make up his mind whether he shall leave Rome at once or not (III, 4). Bérénice's speech at the end of the second act represents with admirable fidelity her uncertainty as to the meaning of Titus's attitude towards her. It is part of her charm that her emotional temperament makes her fluctuate between hope and despair.

This conflict between "the interests, the sentiments, and the passions" of the individual characters, and between all the characters and the great and relentless majesty of Rome, is the whole drama. Except for Antiochus's soliloquy, the opening scenes are rather dull, chiefly because Antiochus's confidant is of an irritating denseness, but the fourth scene, the scene in which Antiochus tells Bérénice the story of his love for her, is of remarkable beauty and pathos. The following lines are perhaps too famous to quote, but I will quote them nevertheless:

> Rome vous vit, Madame, arriver avec lui.
> Dans l'Orient désert quel devint mon ennui!
> Je demeurai longtemps errant dans Césarée,
> Lieux charmants où mon cœur vous avoit adorée.
> Je vous redemandois à vos tristes États;
> Je cherchois en pleurant les traces de vos pas.

Racine

A pendant to this is Bérénice's panegyric of Titus in the next scene. From here onwards the interest never flags. In the second scene of the second act we have the fine dialogue between Titus and his honest confidant, Paulin, in which the emperor determines that it is his duty to dismiss Bérénice. In a striking speech Paulin faithfully interprets to his master the opinion of Rome. Six times, like a solemn bell calling to prayer, the mystic word "Rome" falls from his lips. The result is the scene between Titus and Bérénice (ii, 4), in which Titus hesitates to make known to her his decision. "Rome...l'empire" is all he can stammer and then his courage fails him. "Sortons, Paulin: je ne lui puis rien dire." The great scene in the third act is that between Antiochus and Bérénice, to which I have already referred, and which reaches the height of pathos in the line,

Nous séparer! Qui? Moi? Titus de Bérénice?

The whole of the fourth act is of peculiar beauty and power. I have remarked on Titus's soliloquy with its note of wavering and hesitation. Again the word "Rome" is sounded six times; it is the knell of his love. "Faisons ce que l'honneur exige: Rompons le seul lien...." And then Bérénice bursts in, and we have the finest and most effective scene of the whole act. A message comes from the senate demanding audience. Antiochus counsels escape. But the word "Rome" uttered by Paulin determines Titus.

Il suffit, Paulin; nous allons les entendre.

In the concluding act these constant but unhappy lovers submit to the inevitable. They bow to the decree of the "stern lawgiver" and they part for ever. Love has yielded to duty, but it still reigns unconquered in their hearts. They have gained the victory over themselves, but they came very near to defeat. Not till Bérénice had announced her intention to kill herself, and both Titus and Antiochus had declared that they would not survive her, did she, the most impulsive of the three, recognising the depth of their love, recall them to sanity. The intention of suicide may seem a somewhat clumsy invention, unworthy of Racine's perfect art, but Bérénice's farewell speech is beautiful enough to atone for anything. First she addresses Titus:

> Mon cœur vous est connu, Seigneur, et je puis dire
> Qu'on ne l'a jamais vu soupirer pour l'Empire:
> La grandeur des Romains, la pourpre des Césars,
> N'ont point, vous le savez, attiré mes regards.
> J'aimois, Seigneur, j'aimois, je voulois être aimée.
>
> . . . . .
>
> Je crois, depuis cinq ans jusqu'à ce dernier jour,
> Vous avoir assuré d'un véritable amour.
> Ce n'est pas tout: je veux, en ce moment funeste,
> Par un dernier effort couronner tout le reste:
> Je vivrai, je suivrai vos ordres absolus.
> Adieu, Seigneur, régnez: je ne vous verrai plus.

Then turning to Antiochus:

> Prince, après cet adieu, vous jugez bien vous-même
> Que je ne consens pas de quitter ce que j'aime
> Pour aller loin de Rome écouter d'autres vœux.
> Vivez, et faites-vous un effort généreux.
> Sur Titus et sur moi réglez votre conduite:
> Je l'aime, je le fuis; Titus m'aime, il me quitte;
> Portez loin de mes yeux vos soupirs et vos fers.
> Adieu: servons tous trois d'exemple à l'univers
> De l'amour la plus tendre et la plus malheureuse
> Dont il puisse garder l'histoire douloureuse.
> Tout est prêt. On m'attend. Ne suivez point mes pas.
>   (à Titus)
> Pour la dernière fois, adieu, Seigneur.

ANTIOCHUS.
                              Hélas!

It should be noted that none of these three characters is a complete portrait like Néron or Agrippine. Only a few touches are given. Titus is soft-hearted and a little wanting in moral courage. Antiochus is given to melancholy and self-pity. Bérénice is emotional and impulsive. But she appeals to our imagination more than either of the others and so we can supply for ourselves what is omitted in Racine's presentation of her. She must be counted among his great characters, among those which are most vividly present to us. To have seen and heard Mlle Bartet in the part during the celebration by the Comédie Française of the two-hundredth anniversary of Racine's death (April 26, 1699) must have been a rare treat. Though the three noble lovers have human weaknesses, they are not ordinary folk. They are raised above the multitude by the intensity, the fineness, and the constancy of their love. They have loved for five years without any wavering, and love has called forth all that is best in their noble and generous natures. Especially it has changed Titus from a pleasure-loving youth at the corrupt court of Nero into a triumphant and merciful conqueror, who has counted it his greatest joy to relieve the unfortunate and the distressed. "Je lui dois tout, Paulin." Nor is the story of Titus and Bérénice quite an ordinary one. True, as Brunetière and others have pointed out, it is more or less that of a young man who gives up the woman he loves at his father's bidding or for the sake of the family name; but Rome is something greater than either father or family, and Racine has made this abundantly clear. There is no local colour, as it is ordinarily understood, but Rome is the irresistible force that governs the whole play.

Bérénice was a triumphant success, and Racine recounts with pride that the thirtieth performance was as well attended as the first. It was admirably interpreted. The great Floridor was Titus, Champmeslé, a good actor and a recent acquisition, was Antiochus, and his more famous wife was Bérénice. She and her husband had joined the Hôtel de Bourgogne at Easter, and she had won great approval from Racine for her acting in the rôle of Hermione, in which she replaced Mlle Des Œillets, who had died in October, a month before the production of *Bérénice*. But Bérénice was the first new part in which she was associated with Racine's triumphs. It was to be followed by equal successes in the rôles of Roxane, Monime, Iphigénie, and Phèdre. We may disregard Louis

Racine's ridiculous statement that his father had "formed" her, and that he had to explain every line to her. No doubt they rehearsed her parts together, and no doubt here and there the author corrected her interpretation and made suggestions. But by all accounts she was an actress of genius, and she had had some experience at the Marais when, at the age of twenty-eight, she came to the Hôtel de Bourgogne. Her maiden name was Desmares, and Charles Chevillet, called Champmeslé, was her second husband. She was not exactly beautiful, but she had an agreeable face, a fine figure, much grace and charm, and an incomparable voice, which could be as gentle as it could be full of energy. She practised, though in moderation, the declamatory style which was the tradition of the Hôtel, and which remained so even after Baron had joined the company in 1673. She became Racine's mistress as well as his favourite actress, but, though the *liaison* lasted seven years, it was an ignoble affair and his affections were evidently not seriously engaged. For the lady had several lovers, including Charles de Sévigné, who met together from time to time in friendly convivialities, in which her husband took part. It reminds one of Mme Marneffe.

Though Racine adhered strictly to his conception of tragedy, he varied greatly in his choice of subject, and nearly every play exhibits in this respect a marked contrast to its predecessor. After the study of crime and criminals in *Britannicus* he had presented in *Bérénice* a picture of singularly noble souls. And now after a theme of the greatest simplicity he chooses a plot, which, without being unduly complicated, is the only one in all his tragedies which has any complications at all. However, in the opening scene he has made Acomat, the Sultan's grand vizir, explain the situation in what has been commended as the finest "exposition" in the whole history of the French drama. The subject of *Bajazet* is taken from the recent history of Turkey, the Sultan of the play having died little more than thirty years before its production. This departure from common usage Racine defends on the ground that the distance of place makes up in a measure for the nearness in point of time. The Sultan in question is Amurat IV, who, when the play opens, is engaged in a war against the Persians. He has appointed Roxane, his favourite sultana, regent of the kingdom with full powers and has in particular enjoined her to put to death his brother Bajazet, who is confined in the seraglio, on the slightest suspicion. But Acomat, who, though now in disgrace, can count on a strong following, has plotted with Roxane to depose Amurat and put Bajazet, who is to marry Roxane, on the throne. Acomat himself proposes to marry Atalide the niece of Amurat. Unfortunately for the success of the plot Bajazet and Atalide are in love with one another, and Bajazet has no intention of marrying Roxane. But the sultana is all powerful and is furiously—there is no other word—in love with Bajazet, and for fear of her vengeance the lovers have agreed to pretend that Bajazet returns her love, and this she interprets to mean that he will accept her offer of marriage. Thus the dramatic interest of the play lies in the conflict between Roxane on the one hand and Bajazet and Atalide on the other, while Acomat in the background tries to guide events with a view solely to his own interests. The plot is thoroughly Turkish in character and the whole atmosphere—the intrigues, the Oriental despotism, the indifference to life and death, the disregard of truth—is equally Turkish. Yet Corneille said in confidence to Segrais, "There is not a single character that has the sentiments that one ought to have or has at Constantinople; beneath a Turkish dress they all have purely French sentiments". And Mme de Sévigné wrote to her daughter that "the manners of the Turks are ill-observed". Roxane and Acomat, at any rate, are thoroughly Turkish characters in the sense that, though they have traits which you might find anywhere, these could not have been so completely developed or so freely expressed except in an environment of Oriental despotism.

In pursuance of his plot Acomat had spoken so warmly

to Roxane of Bajazet's attractions ("je lui vantai ses charmes") that her only desire was to see him. She saw him and "he pleased her", but, in spite of his long-continued deception, she does not feel sure that he returns her love. Though her love for him is largely sensuous, it is also partly of the heart. In her first scene with him (II, 1) after threatening him with death if he refuses to marry her, she suddenly says, "Je sens que je vous aime", and after another threat,

> Ne désespérez point une amante en furie.
> S'il m'échappoit un mot, c'est fait de votre vie.

she becomes really pathetic:

> Crois-tu...que...
> Je puisse désormais souffrir une autre idée,
> Ni que je vive enfin, si je ne vis pour toi?
>
> .   .   .   .   .
>
> De toi dépend ma joie et ma félicité:
> De ma sanglante mort ta mort sera suivie.

Her moods alternate from hope to despair (III, 7), and even after the cruel ruse by which she detects Atalide's love for Bajazet she determines after much hesitation to let the plot go forward. If, when she has raised him to the throne, she argues, he chooses Atalide, and not her, for his wife, she can kill them both and herself afterwards. That is her intention, but the discovery of a letter from Bajazet to Atalide, in which he speaks of eternal love, arouses the tigress in her nature. She sends for him, prepared to confront him with the incriminating letter and at the same time with an order just received from Amurat to put him at once to death. Orcan, the African negro who brought the order, is to wait with his mutes outside her apartment and, when Bajazet leaves it, to strangle him in the approved Turkish fashion. As soon as Bajazet appears, she accuses him with furious insolence of his long deception, but she still offers him his life on two conditions. He must see Atalide strangled before his eyes and he must promise to marry Roxane. Bajazet of course refuses, but pleads for Atalide's life. His plea is cut short by the one word "Sortez", and he goes to his doom. Then Atalide, ignorant of his death, takes to herself all the blame for their deception, and, having promised to kill herself, implores Roxane to forgive Bajazet. With devilish mockery the sultana refuses her sacrifice. She shall be united to her lover, she says, by eternal ties. She is so united, but by her own hand, after hearing of Roxane's assassination by Orcan and of her lover's fate.

Roxane must be a difficult part to interpret satisfactorily, and when Rachel, as a girl of seventeen, appeared in it for the first time, she met with a good deal of criticism in spite of her triumphs in other Racinian rôles. It appears from Alfred de Musset's protest against these criticisms that, breaking with the traditional interpretation, she recognised that Roxane's desire for Bajazet is not wholly sensual, and that there is real pathos in her appeal for his love. It is not surprising that Bajazet confronted with the alternative of marriage or death—"Épouse-moi ou je te tue"—should have deceived her; deceived she was, and her furious reaction, when she discovered the deception, is natural in one who from a slave had suddenly risen to the position of favourite sultana and regent of the kingdom with unlimited powers. Alike in her imperious arrogance, her ungoverned fury, and the cruel thoroughness of her vengeance, she is a true Oriental.

Acomat is equally Oriental and he is a conception of genius, but when once conceived his actual creation was not perhaps difficult. He is a man who devotes his great abilities as soldier, politician, and diplomatist solely and entirely to the acquisition of power and the furtherance of his own interests. He has no love for his country; he is quite unscrupulous; and he has all an Oriental's disregard for human life:

Cet esclave n'est plus: un ordre, cher Osmin,
L'a fait précipiter dans le fond de l'Euxin.

One can picture to one's self the caressing gesture with which here and elsewhere he says "cher Osmin". Yet with all his cleverness he is too prone to regard other people as mere pawns in his game. Above all he forgets the claims of the heart and the possibility of Bajazet and Atalide being in love. He himself recognises his oversight:

> Prince aveugle! ou plutôt trop aveugle ministre!
> Il te sied bien d'avoir en de si jeunes mains,
> Chargé d'ans et d'honneurs, confié tes desseins,
> Et laissé d'un Visir la fortune flottante
> Suivre de ces amants la conduite imprudente!

When his plot fails, he sails away in his ships leaving the dead behind him.

Roxane and Acomat fit in perfectly with the Turkish atmosphere, but Bajazet does not. It is true that a man between two women is always in an awkward position and is a figure for comedy rather than for tragedy. But the difficulty with regard to Bajazet also is that, while in his first interview with Roxane he fences with her like an Oriental, in the fine scene with Atalide which concludes the second act he talks like an honourable gentleman with Western ideas of truth and a hatred of Oriental lying. Atalide has more of our sympathy, partly because we prefer her straightforward lying to his prevarication, partly because she has not the invidious task of pretending to be in love. From the scene with Bajazet (II, 5) to the equally fine scene in which she faces Roxane (III, 6) she is continuously on the stage, and from here onwards the drama moves so rapidly and with such thrilling interest that we are no longer disposed to criticise. As for "la grande tuerie" for which Mme de Sévigné cannot see any reason, and which includes the deaths not only of Bajazet and Roxane and Atalide, but also of the dead and dying whom Bajazet "forced to accompany his shade", it is all part of the Turkish atmosphere. On this count Mme de Sévigné could not complain that "the customs of the Turks were ill-observed".

Of all Racine's tragedies from *Andromaque* onwards the one that shews the plainest marks of Corneille's influence is

Mithridate. The long speeches, of which three are narratives and one is Mithridate's exposition of his great plan for marching on Rome; the character of Monime with her strength of will and her noble and dignified utterances; and the happy ending, are all Cornelian features. We may therefore accept as extremely plausible Lemaître's supposition that the piece was primarily inspired by a desire to rival Corneille on his own ground. Racine would shew the world that he could handle a great historical subject as well as the older man and compose speeches of as weighty eloquence. So he chose for a hero Mithridates, the great Oriental king who waged war against the Romans for forty years, the greatest king, says Cicero, after Alexander. And turning over the historians—Plutarch, Dio Cassius, Appian, Florus—he found mention of two of his sons, Xiphares and Pharnaces, and, among his many wives and concubines, Monime.

With these four characters he constructed his tragedy, making the struggle with Rome a background for a domestic drama of love and jealousy. Some of the critics of his *Alexandre* had objected that he had made Alexander in love, others that he had not made him a real lover. Well, in spite of the critics he would make Mithridates in love, but his love should have the note of real passion, and his two sons should be his rivals. He would portray him both as a great soldier and statesman, fighting to the last against the might of Rome, and as an elderly, doubting, jealous, and tyrannical lover. It was no easy task either to combine these two aspects of the man in a single portrait or to give unity to the double action of his drama, and he only partially succeeded. There are, it seems to me, two reasons for this. In the first place it is evident that Racine took far more interest in the domestic than in the political side of his story. The great speech at the opening of the third act, in which Mithridate unfolds to his sons his grandiose plan of marching into Italy with an army collected from every nation that was actually or potentially hostile to Rome, is a most able performance, in which no doubt Racine took immense pride. But it is too long and, what is a greater fault, it is out of scale. The real interest of the drama is elsewhere. We only care for Mithridate's success or failure so far as it affects the fortunes of Xipharès and Monime. A stronger reason, and one which, I think, has not been noticed by critics, is that Mithridate is a character with whom we can have little sympathy. In the very first scene Xipharès reminds Arbate of the number of mistresses that he had put to death, and in the fifth scene we are told that he had done the same to two of his sons.

> Vous dépendez ici d'une main violente,
> Que le sang le plus cher rarement épouvante;
> Et je n'ose vous dire à quelle cruauté
> Mithridate jaloux s'est souvent emporté.

Such is the warning that Xipharès, who is a loyal and admiring son, feels bound to give to Monime. It may be said that an Oriental despot was bound to be cruel and bloodthirsty and that, as a historical fact, Mithridates was much worse than Racine has painted him. But it surely was not necessary that Racine should emphasise this ferocious side of his character. It would have been quite enough to represent him as a tyrant who shewed no mercy when his commands or wishes were disregarded. Moreover, in his relations towards Monime he is cunning as well as tyrannical. Another Oriental trait, it may be said; but the mean subterfuge by which he elicits her avowal that she and Xipharès love one another is unworthy of a tragic hero and has rightly been called a "stratagem of comedy". Even in the fine soliloquy of the fifth scene of the fourth act, in which he wavers between putting the lovers to death and consenting to their marriage, it is his need for his son's help in his contest with Rome, and not affection, that restrains him, so that the appeal that he here makes to our sympathy is very limited.

There is little to say about either Xipharès or Pharnace. There is nothing of the Oriental in Xipharès. Like Oreste, he regards himself as singled out by destiny for misfortune, but otherwise he is a typical hero of Western chivalry; a fine soldier, a loyal son, an ardent but respectful lover; in fact a Cid, but with none of the Cid's glamour. Pharnace is a mere blusterer, without a single good quality. The one character that is really attractive, the one character that really lives for us, is Monime. With her maidenly reserve, her calm dignity, her resolute courage, her firm determination to be "mistress of her soul", she is a beautiful and noble figure. With what delicacy she hints to Xipharès that he is not wholly indifferent to her!

> Mon cœur, affermi,
> N'a rien dit, ou du moins n'a parlé qu'à demi.

When Mithridate bids her prepare for her immediate marriage with him, she replies simply that she will obey him. "Seigneur, vous pouvez tout....Je ne vous répondrai qu'en vous obéissant." But when Xipharès, under the false impression that she is in love with his brother, questions her, she avows her love. But she reminds him that she belongs to his father and that henceforth they must avoid one another:

> Souvenez-vous, Prince, de m'éviter;
> Et méritez les pleurs que vous m'allez coûter.

Then after Mithridate's unworthy stratagem her attitude entirely changes. She will not marry a barbarian and a tyrant, whose hand will be red with the blood of her lover, and she faces him with cold scorn:

> Quoi, Seigneur! vous m'auriez donc trompée?

Her speeches in answer to his reproaches and threats have a noble dignity, which is very impressive. In her control of her emotions she resembles a Cornelian heroine, but she is not, like most of these, coldly superior to human weaknesses. She imposes her will on others, not by vehement self-assertion, but by quiet steadfastness. Though in Xipharès's presence she is reticent in the expression of her love, it is deeply rooted in her soul. When she believes that he has been put to death she tries to hang herself rather than marry his murderer, and when poison is sent her by the tyrant's order, she welcomes it. But just as she is putting it to her lips, she is stopped by the cry of "Arrêtez! arrêtez!" from Mithridate's confidant and messenger. He has come with the news that the great king has been attacked by the Romans, that he is at the point of death, and that he is being carried in by his soldiers, accompanied by Xipharès. "Xipharès! Ah, grands dieux", "Xipharès vit encor", is Monime's cry, and the contrast with her "Xipharès ne vit plus", twice repeated, after her failure to hang herself, is most effective. Indeed, in this fifth act there are more sudden appeals to the emotions, more striking dramatic effects than is usual with Racine. But at the most thrilling moment we are pulled up by Arcas's long narrative of Mithridate's last encounter with the Romans. Need it have been so long? Or is it that Racine wishes to divert our interest from the lovers to the dying Mithridate? If so, he has not been altogether successful. We sympathise here to some extent with the great king, who in his last breath shews an unexpected spirit of forgiveness and generosity. But, although Xipharès and Monime are kept in the background, our real sympathies remain with them, and in spite of the hero's death the tragedy for us ends happily.

Iphigénie, which was specially performed before the court at Versailles on August 18, 1674 and given to the public at the Hôtel de Bourgogne in the winter of 1674–1675, resembles *Mithridate* in its happy ending, which in both cases is brought about by the sudden rescue of the heroine from the very jaws of death. In both plays too the heroine—for so Monime and Iphigénie may be called—outshines all the other characters. In both too the psychological interest is chiefly in the portrayal of a great man's weakness. But the inspiration of the two tragedies is very different. In *Mithridate*, as in *Britannicus* and *Bérénice*, Racine has gone to Roman history for his subject and has made the majesty of Rome not only a background for his drama but a real influence on its

development. In *Iphigénie* he has returned to the sources
which had inspired him so well in *Andromaque*, to Greece and
Euripides and Homer. It was a bold act to choose the sacrifice of Iphigenia for his subject, but the sixteenth-century
Beza's play of *Abraham sacrifiant*, in which the actual sacrifice
is portrayed with extraordinary pathos, had been very
popular, and George Buchanan's Latin tragedy of *Jephthes*,
with its similar subject, has considerable dramatic merit. In
Euripides's *Iphigenia at Aulis* the doomed maiden is carried
off in a cloud by Artemis and a doe is substituted for her, but
Racine believed, as he says in his preface, that such a meta-
morphosis would have seemed too absurd and too incredible
to a modern audience, and that it was equally impossible "to
sully the stage with the horrible murder of so virtuous and
so amiable a person as Iphigénie". Lemaître thinks that the
idea of a human sacrifice would not have been so insupport-
able to Racine's audience as he imagines. This is possible, but
Racine could neither have represented the sacrifice as actually
taking place, nor have adopted the version followed by
Euripides, without treating his subject from the point of
view of Greek religion and giving a thoroughly Greek aspect
to his play, just as Beza has provided for his *Abraham sacrifiant* a thoroughly Biblical setting. But this would have been
entirely contrary to Racine's practice of portraying men as
they are. He therefore gladly availed himself of a version of
the story which declared that the Iphigenia who was sacri-
ficed at Aulis was the daughter not of Agamemnon but of
Theseus and Helen.

Racine takes an evident pleasure in probing the weaknesses
of great men, and he does not spare Agamemnon. In the opening scene in the course of a confidential conversation with his
servant Arcas he naïvely confesses, that not only the appeal to
his honour and his patriotism moves him to obey the terrible
command, but also his pride in his power and position:

> Ces noms de roi des rois, et de chef de la Grèce,
> Chatouilloient de mon cœur l'orgueilleuse foiblesse.

So *en pleurant* he gave the order for his daughter's sacrifice. But when the play opens, he has repented of this step and he sends Arcas to stop Clytemnestre and Iphigénie from coming to Aulis. This means that the expedition must be given up. But Ulysse and Achille resist this, and Agamemnon's arguments are so transparently feeble that he is obliged to compromise. If Iphigénie comes to Aulis, he will keep his promise, but if not, the Greeks must accept this solution as coming from some kinder god. This manœuvre—Agamemnon has said nothing about his order to Arcas—is unsuccessful, for the next moment another servant announces the arrival of Clytemnestre and Iphigénie. All that is left to Agamemnon is to practise his deceit on them. This is the position at the end of the first act. In the second act Agamemnon only appears in a touching scene between himself and Iphigénie, but in the third act he is busy deceiving not only his wife and daughter but Achille. Then Arcas reveals the truth and Agamemnon has to answer for his conduct. His reply to Iphigénie's noble pleading gives the measure of his weakness and self-deception. He makes a merit of his endeavours to stop their coming to Aulis, and throws the blame for its failure on the gods; he pleads the feebleness of his power as commander-in-chief and the impossibility of arresting the popular violence; and he concludes with the weak man's cry,

> Du coup qui vous attend vous mourrez moins que moi.

His speech is followed by violent reproaches from Clytemnestre and threats of force from Achille, which have their effect. In a remarkable monologue Agamemnon expresses the fluctuating sentiments of a man swayed by many motives. He will not be browbeaten by the insolent Achille.—But can he pronounce the order for his daughter's death?—Her intrepid mother will defend her child against a murderous father. Perhaps the soldiers will take her side.—Then, there is Achille with his threats.—No, he cannot do it; let Iphigénie live.—But shall he surrender to Achille and his reckless pride?—No, his daughter shall live, but she shall not marry Achille. It is a wonderful picture—a picture, as M. Truc truly says, rather than a psychological analysis—of a mind at war with itself and tortured by conflicting emotions.

Clytemnestre is the type of a mother fighting for her child. When she first hears of the intended sacrifice she turns to Achille with a pathetic appeal:

> Elle n'a que vous seul: vous êtes en ces lieux
> Son père, son époux, son asile, ses dieux.

But after listening to Agamemnon's feeble and insincere defence of his conduct, she blazes forth in a denunciation which for all its fury goes straight to the mark:

> Pourquoi feindre à nos yeux une fausse tristesse?

And she reproaches him with,

> Cette soif de régner, que rien ne peut éteindre,
> L'orgueil de voir vingt rois vous servir et vous craindre,
> Tous les droits de l'Empire en vos mains confiés,
> Cruel! c'est à ces dieux que vous sacrifiez.

Irascibility is the first quality that a lover of Homer like Racine would naturally assign to Achille, and accordingly in the first scene in which he appears (I, 2) he is represented as firing up at Ulysse's suggestion that he is wanting in patriotism. We also see him as an impetuous and imperious young lover, but his love-making, though it leaves no doubt of his ardour or sincerity, is not much in evidence. In fact he does not appear at all decisively till the fine scene with Iphigénie (III, 6), in which with absolute self-confidence he expresses his determination not only to defend her but to punish her would-be murderers:

> Est-ce à moi que l'on parle, et connaît-on Achille?

He is emphatically a man of action:

> Il faut des actions, et non pas des paroles,

and he has no fears as to the result.

> Votre fille vivra, je puis vous le prédire.
> Croyez du moins, croyez que, tant que je respire,
> Les dieux auront en vain ordonné son trépas:
> Cet oracle est plus sûr que celui de Calchas.

His interview with Agamemnon is admirably rendered. He begins on a calm note, but Agamemnon's haughtiness soon rouses him to anger, and he is not in the least abashed by the air of superiority which the commander-in-chief assumes. It is not to redress *his* wrongs that the army was assembled:

> Je ne connois Priam, Hélène, ni Pâris;
> Je voulois votre fille, et ne pars qu'à ce prix.

In the last scene in which he appears (v, 2), after in vain calling upon Iphigénie to take refuge in his tents under the protection of his soldiers, he strides forth breathing fury and vengeance.

> Vous allez à l'autel; et moi, j'y cours, Madame.
> Si de sang et de morts le ciel est affamé,
> Jamais de plus de sang ses autels n'ont fumé.
> A mon aveugle amour tout sera légitime.
> Le prêtre deviendra la première victime;
> Le bûcher, par mes mains détruit et renversé,
> Dans le sang des bourreaux nagera dispersé,
> Et si dans les horreurs de ce désordre extrême
> Votre père frappé tombe et périt lui-même,
> Alors, de vos respects voyant les tristes fruits,
> Reconnoissez les coups que vous aurez conduits.

Achille is an admirable foil to the beautiful, gentle, and self-controlled Iphigénie. Just as Homer gives an unforgettable impression of Helen's beauty by describing its effect on the Trojan leaders, so Racine represents the soldiers as lost in admiration for the beauty of Iphigénie and offering vows for her happiness. She is more dignified and of higher courage than Euripides's Iphigenia, and for all her gentleness she can be moved to anger, as when she discovers that Ériphile is in love with Achille and aspires to be her rival.

But her loftiest virtue is her loyalty to her father. "Songez",
she says to Achille, "quoique il ait fait, songez qu'il est mon
père", and she repeats:

> C'est mon père, Seigneur, je vous le dis encore,
> Mais un père que j'aime, un père que j'adore,
> Qui me chérit lui-même, et dont jusqu'à ce jour
> Je n'ai jamais reçu que des marques d'amour.

In the scene with her father, when concealment of his intentions is no longer possible, she is admirable. She professes
her perfect readiness to obey him, but she pleads, not for herself, but for her mother and her lover. If we compare this
scene (IV, 4) with the corresponding scene in Euripides, from
which Racine has borrowed, we recognise her superiority to
her Greek original. She is equally pathetic, but she is less of
the suppliant, more the royal maiden who knows her duty
and will not shrink from it. The last words that she utters in
the play are truly sublime:

> D'un peuple impatient vous entendez la voix.
> Daignez m'ouvrir vos bras pour la dernière fois,
> Madame; et rappelant votre vertu sublime...
> Eurybate, à l'autel conduisez la victime.

It is one of the noticeable features of *Iphigénie* that it has
more characters that are truly individual than we usually find
in Racine. To the four that have been already considered we
must add Ériphile, that unhappy young woman whom Racine
unearthed in order to provide a more plausible substitute for
Iphigénie than a doe. She is original and interesting, but it
appears as if Racine had deliberately wished to deprive her
of our sympathies. He has almost succeeded, for the only
thing that arouses in us any sympathy is that nobody wants
her. She evidently has this feeling about herself, and combined with egotism and self-centredness it makes her a remarkable study in the passion of envy. She is envious of
Iphigénie, not only because she is intensely jealous of her—
her love for Achille is almost hysterical—but because she can-

not bear to see anyone happy. In the first scene of the fourth act this envy swells into a murderous hate, and she reveals the attempted flight of Clytemnestre and her daughter to the Greeks, only to perish herself by her own hand, when Calchas proclaims that she too is of the blood of Helen and that she was called Iphigénie at her birth.

The *dénouement* is ingenious, but it is not altogether satisfying. Certainly the account of it given by Ulysse is neither so beautiful nor so affecting as the corresponding narrative by the messenger in Euripides. Yet in Ulysse's speech there are more poetical lines than in any other of Racine's tragedies except *Phèdre*. Ulysse is a minor character, who only appears in this last scene and in two scenes of the first act, but he too has individuality. He is a statesman who has national interests at heart, and he impresses them upon Agamemnon with great tact and considerable sympathy. In his sagacity and eloquence he agrees with the Ulysses of tradition.

There are thus six characters in the play whom Racine has individualised, and in no other play, except *Athalie*, are there more than four. There are also of course the usual confidants. In the fifth scene of the third act no less than seven characters are on the stage at once, and the numbers are greatly increased in the fourth and fifth acts by the guards, whom Agamemnon summons—"Holà! Gardes, à moi!"—after Achille's menacing attitude. This effective use of a sudden dramatic movement is also made at the entry of Ulysse in the last scene of all, when Clytemnestre's despairing cry of

> Mais, Dieux! ne vois-je pas Ulysse?
> C'est lui: ma fille est morte! Arcas, il n'est plus temps

is immediately answered by "Non, votre fille vit".

Besides the increase in the number of characters and the limited use of *coups-de-théâtre*, there are other signs that Racine was feeling his way in *Iphigénie* towards a larger and a more spectacular conception of classical tragedy. Its first production at Versailles was in a temporary open-air theatre, the scenery for which was harmonised with the long alley of the Orangerie with its double row of orange and pomegranate trees, ending in a marble portico.

Sarcey, who in his early days thought Racine deficient in the qualities of a playwright with little sense of stage construction, cannot speak too highly of the construction of *Iphigénie*; Scribe, he says, could not have done it better. The first act, in which Agamemnon's terrible dilemma is put before us with incomparable force and lucidity, is a masterpiece of exposition. In the second act Iphigénie and Ériphile are introduced; Iphigénie remains on the stage for the first six scenes, Ériphile throughout the act. Clytemnestre takes part in one short scene, but she does not become prominent till the third act. With the introduction of each new character Agamemnon's problem becomes more difficult, and in the fifth scene of the third act, as we have seen, his web of intrigue is torn to pieces. The next scene is a particularly fine one, and to the conflict which awaits Agamemnon is now added a conflict between Achille and Iphigénie. The whole fourth act is alive with movement—movement of the soul, but vividly represented by emphasis of speech and gesture. In the fifth act Agamemnon finds no place. Our last glimpse of him is as he stands near the sacrificial altar with his face covered, ὀμμάτων πέπλον προθείς ("s'est voilé le visage"). Visitors to Naples will remember the picture from the House of the Tragic Poet at Pompeii (Bulwer's House of Glaucus), in which Agamemnon is represented in an identical attitude. It is a copy—at any rate so far as this figure is concerned—of a celebrated picture by the Greek painter, Timanthes, who painted in the middle of the fourth century B.C. and who must have taken the idea from Euripides. The latter died in 406 B.C. and his *Iphigeneia* was produced soon afterwards. The covered face, though it represents Agamemnon's feelings as a father, seems in Racine's play as if it were symbolical of the ignoble part that he had played. For his wavering between two courses is largely the result of pressure from without—pressure in one direction from Ulysse and the leaders of the army, and in the other from Clytemnestre and Achille. It is an admirable picture of human weakness, of which the first hint is given, when Agamemnon in almost his first speech says:

Charmé de mon pouvoir et plein de ma grandeur.

Behind his glamour as king of kings and leader of a great army we see an ordinary commonplace mortal, moved by ambition of no lofty kind and lacking the strength of will to carry through what he proposes. He might be a modern monarch or landowner seeking to preserve his kingdom or his acres by the sacrifice of his daughter to a loveless marriage. The Greek legend which Racine took as his theme pointed to a nobler conflict in Agamemnon's soul, and the theme perhaps is not very well suited to Racine's realistic conception of tragedy, to his desire to paint men as they are. But in spite of this initial difficulty he has produced a very fine play.

Lemaître gives as his reason for liking *Mithridate* and *Iphigénie* less than some of Racine's other tragedies that they are the two in which, consciously or otherwise, he has most closely conformed to the manners and taste of his age. They bear more than the others the stamp of Versailles and the court of Louis XIV. He calls *Iphigénie* the "royal tragedy". But the high rank of the characters in *Iphigénie* does not lessen their humanity. Clytemnestre tells Agamemnon what she thinks of his conduct and character with a blunt freedom that any wife might use. Both *Mithridate* and *Iphigénie* were highly successful when produced—partly perhaps because they were the favourites of Louis XIV. With Mlle de Champmeslé in the part of Iphigénie, and Baron, who had joined the Hôtel de Bourgogne after Molière's death, in that of Achille, *Iphigénie* had a long run. And it remained on the programme for many years. Adrienne Lecouvreur during the thirteen years of her too short career acted in all Racine's tragedies, but most often in *Iphigénie*.

For *Phèdre*, which was produced on January 1, 1667, Racine had recourse again to Greek legend and Euripides, supplementing the latter with Seneca. We may partly ascribe to this renewed draught of Greek inspiration the marked increase in the use of deeply poetical language, of which there are, as we have seen already, instances in *Iphigénie*. Four speeches, that of Phèdre in the third scene of the first act, that of Hippolyte in the second scene of the second act, that of Phèdre again in the sixth scene of the fourth act, and the much-discussed narrative of Théramène in the last act, stand out as full of poetical beauty. Here are two examples from Hippolyte's speech:

> Dans le fond des forêts votre image me suit;
> La lumière du jour, les ombres de la nuit,
> Tout retrace à mes yeux les charmes que j'évite;
> Tout vous livre à l'envi le rebelle Hippolyte.

and

> Mes seuls gémissements font retentir les bois,
> Et mes coursiers oisifs ont oublié ma voix.

In the opening scene and elsewhere proper names which combine associations of place with those of legend are happily used to stir the imagination in quite a Miltonic manner. They help to produce the atmosphere of legend and poetry in which Racine has bathed his story and so lifted it from the region of horror and fear to that of terror and pity. Théramène's

> J'ai demandé Thésée aux peuples de ces bords
> Où l'on voit l'Achéron se perdre chez les morts;
> J'ai visité l'Élide, et laissant le Ténare,
> Passé jusqu'à la mer qui vit tomber Icare.

is matched by Hippolyte's

> Les monstres étouffés, et les brigands punis,
> Procuste, Cercyon, et Sciron, et Sinnis,
> Et les os dispersés du géant d'Épidaure,
> Et la Crète fumant du sang du Minotaure.

In one important respect *Phèdre* presents a direct contrast to *Iphigénie*. In the latter play there are as many as six characters of more or less importance; in *Phèdre* there is only one, or rather the character of Phèdre overshadows all the others. They seem only to exist for the sake of throwing light on the working of her passion. But, except for Thésée, who, as Brunetière says, is the least successful of all Racine's rôles, they are sufficiently well delineated. Hippolyte makes a distinct appeal to our imagination. He is the true son of his Amazon mother, a handsome and graceful figure, now hunting in the forest, now driving his car at headlong speed by the sea-shore, now taming an unbroken colt. In contrast to his father, that prince of inconstant lovers, he has the reputation of being "an implacable enemy to love", but when the play opens, he has succumbed to its sway, and the poetical language in which he avows to Aricie his feeling for her (II, 2) is eloquent of its genuine intensity. The part, we may be almost sure, was created by Baron and in his hands it must have been imposing and attractive. The introduction of the love element has been criticised, notably by Fénelon, but, apart from the human interest which it adds to Hippolyte's character, it is of importance from its effect on Phèdre. Aricie has not much individuality, but she preserves in captivity the high spirit of her ancestors. She prefers the conquest of a heart as inaccessible as Hippolyte's to that of one "which is open to all the world", and in the scenes with Hippolyte (II, 2; V, 1) and Thésée (V, 3) she shews admirable dignity and self-control.

Œnone is almost a part of Phèdre; she is the embodiment of her evil thoughts, putting them into words before Phèdre can utter them. Nothing has any value for her in comparison with Phèdre's life:

> Votre vie est pour moi d'un prix à qui tout cède,

and to save her honour she will sacrifice everything, even virtue. In considering Phèdre herself one may start from

Racine

Brunetière's remark that she is "neither wholly pagan nor wholly Christian". This is true enough, but, put in this way, it is rather misleading, for there is much in her that is neither pagan nor Christian. Granddaughter of Zeus on one side and the Sun on the other, daughter of Minos and Pasiphae—of Minos the judge of Hell and Pasiphae that monstrous product of Greek legend—she has the awe and fear of her dread ancestry ever before her. She is also morbidly obsessed by the idea that Venus has specially marked her for her prey and that it is useless to struggle against her destiny. Yet she has struggled hard, for she has a sense of sin that is almost Christian. But, pagan or Christian, she is before all things a human being, a prey to the most tyrannous and the most relentless of human passions. In her despair she has been starving herself to death. When the play opens, she enters tottering on her nurse's arms and with her hand over her eyes drops exhausted on to a seat:

> N'allons point plus avant. Demeurons, chère Œnone.
> Je ne me soutiens plus; ma force m'abandonne.
> Mes yeux sont éblouis du jour que je revoi,
> Et mes genoux tremblants se dérobent sous moi.

It is an extraordinarily effective entry. No other character in Racine makes the same distinctly physical impression upon the reader and one which he retains throughout the play. It is interesting to compare the great scene that follows (1, 3) with the corresponding one in Euripides, from which it is imitated. The language of Euripides, of which the first part is written in lyrical measures, is more poetical throughout, but, as one would expect, his scene is far inferior in dramatic power and especially in the indication of dramatic action. In the next great scene (II, 5), in which after the report of Thésée's death Phèdre avows her love to Hippolyte, Racine leaves Euripides for Seneca, particularly in the speech beginning, "Oui, Prince, je languis, je brûle pour Thésée". In the third act, in which Racine still follows Seneca rather than Euripides, Phèdre, though she has been repulsed with horror

55

by Hippolyte, despairs more than ever of escaping from her "shameful yoke". She has "abandoned the empire of her senses", but in spite of her shame she still has hope and she appeals to her nurse to help her:

> Sers ma fureur, Œnone, et non point ma raison.

and then, when left to herself, she cries in her bitterness:

> O toi, qui vois la honte où je suis descendue,
> Implacable Vénus, suis-je assez confondue!
> Tu ne saurois plus loin pousser ta cruauté.
> Ton triomphe est parfait; tous tes traits ont porté.

Œnone returns with the news that Thésée is alive and has arrived at Trœzen. A terrible scene follows (III, 3). Divining her mistress's thoughts before they are spoken, and unaware of Hippolyte's determination to be silent, Œnone proposes that she shall forestall him by denouncing him to his father as the wrongdoer. Phèdre consents:

> Fais ce que tu voudras, je m'abandonne à toi.
> Dans le trouble où je suis, je ne puis rien pour moi.

But, when it is too late to stay Thésée's vengeance, she goes to him with an appeal to spare Hippolyte's life and learns for the first time of his love for Aricie. In a short and powerful soliloquy she gives expression to her jealousy:

> Hippolyte est sensible, et ne sent rien pour moi!
> Aricie a son cœur! Aricie a sa foi!

The scene which follows between Phèdre and Œnone is tremendous. Of Phèdre's three great speeches the first is a picture of the happy lovers drawn by jealousy:

> Dans le fond des fôrets alloient-ils se cacher?
>
> .   .   .   .   .
>
> Tous les jours se levoient clairs et sereins pour eux!

The second is a cry of wild despair and dreadful foreboding:

> Misérable! et je vis? et je soutiens la vue
> De ce sacré soleil dont je suis descendue?

J'ai pour aïeul le père et le maître des Dieux;
Le ciel, tout l'univers est plein de mes aïeux:
Où me cacher? Fuyons dans la nuit infernale.
Mais que dis-je? mon père y tient l'urne fatale;
Le sort, dit-on, l'a mise en ses sévères mains:
Minos juge aux enfers tous les pâles humains.
Ah! combien frémira son ombre épouvantée,
Lorsqu'il verra sa fille à ses yeux présentée,
Contrainte d'avouer tant de forfaits divers,
Et des crimes peut-être inconnus aux enfers!

The third is a terrible outburst of imprecation against
Œnone. Each speech has its own distinctive character, and
each is a masterpiece. Between them they present an unforgettable picture of human nature in its direst straits, a
picture which shews profound knowledge of the human
heart combined with the vision of a great poet. And the
wonder is that, as Phèdre's passion drags her lower and
lower from one wickedness to another, our pity for her in-
creases. We can even forgive her her cruel treatment of
Œnone. For it is a mistake to regard Œnone as just a temp-
tress who is without moral sense. Though the proposal to
accuse Hippolyte comes from her, it is prompted by her
mistress's outburst of hate and it is the tribute of a boundless
devotion. Yet Phèdre's act is true to human nature; it is the
act of a woman whom shame and remorse have made furious
beyond all reason. Her

Malheureuse! Voilà comme tu m'as perdue,

is the pendant of Hermione's

Tais-toi, perfide,
Et n'impute qu'à toi ta lâche parricide.

—There is nothing left to her but to confess and die.

But the very fact that she confesses distinguishes her from
the Phaedra of Euripides, whose accusation of Hippolytus in
writing is found in her hand after she had hanged herself—a
deliberate attempt to give it a greater semblance of truth.

57

The confession in itself is a sign of Phèdre's consciousness of sin and of the beginnings, at any rate, of penitence. It is a vaguely Christian act, but there is nothing especially Jansenist about it. The view of some critics, perhaps of most, and notably of Lemaître, that the play is intended to be an illustration of the Port-Royal dogma that to do good without grace is impossible for the human will and that Phèdre in the words of Chateaubriand is "la chrétienne réprouvée", seems to me untenable. I prefer the contrary view of M. Truc, whose understanding of Racine on this as on many points keeps pace with his admiration.

The rôle of Phèdre is the Mecca of French actresses. To attempt it is their greatest ambition, to succeed in it is their greatest glory. The creatress of the part, Mlle Champmeslé, died in 1698. Her successor was Mlle Duclos, whose majestic appearance and superb voice were not at the service of a high intelligence, but who for twenty years held her audience. From 1717 to 1730 the great classical rôles were filled, as we have seen, by Adrienne Lecouvreur, but she does not appear to have specially identified herself with Phèdre. Three years after her early death, that is in 1733, Mlle Dumesnil, a brilliant but unequal actress who trusted more to inspiration than to study, made her *début*. Gray saw her as Phèdre in 1739 and in a letter to Ashton says that "she affected me so strongly that I can't help prattling about her even to you, that do not care two Pence". His friend, Horace Walpole, after seeing Mrs Siddons in one of her great parts in 1782, the year of her re-engagement at Drury Lane, writes that he might have thought her marvellous if he had not remembered the Dumesnil. Her rival, Mlle Clairon, made her *début* at the Comédie Française in 1743 and insisted on making it with Phèdre. Her success completely justified her audacity. In her memoirs she has left some interesting notes on the part. She says with much truth that an actress has only to follow Racine's indications—that is, of course, if she has the necessary powers of expression—and that she must not attempt to

improve on them. She adds that she always found Phèdre's
last speech to Hippolyte in the fifth scene of the second act
very difficult to interpret, and that her rendering of it never
did justice either to the author or to her own ideal.

A hundred years later than Mlle Clairon, on January 21,
1843, Rachel made her first appearance in the part, but it was
not her *début*, for she had begun her career in the summer of
1838, when she was only seventeen, and since then had played
Hermione, Ériphile, Monime, and Roxane. Charlotte Brontë
saw her as Phèdre in London in 1851 and has recorded her
impressions in two letters and also in *Villette*. She was at
once thrilled and perturbed by "the tremendous force with
which she expressed the very worst passions". She made her
"shudder to the marrow of her bones". The Phèdre of the
next generation was Sarah Bernhardt, and to her splendid
powers Lytton Strachey and Mr Maurice Baring have
eloquently testified. It is no doubt due to the tradition of all
these great actresses that *Phèdre* has come to be regarded as
a one-part play. We have seen the same thing happen to
Hamlet, and with much less justification.

After *Phèdre* Racine, in the height of his powers, retired
from the stage. There has been considerable discussion as to
his reasons. Some have supposed that the malicious plot
which had caused an almost complete fiasco of the first
performances of *Phèdre* had thoroughly disgusted him. But
though, as we have seen, he was sensible and irritable beyond
the average artist, he must have been aware that this attack
of his enemies was too puerile to damage either his reputation
or his success. For my part I subscribe unreservedly to the
view of M. Truc that the decisive reason was his "conversion". Of the moral struggle that led up to it we know
nothing, but we may guess that his early religious training
under the strict discipline of Port-Royal and the sorrowful
reproaches which his aunt, Sister Agnes, sent him at the beginning of his dramatic career, so long forgotten, now came
back to his mind. And with these memories there must have

come a feeling of remorse for "the fifteen years of going astray (*égarement*)", the years which include his *liaisons* with Mlle Du Parc and Mlle de Champmeslé. But the actual "conversion" was probably sudden, like those of Conti and Mme de Longueville and other well-known persons of the seventeenth century. If it was sudden, it was thorough, for his first idea was to become a Carthusian monk. But he was dissuaded by his confessor, who advised him to marry instead. He followed his advice, and the marriage took place on June 1, 1677, exactly seventeen months after the production of *Phèdre*.

As a husband and father he led an exemplary life and he wrote no more for the theatre. But at Mme de Maintenon's request he produced in 1689 a biblical play to be acted by the pupils of Saint-Cyr. With his usual skill and tact he extracted out of the book of *Esther*, which, it is generally agreed, has less in it of the spirit of the Gospel than any other book in the Bible, a moving and attractive religious drama—and this, without any alteration of the circumstances of the narrative, by the simple process of embellishing the characters of Assuérus (Xerxes), Mardochée, and Esther and by omitting all mention of the permission given to the Jews to massacre their enemies, especially of Esther's bloodthirsty petition to grant them an additional day. The story in the Bible reads like an Arabian Night. In Racine's play it still reads like an Arabian Night, but like one written by a devout Christian. There is no real attempt at characterisation, but there are touches of character in the scene (III, 1) between Aman and his wife, especially in her last speech beginning,

> Seigneur, nous sommes seuls. Que sert de se flatter?
> Ce zèle que pour lui vous fîtes éclater,
> Ce soin d'immoler tout à son pouvoir suprême,
> Entre nous, avoient-ils d'autre objet que vous-même?
> Et sans chercher plus loin, tous ces Juifs désolés,
> N'est-ce pas à vous seul que vous les immolez?

This is the old Racine probing into human nature.

Racine

Even a foreigner can appreciate the beauty of the style and the music of the verse. There are no striking passages of great poetry such as there are in *Phèdre*, but the verse flows on like a limpid stream, making music as it flows. Specially famous is Esther's prayer, which forms the fourth scene of the first act. The choruses too demand a word of notice. Mme de Maintenon had asked that singing should be combined with the dialogue, and this gave Racine the opportunity of putting into execution a design which he had often had in his head, namely of linking the chorus with the action as in Greek tragedy. Though the choruses shew little real lyrical power, they are a very skilful and agreeable arrangement of passages from the Psalms and the Prophets and serve perfectly well as words for music.

Athalie, which after some difficulties was produced in January 1691, is a great religious drama. Sarcey, in his over-insistence on the universal character of Racine's tragedies, on their freedom from limitations of date and place and social rank, was wrong when he saw in *Athalie* only the drama of a successful conspiracy against a usurper, organised and led by an ambitious priest. No—*Athalie* is much more than this. It is the triumph of true religion over false, and the protagonist, as Sainte-Beuve pointed out in his *Port-Royal* and as M. Truc has eloquently maintained in his recent book on Racine, is not Joad but God. The first chorus and the last are given wholly to the praise of God:

> Tout l'univers est plein de sa magnificence:
> Qu'on l'adore ce Dieu, qu'on l'invoque à jamais!
> Son empire a des temps précédé la naissance;
> Chantons, publions ses bienfaits.

"C'est Dieu pour qui vous combattez" sing the chorus just before the combat, and Athalie, when she recognises her defeat, cries out "Dieu des Juifs, tu l'emportes!" and

> Impitoyable Dieu, toi seul as tout conduit.

Joad is far from being the ambitious priest that Sarcey would

61

make him, plotting for the restoration of Joas in order that
he might exercise autocratic power in the boy's name, just as
Mazarin did in the name of Louis XIV. He is confident in
his cause and he inspires others with the same confidence because he believes that his cause is God's. Almost his first
words are

> Je crains Dieu, cher Abner, et n'ai point d'autre crainte.

He is the dominating figure throughout the first act. The first
scene, with Abner, gives us an idea of his skill in influencing
others. Abner is described as "one of the principal officers
of the kings of Judah", but we learn from Joad that he had
been commander-in-chief. He has the characteristics of a
soldier; he is loyal to Athalie, usurper though she is, but his
loyalty is complicated by his devotion to the true religion, and
he only recognises Athalie because he believes that the royal
line is extinct. His intelligence is limited and he has no
initiative. Joad's handling of him is masterly. He begins
by paying him perfectly sincere compliments on his loyalty
and good service, but he goes on to point out that silent dis-
approval of the Baal-worshipping usurper is not enough. The
God of Israel calls on him to take action and break off all
compromise with impiety. And when Abner hazards the supposition that "some drop of royal blood might have escaped
Athalie's fury", Joad elicits from him a cry of joy that if this
were true he would recognise his king with ardour. The
next scene opens with Joad's announcement to Josabeth that
the crisis is reached:

> Les temps sont accomplis, Princesse: il faut parler.

Josabeth makes an admirable compliment to her husband
Joad. She is devoted to her nephew Joas, whom she loves
equally with her own children. But her love makes her
fearful for him, and she is by nature timid as well as tender.
The result is a character of much charm. There is charm
too in Joad's treatment of her. He never forgets that
she is of royal birth, but he expects from her a wife's

Racine

obedience and he does not hesitate to rebuke her when in her fear for Joas she seems to question his decision—"Quoi! déjà votre foi s'affoiblit?" But he has complete confidence in her and he carefully unfolds his plans to her and gives his reasons for his belief in success, the chief reason being that God is on their side:

> Et comptez-vous pour rien Dieu, qui combat pour nous?

When confronted with Athalie's emissary, Mathan, she meets him with courage and discretion.

It will have been observed that Racine's dramas are generally constructed on a more or less symmetrical plan. So in *Athalie*, while Joad is the principal figure in the first act, the second is dominated by Athalie. We have learnt a good deal about her already. She is haughty—"la superbe Athalie"— cruel, bloodthirsty, avaricious. But her first words in the play (II, 3) shew that she is not the woman she was. She has begun to weaken:

> Non, je ne puis: tu vois mon trouble et ma foiblesse.
> Va, fais dire à Mathan qu'il vienne, qu'il se presse;
> Heureuse si je puis trouver par son secours
> Cette paix que je cherche, et qui me fuit toujours!

She has been troubled by a dream, which she relates to Abner, whom she flatters by praising his loyalty to his God and his king, and to Mathan, the apostate priest of Baal. Either the dream itself or the trouble that it causes her is evidently the result partly of remorse for the wholesale massacre of her children and partly of fear that the massacre has not been complete. During her interrogation of Joas (II, 7) she is moved by his childish grace and the gentleness of his voice—"Je serais sensible à la pitié?" But she soon returns to her imperious tone and she roughly reproaches Josabeth for having brought the boy up in horror of her. The speech in which she boasts of her crimes is a superb outburst of savage hatred, and she leaves the temple with a final sneer at Josabeth's God and the promised offspring of David. Faguet compares her with

63

Agrippine, but except that they are both ambitious and unscrupulous there is little likeness between them. Agrippine
only cares for the semblance of station and power, but
Athalie justly claims that for six years she has ruled her kingdom well, that she has made it respected by its neighbours
and rivals, and that it enjoys a profound peace. In her
courage, her ability, and her ruthlessness she resembles Lady
Macbeth. She resembles her also in her remorse.

> Ce n'est plus cette reine éclairée, intrépide,
> Élevée au-dessus de son sexe timide,
> Qui d'abord accabloit ses ennemis surpris,
> Et d'un instant perdu connaissoit tout le prix.
> La peur d'un vain remords trouble cette grande ame;
> Elle flotte, elle hésite; en un mot, elle est femme.

This is what Mathan says of her to his confidant Nabal, and
almost the same words might have been used of Lady Macbeth. Mathan is one of the few characters in Racine who
have not a single good or even attractive quality. His
apostasy is due solely to past rivalry with Joad, arising out of
some unimportant detail of ritual. He is ambitious, self-
seeking, unscrupulous, unforgiving, but one loathes him
most for the cunning flattery and subservience by which he
has wormed himself into Athalie's favour. He only appears
in the third act, his last appearance being in a short scene with
Joad (III, 5) before whose menacing command,

> Sors donc de devant moi, monstre d'impiété.

he leaves the temple stammering with confusion.

We must now return to Joad, who from here onwards
dominates the play. He gives orders to the commanders of
his Levite army with the authority of a born leader and the
decisive brevity of a commander-in-chief. He is at once a
Chatham and a Wellington. The fourth act is occupied with
his final preparations for resisting Athalie's impending attempt to carry off Joas. Recognising that the moment has
come for bold action, he first reveals with due solemnity the

secret of his birth to the mysterious child and then he presents him to the five leaders of the Levites and commends him to their care in an impassioned speech, which shews that to his other gifts he unites that of a great orator. Joas fits admirably the part that he has to play. Already in the scene with Athalie (II, 7) he has shewn courage and readiness in answering her questions, and he now behaves with modesty and dignity in his new position, not forgetting his affection for his mother and his playmate, Zacharie, the son of Joad and Josabeth.

The final act opens with a short scene between the two children, Zacharie and his sister, and then Abner appears with an ultimatum from Athalie (V, 2). Joad here shews wonderful astuteness. Now is the moment to win over Abner. But Joad does not take the initiative by revealing to him the secret. He leaves it to Abner to declare of his own free will that he will join in the defence against any attack by force. He has thus become "a conspirator" as Faguet calls him "in spite of himself". Joad, now feeling secure of Abner's help, prepares a trap for Athalie.—There is no mention of this in the Bible.—Let her come to the temple, attended only by a small escort, and he will admit her. He has just time to make his final preparations, to give orders to his commanders, to conceal the priests and Levites from view, and to hide Joas behind a curtain, when Athalie appears. She has recovered all her insolent pride. "Te voilà, séducteur", is her salutation. Joad says little, but acts:

> Soldats du Dieu vivant, défendez votre roi.

The curtain is drawn back and Joas is discovered on a throne. Then the stage opens at the back and the interior of the temple is disclosed with armed Levites entering from all sides. Athalie recognises that she is defeated and that death awaits her. But she does not lose courage; her last words are an imprecation and a cry for vengeance.

This fifth scene shews a great stride forward in the direction of that spectacular effect which was foreshadowed, as we saw, in *Iphigénie*. First, note the crowded stage—Athalie and her escort, Joad, Josabeth, and, when the curtain has been drawn aside, Joas, his nurse, Zacharie, Salomith, Azarias and the Levites. Next note the continual movement and the great dramatic moments—the entry of Athalie with her menacing gesture, the sudden discovery of the impressively staged group behind the curtain, the ringing tones of Joad answered by the "Perfide!" of Athalie, her appeal to her guards and the counter-appeal of Joad, the opening out of the temple and the pouring in of the armed Levites, Athalie's despair, her call to Abner:

> Laisse là ton Dieu, traître,
> Et venge-moi.
> ABNER.   Sur qui? Sur Joas! sur mon maître!

The most ardent romanticist could not desire a more spectacular or a more thrilling effect.

Racine has made the chorus a really integral part of the play, bringing it on and taking it off the stage as the action requires. From the seventh scene of the third act onwards, after the gates of the temple have been closed, it remains on the stage continuously. As in Æschylus and Sophocles, but not in Euripides, the words of the chorus bear on the action of the play. At the end of the first act the subject is the praise of God; at the end of the second the mysterious and courageous child, who has just been questioned by Athalie. After the third act, they sing in anticipation of the conflict. We hear two voices, one of fear, the other of hope, and then a third joins in, bidding them trust in God. After the fourth act they express trepidation and uncertainty as to the result. But when the conflict is over and God has avenged the innocent, the last word is not with the chorus, but with Joad.

Racine lived for eight years after the production of *Athalie*, greatly attached to his home and family and with an assured footing at the court. He died on April 21, 1699. Saint-Simon's epitaph cannot be bettered:

Personne n'avait plus de fond d'esprit, ni plus agréablement tourné; rien du poète dans son commerce, et tout de l'honnête homme, de l'homme modeste, et sur la fin, de l'homme de bien.

Sarcey, as we have seen, regarded Joad as an ambitious priest organising a conspiracy in his own interests, and the trap which he set for Athalie has been roundly condemned. Such judgments, whether we agree with them or not, prove at any rate that Joad is not an idealised hero "sprung from the imagination", but a real "man portrayed after nature". He has not the impassive superiority that irritates us in Nicomède, the hero of Corneille's political play. He has a warm heart as well as a cool head, and he can be moved to anger as well as to tenderness. So too with Monime and Iphigénie. Of high courage and a strong sense of duty, they face death rather than live ignobly. But they are not Cornélies or Pulchéries. They are heroines, if you like, but they are true to nature. Neither they, nor the equally noble but less important Junie, nor the resolute and magnanimous Xipharès. and Hippolyte, are exceptions to Racine's realism in the treatment of character.

He is rightly acclaimed as a great psychologist, by which is meant, not that he was a scientific student of the human soul, but that he was a close, subtle, and penetrating observer of it. He does not collect data in order to present them in an orderly form and come to a reasoned conclusion about them; but as the result of observation and with the help of his creative imagination he gives us pictures of souls in action. Sometimes it is the picture of a single passion, sometimes of a whole character. In *Andromaque* and *Phèdre* he deals chiefly with passion; in *Britannicus* and *Athalie* chiefly with character. In the other tragedies passion and character are equally represented. Mithridate and Eriphile are studies of jealousy, but they are also studies of character. Mithridate is at once an Oriental despot, the upholder of his country's liberty against Rome, and a jealous elderly lover; Ériphile is a lonely, envious, hysterical girl as well as the victim of an unhappy passion.

But a first-rate psychologist like Racine cannot of course portray a passion without giving some indication of the character behind it. For upon character as well as upon circumstances the issue of the passion depends. Hermione suffers as much from wounded pride and vanity—"spretae iniuria formae"—as from unrequited love. She is vain, hard, and undisciplined. She has a shallow nature. Roxane is a typical product of an Oriental harem, sensuous, cruel, and intoxicated by her sudden rise to autocratic power. But she is not wholly animal, for there is a touch of real love in her passion. Phèdre's passion has absorbed her whole character, till it drives her headlong from one crime to another. Yet she preserves a certain individuality. She is held back, first by a sense of sin and then by remorse, till the feelings of awe and horror inspired by her dread ancestry terrify her into further crime.

Racine does not depict love only as a furious and crime-provoking passion. He gives us five pairs of youthful lovers, who are innocent and self-controlled, but whose love is "strong as death". In fact all, except Aricie and Junie, who becomes a Vestal Virgin, face death rather than be untrue to love, and four of them pay for it with their lives. Equally true are Titus and Bérénice, lovers of maturer age and longer probation, but they stand on a different footing, for their fate is in their own hands and their conflict is not with the machinations of cruel and jealous foes, but with duty.

It is in *Britannicus* and *Athalie* that Racine's power of portraying character is most fully displayed. Néron and Agrippine, Joad and Athalie are among his greatest creations. Néron is especially remarkable. In most plays, even in those in which the action is spread over a long period, the characters are the same at the end as they are at the beginning. They may reveal themselves as the play proceeds, but they can hardly be said to develop. But Néron within a few short hours is transformed from a timid love-sick boy into a brutal and callous criminal. On the other hand, Agrippine, Athalie, and Joad are what are sometimes called static characters, but Racine has caught them, so to speak, at the psychological moment, that is to say at the moment when the latent conflict between Agrippine and Néron in the one play and between Athalie and Joad in the other is on the point of becoming open warfare. This advent of the crisis has the effect of bringing out the strength in Joad's character and the weakness in Agrippine's and Athalie's, both of whom meet with defeat in a combat to which they are no longer equal.

These four great characters are remarkable both for the total impression that they make on us—and be it remembered that Athalie only appears in seven scenes, of which three are very short—and for the subtle and careful observation of their individual characteristics. Less complex, less closely studied, but admirable in their almost instant appeal, are Abner, the typical soldier, Mathan, the typical renegade, and above all Acomat with his bland demeanour and his cool calculating devotion to his own interests. Narcisse and Burrhus have been highly praised, but it seems to me that Narcisse is rather a personification of evil than real flesh and blood, and that Burrhus is wanting in consistency and not particularly impressive. Nor, as I have already pointed out, has Racine been altogether successful with Mithridate. On the other hand he has succeeded with Agamemnon because he has made no attempt to portray him as a great king or a great commander, but wholly as a father, torn between his love for his daughter and his rather petty and self-regarding ambition. He lacks indeed the unifying touch of imagination, but in no character has Racine shewn greater subtlety in probing the motives, conscious and unconscious, that prompt a man to action.

He is also a first-rate example of Racine's skill in portraying hesitations and fluctuations between two possible courses of action. Conflict is the making of drama, but, whereas in most of Corneille's plays, especially in his later ones, the conflict is between two opposing wills, in Racine, more often than not, it is within the breast of a single individual. Instances in addition to Agamemnon are Néron, Roxane, Mithridate, and even Athalie, though in all of them the spirit of evil prevails after but a feeble resistance. In Racine's first great play the internal conflict is not so much between evil and good as between two appeals to self-interest. Each of the characters knows what he or she wants; Oreste wants Hermione, Hermione wants Pyrrhus, Pyrrhus wants Andromaque, and Andromaque wants at once to be faithful to her husband's memory and to secure the safety of her son. But all except Andromaque are tossed to and fro by passion and self-interest. It is partly by contrast with these undisciplined self-seekers that Andromaque stands forth as a great character. Like Monime and Iphigénie she rises to greatness by reason of her constancy and courage in cruelly adverse circumstances, and in her unswerving fidelity to her high ideals.

But the tragedy in which Racine most excels in portraying the inner conflict of souls is *Bérénice*. It is not only the motive-power of the drama, but it is the whole drama. In his first appearance on the stage (II, I) Titus makes up his mind to dismiss Bérénice, and the rest of the play consists in his unmaking it and making it up again, and in the corresponding conflict in the breast of Bérénice. Whatever human weakness their indecision reveals, it is wholly free from self-interest, and we follow their hesitation between duty and true love with whole-hearted sympathy. The beauty of the scenes to which it gives rise is a noble testimony to Racine's power of giving dramatic life to the movements of the soul.

To say that Racine is a great dramatist is a truism. Had he not been one, he would not have remained a living force on the stage. But it may be worth while to point out some of the qualities which give him this greatness. In the first place, his plays are extraordinarily well constructed. I have mentioned Scribe's admiration for *Andromaque* and I added that the only criticism that could be made on its structure was that it conforms rather too closely to its cleverly devised plan. *Britannicus* and *Athalie* are on broader lines, but with a similar feeling for symmetry. In each play the two protagonists dominate the first and second act respectively; in *Britannicus* Agrippine dominates the first act and Néron the second; in *Athalie* Joad the first act and Athalie the second. In *Phèdre* the honours of the first act are divided between Hippolyte and Phèdre, with Œnone as a connecting link between them. The report of Thésée's death and his subsequent reappearance are severely condemned by Brunetière as external expedients (*moyens extérieurs*), from which French tragedy from the *Cid* to *Andromaque* had gradually freed itself. How different, he says, from *Andromaque* and *Bérénice* and *Iphigénie*, in which everything comes from the characters themselves, and nothing from without! His objection seems to me pedantic, for Racine's theme is the presentation in a dramatic form of Phèdre's passion, and for this both the report and its contradiction are of the greatest importance. Moreover they arise naturally out of the situation. But Brunetière is indignant at the high rank that is usually accorded to *Phèdre*. Though Racine himself thought it his best play, Brunetière, with his love of tracing the growth and decline of *genres littéraires*, while fully appreciating its beauties of detail, sees in it the beginning of the decline of French tragedy. A single character, love as the sole theme, romanticism, lyricism, descriptive passages—what are these, he asks, but signs that French tragedy is on its way to being transformed into opera?

The expedient of a false report of death had already been employed by Racine in *Mithridate*. It serves to reveal the characters and intentions of Xipharès and Pharnace and it prompts Monime to hint delicately that Xipharès is not indifferent to her. But as a whole *Mithridate* is the least successfully constructed of Racine's tragedies. The first act hangs fire, and throughout the play there are too many long speeches. The last two acts, however, especially the last, are very effective. *Iphigénie*, on the other hand, is a masterpiece of construction from beginning to end. From the first scene, in which Agamemnon confides to Arcas the cruel dilemma in which he has been placed, to the last, in which it is solved, the central theme is kept steadily before us. The love of Achille and Iphigénie and the jealous passion of Ériphile, important though they are for the development of the play, are not allowed to become too prominent. All the characters, including Ulysse, contribute to the working out of the solution, and it is through the characters alone, and not with the help of any outside expedient, that the *dénouement* is reached.

Whether the conception of Ériphile as a substitute for Euripides's miraculous doe commends itself to us or not, her death by her own hand arises naturally out of the drama. And it may be said generally of Racine's *dénouements* that they are always natural and always definite. They are not mechanical, neither do they leave the characters, so to speak, in the air. Particularly fine is the *dénouement* of Athalie, for it is at once dramatic and spectacular.

Racine begins his plays as skilfully as he ends them. The first scene invariably consists of a dialogue between one of the principal characters and a confidant—in *Athalie* Abner takes the place of a confidant—which serves not only to explain the situation but to arouse our interest so that we look forward with keen anticipation to the unfolding of the drama. These "expositions" are always admirable, but the finest of all is that of *Bajazet*, in which Acomat and his confidant, Osman, in the course of a natural conversation tell the complicated story of an Oriental intrigue with perfect clarity. It is in Vinet's words "un modèle achevé d'exposition dramatique".

Racine had in full measure that feeling for movement

which is the mark of a true dramatist. But his dramas move, not, like Corneille's, in a straight line of continuous progress, but in irregular zigzags, determined by the fluctuating emotions and intentions of his characters. Our interest never flags, but becomes more and more intense with each act and each scene. Racine makes considerable use—more than Corneille—of that favourite but tiresome character of French classical tragedy, the confidant. In *Andromaque*, *Bérénice* and *Phèdre* all the principal characters have a confidant apiece. The confidant is usually a dummy, and if he or she ventures to give advice it is seldom or never followed. This is noticeably the case in *Andromaque*. Sometimes the confidant has a certain individuality, as for instance Pylade, the bosom friend of Oreste, who sacrifices his prudence to his friendship, Théramène, the governor of Hippolyte, and Œnone. In *Britannicus* and *Athalie*, the dramas of character, there is only one confidant, the characters being chiefly revealed by their reaction on one another.

Another method of laying bare the workings of the soul, and one equally out of favour at the present day, is that of soliloquy. But soliloquy is a perfectly justifiable stage convention, and Racine often uses it with magnificent effect, generally for the purpose of exposing the irresolution of the speaker as he is swayed from one motive to another. Perhaps the finest of all the soliloquies of this sort is that of Mithridate (IV, 5), which, as M. Truc says, is "no longer an analysis, but the photograph of a soul"—"Et c'est là tout Racine". Equally fine as a picture of irresolution and conflicting motives, but less animated by strong passion, is Agamemnon's soliloquy in *Iphigénie* (IV, 8), the first words of which, "Que vais-je faire", recall Hermione's famous soliloquy:

Où suis-je? Qu'ai-je fait? Que dois-je faire encore?

in which tossed between love and hate she runs through the whole gamut of the primitive emotions. Of rather a different character are the two soliloquies of Roxane (*Bajazet*, III, 7 and IV, 4) and that of Mithridate (III, 4), in which they make up their minds to a certain course of action, and that of Phèdre (IV, 5) when she learns that Hippolyte is in love with Aricie. No doubt Racine learnt much from Corneille, who was a master of dramatic construction, and his own strict adherence to the "rules", which makes for concentration, must have made his task easier. But he had an innate gift for form and order and perfect workmanship.

One is so accustomed to regard Racine's style as a model of correctness that one is surprised to learn that in his own day and throughout the eighteenth century he was either criticised or applauded as an innovator. "Novelty" was one of the faults with which he was charged by Subligny in *La folle querelle*. In 1738 the Abbé d'Olivet, though he regarded him as being with Boileau "at the head of our classical authors", criticised minutely his grammar and his syntax. On the other hand La Motte and La Harpe, especially the latter, praised him unreservedly for his boldness in adding to the resources of the language, and Louis Racine, the poet's son, after quoting La Motte, writes as follows:

> Voilà donc un écrivain qui, sans jamais hasarder un mot nouveau, ni un mot qui ne soit plus en usage, invente pour ainsi dire une langue par des alliances de mots, que dans les endroits surtout où il fait parler les passions dans toute leur vivacité, il sait unir si habilement, que le temps ayant confirmé ces alliances qui étonnèrent d'abord, nous ne nous apercevons plus aujourd'hui de la hardiesse de celui qui les risqua.

"Alliances de mots qui étonnèrent d'abord." These were sometimes of an adjective with a substantive, as

> N'en attendez jamais qu'une paix sanguinaire,

sometimes of a substantive with a verb, as

> Quel est ce glaive enfin qui marche devant eux?

This was one of the bold novelties introduced by Racine. Others were the use of words in an unusual though legitimate sense, the violation of the accepted rules of grammar and syntax, and the unexpected use of familiar words and phrases. But all these methods were employed with consummate tact and judgment. He knew the French language as well as any man, but he realised that the spirit was more important than the letter and that occasionally he could interpret his meaning—or rather the meaning of his characters —more faithfully by breaking the rules than by observing them. "The real novelty of his style", rightly says M. Truc, "is in his psychology." He is equally a psychologist in his use of imagery. In *Alexandre le Grand*, having thrown off the influence of Corneille and developed a style of his own, he uses imagery more frequently and of a more ornamental character than in his later plays. In *Andromaque* he uses it much more sparingly but with far greater subtlety. It now helps to bring out the thought, the mood, and even the character of the speaker. In the admirable study which precedes M. Marty-Laveaux's *Lexique* (*Œuvres*, VIII) M. Mesnard declares that the four principal characters of *Andromaque* are differentiated by the style of their speeches, and though a foreigner may not be able to detect the differences very readily, he can at any rate recognise that in a general way this is true. In *Britannicus* Racine's progress in the knowledge of human nature is reflected in the greater firmness, precision, and pregnancy of his diction. We notice this in the very first scene, in which not only is the situation explained with equal brevity and clarity, but Agrippine and even the absent Néron already become living figures. Yet there are very few images, not more than half a dozen in 128 lines, the most arresting being Agrippine's

> Je m'assure un port dans la tempête.
> Néron m'échappera, si ce frein ne l'arrête.

In *Bérénice* the style is even less imaginative, and in Sainte-Beuve's words may be said to "raser la prose". Yet it is extremely beautiful, and its very simplicity expresses far better than a more ornate style could do the absolute sincerity and the profound passion of all three characters. Shakespeare, it will be remembered, in moments of intense emotion is absolutely simple. The heightening of the poetic diction here and there in *Iphigénie* may be due to the influence of Greece and Euripides, but in *Phèdre*, where in whole speeches, as for instance in Hippolyte's first long speech, the style becomes unusually concrete and full of imagery, there is surely another reason at work. Is it not that Racine in order to express with the utmost intensity the dark doom-laden passion of Phèdre, and, in contrast with it, the manly purity of Hippolyte, has here drawn more largely upon the resources of the poetic imagination? *Esther* and *Athalie*, with their biblical inspiration, demanded a different style. *Esther* excels in the tranquil and pellucid flow of its language and the entrancing music of its verse. *Athalie* resembles *Britannicus* and even surpasses it in concentrated vigour and imaginative pregnancy. A single line, already quoted,

Je crains Dieu, cher Abner, et n'ai point d'autre crainte.

which some critics acclaim as the finest line Racine ever wrote, gives the key-note of a whole character, and another single line,

Et du temple déjà l'aube blanchit le faîte,

calls up a picture that no painter could rival.

This power of compressing a world of meaning in a "lonely word" is all the more wonderful when one considers the smallness of Racine's vocabulary, the result of that purification of the French language which had been going on since the beginning of the century under the influence of Malherbe, Vaugelas, and the Hôtel de Rambouillet, and which had caused Fénelon to say, "On a appauvri, desséché et gêné notre langue". This carefully pruned vocabulary compelled Racine not only to use words, as we have seen, in unusual meanings and collocations, but to choose the best words, that is to say, the words best fitted to stimulate the imaginative vision or to express delicate shades of thought or emotion.

I have already paid a tribute in my brief mention of *Esther* to the music of Racine's verse. Its high quality is recognised by all Frenchmen, and even a foreigner can appreciate it. Of the values of vowel and consonantal sounds and of the art of interlacing words of varying lengths Racine knew all that there was to know. Nor does he conform slavishly to the tyranny of the classical Alexandrine. When occasion requires, he varies its monotony either by shifting the place of the caesura, or by the use of *enjambement* or the overflow of one line into another. But he does this not merely from a desire for variety or from any motive of virtuosity, but solely because he wishes to heighten or intensify the dramatic or psychological situation.

In the house of poetry there are many mansions, and Racine has an assured place in it as a consummate master of language and metre. It is well to remember this, because some English critics, accustomed to the wealth of metaphor and simile in the plays of Shakespeare and other Elizabethans, have greatly undervalued, if they have not altogether questioned, the poetical side of Racine's art. Some of his plays have certainly more poetry in them than others. In *Iphigénie* and *Phèdre* the whole conception and atmosphere is markedly more poetical, and as a result their style is more imaginative. Most of the passages and single lines that lovers of Racine quote as instances of his poetic endowment come from *Phèdre* or *Iphigénie*. But if Racine was a poet, he was first and foremost a dramatist and psychologist. The making of his play and the portrayal with absolute fidelity of passion and character were for him paramount, and to these tasks his poetic art was unreservedly dedicated.

II

Marivaux

Marivaux's comedies were not greatly in favour with contemporary critics and some of them were badly received. During the last twenty-three years of his life he produced very little, and his death passed almost unnoticed, even by literary journals. It is true that D'Alembert, the Secretary of the Académie Française, favoured him with one of his longest *éloges*—written about ten years after his death—but he apologises for its length, in comparison with that of Boileau, Massillon, Bossuet, and several other Academicians "greatly superior to Marivaux", on the ground of the great number of his works and the many various traits of his character. He does scant justice to his comedies, which he regards as inferior to his novels. Forty years later, Mlle Mars restored some of them to the repertory and continued to act in them till her retirement in 1841. Indeed, she chose the part of Silvia in *Le Jeu de l'Amour et du Hasard* for her farewell performance, and when she reappeared (as actresses are wont to do) a fortnight later, it was in the part of Araminte.

But though some of Marivaux's comedies found favour with the public, critics still ignored him or treated him with contempt. But in 1854 the tide turned. In that year Sainte-Beuve devoted two *causeries* to him, praising his comedies not only for their delicacy and ingenuity but for their originality and creative power, and pronouncing as his considered verdict that he would live and leave more than a name. Théophile Gautier in his *Histoire de l'art dramatique en France depuis vingt-cinq ans*, discussing the comedies at greater length, was more whole-hearted in his admiration. It was natural that these two men, who, having been fervent Romanticists in their youth, had now become the leaders of the reaction towards Realism, should give a sympathetic welcome to Marivaux's careful and accurate observation of ordinary social life.

At any rate, Marivaux's restoration to favour had begun, and it was lasting, if not complete. Sarcey, writing in 1880, says that during his career of twenty years or more as a dramatic critic he had watched Marivaux's reputation steadily growing. In the same year the Académie Française announced his *éloge* as the subject for the prize of eloquence. The prize was won by M. de Lescure, who published his successful essay as an introduction to a selection from Marivaux's comedies. The interest aroused by the competition was also responsible for Fleury's *Marivaux et le marivaudage* and Larroumet's *Marivaux, sa vie et ses œuvres*. The latter, which was first published in 1882, and of which there was a second edition in 1894, has come to be recognised as the authoritative work on Marivaux.

Marivaux's life was quiet and uneventful. He never joined the struggle for a place in the sun. He preferred to keep his dignity and to remain in the shade. Pierre Carlet de Chamblain de Marivaux—to give him his full name—belonged to a Norman family which had for some generations followed the profession of law and which, as was not uncommon with the *noblesse de robe*, had tacked more than one appendage to their patronymic of Carlet. Marivaux's father, however, had deserted the law for finance, and though Marivaux was born in Paris—the date of his birth is 1688—he spent his boyhood and youth at Riom and Limoges, where his father's duties had called him. After an education which included Latin but not Greek, he became, like so many French dramatists, a law-student, and possibly he took his degrees. But he never practised. In 1712, when he was twenty-four, or a year or two earlier, he came to Paris with a view to a literary career, but his first efforts, which consisted largely of tasteless burlesques, had neither merit nor promise. It was not till March 1720 that he began his true career with a comedy entitled *L'Amour et la Vérité*, which was a complete failure. Nothing daunted, he set to work on a tragedy, *Annibal*, which was produced at the Théâtre-Français nine months later, but only had three public performances. Two months before this second failure, however, another comedy, *Arlequin poli par l'Amour*, had been a real, if not a brilliant, success, at the theatre of the Italians.

In the following year (1721) he married an "amiable and virtuous" young woman of good family, whom "he loved with all his heart". Her death two years later left him for long inconsolable. This was not his only misfortune. His father had bequeathed him a respectable fortune, but in an evil day he yielded to the pressure of his friends and invested it in Law's System. In a short time it was doubled and then the crash came. When the long liquidation was completed Marivaux found that he had little or nothing left. I have given the dates as I find them in Marivaux's biographers, but the facts are not quite clear. Before the end of 1719 many shareholders in the System had sold their shares, but in the following January the shares were still rising, and it was not till May 1720 that the *débâcle* began. In December Law fled, penniless, from France and a month later the liquidation began and was not completed till 1722. Marivaux must have bought his shares not later than January 1720, but by the following May, that is to say before the alleged date of his marriage, he must have been prepared for the worst. Perhaps he still hoped to save some of his capital from the wreck and in that hope married. He says himself in a letter written nearly twenty years later that not a "crumb" was left to him, but we may set against this a statement that he did not invest the whole of his fortune in the System. When some thirty-five years later he and Mlle de Saint-Jean bought a joint annuity, he was able to contribute 8000 *livres*.

Be this as it may, he was almost penniless in 1722 and he had to earn his living by his pen, and from that year till 1740, except for one year (1726), he produced a play every year.

Marivaux

But he did not confine himself to plays. Encouraged by the success of Steele and Addison's *Spectator*, he began in 1722 *Le Spectateur français*, which was intended to be a weekly journal, but which, when abandoned in the following year, had only reached its twenty-fifth number. Even more un-punctual in their appearances were *L'Indigent philosophe*, of which seven numbers were published in 1728, and *Le Cabinet du Philosophe*, which appeared eleven times in 1734. Though the moral essays of which these periodicals consisted were by no means wanting in merit, they were received without enthusiasm and from the pecuniary point of view they were a failure. Much more successful were the novels, *La Vie de Marianne* (1731–1741) and *Le Paysan parvenu* (1735), but it is characteristic of Marivaux that he began the second novel while he was in the middle of the first, and that he never finished either. It was not that he was lazy or idle, but he could not persist in a straight course; he preferred to wander, as the whim took him, along innumerable by-paths. The *esprit de réflexion*, of which he speaks at the beginning of *Le Paysan parvenu*, was too strong for him.

But in all his writings, whether comedies or novels or moral essays, he shewed the same faculty for careful and delicate observation. And for this he had excellent oppor-tunity in the various salons that he frequented from about 1720 onwards. His first hostess was Mme de Lambert, who received every Tuesday and Wednesday, Tuesday being the day for men of letters. Her particular stars were Fontenelle and La Motte, with whom Marivaux had made friends soon after his first arrival in Paris. Montesquieu joined the circle a year or two later than Marivaux. After Mme de Lambert's death in 1733, "the Tuesdays", in the words of the Abbé Trublet, "were at Mme de Tencin's". She had held a salon since 1726 and for some years previously had received a few intimate friends. Among these were Fontenelle and La Motte, and it was probably they who introduced Marivaux to her. At any rate he was among the privileged few who had the honour of dining with her before the rest of the guests arrived.

She had been notorious for her love affairs and her political and financial intrigues, but at the age of forty-five, after a terrible scandal caused by her lover and fellow-speculator committing suicide at her house, she exchanged the rôle of a *femme galante* for that of a *femme d'esprit* and a pillar of the Church. It was characteristic of the eighteenth century that her former life was forgotten and that her salon was frequented, not only by most of the leading French men of letters, but by distinguished strangers like Bolingbroke and Chesterfield. She had at any rate the virtue of being a good friend to her " *bêtes* ", and it was owing to her untiring efforts that Marivaux was elected unanimously to the Academy in December 1742. Among the rival candidates was Voltaire, who had the support of the Duc de Richelieu till the Duke was won over by Mme de Tencin's pertinacity. Marivaux's name had been put forward on two previous occasions, but strong objections had been made to him on the score of his style.

Though he had twenty more years to live, his dramatic career was practically at an end. A comedy, *La Dispute*, was produced at the Théâtre-Français in 1744, but was withdrawn after a single performance. Two years later *Le Préjugé vaincu*, thanks to the acting of Mlle Gaussin, the most beautiful and graceful actress of the eighteenth century, and Mlle Dangeville, "the inimitable", who charmed Paris for thirty-three years in the rôles of *soubrettes*, had more success, but it only reached seven performances, and it is after all a slight and rather feeble comedy.

In 1749 Mme de Tencin died and the succession to her salon passed to her neighbour in the Rue Saint-Honoré, Mme Geoffrin, who had for the last twelve years or more been in the habit of receiving a few friends to dinner at one o'clock every Wednesday. Among the distinguished clients whom she inherited from Mme de Tencin were Fontenelle, Montesquieu, Mairan, Piron, and Marivaux, and to these she soon added the leading Encyclopædists. Marivaux was not altogether at home in the new salon. His sensitive nature was ruffled by Mme Geoffrin's brusque manners and despotic, though kind-hearted, rule. But when his susceptibility was wounded he could find a welcome in other salons—in that of Mme Du Deffand, who by what proved to be a strange irony enlarged her boundaries by the admission of men of letters, in order that she might see more of D'Alembert, or in that of Mme Du Boccage, whose poetry was the admiration of her contemporaries, but of whom nothing survives but her letters to her sister. He was sometimes too to be found at the gay supper-parties of Mlle Quinault, the actress, whose guests, mostly leading figures in the social and literary worlds, gave themselves the name of *Société du Bout du banc*.

In all these salons the conversation was remarkable for its wit. This is not surprising, seeing that the note was given by men like Fontenelle, La Motte (who, however, died in 1731 before Mme de Tencin's salon was definitely organised), and Montesquieu. Marivaux's share in the conversation has been noted by Marmontel, who dined for the first time with Mme de Tencin in the year of her death. According to him there was a strong element of artificiality in the conversation. "C'était à qui saisirait le plus vite, et comme à la volée, le moment de placer son mot, son conte, son anecdote, sa maxime ou son trait léger et piquant....Dans Marivaux, l'impatience de faire preuve de finesse et de sagacité perçait visiblement." Duclos, writing eight years earlier (1741), but evidently in a hostile spirit, declares that the whole salon was dominated by *la nécessité d'avoir toujours l'esprit*. According to D'Alembert, who frequented Mme Du Deffand's salon, Marivaux makes his characters talk as he talked himself. Marivaux would have agreed to this, for he says in the preface to *Les Serments Indiscrets* that he tried to reproduce the general tone of conversation. And in his account of the dinner-party at Mme de Dorsin's he makes Marianne say that what struck her in the conversation was not the wit, though this was out of the common, but the effortless and natural ease with which it was carried on. It is generally agreed that Mme de Dorsin is a portrait of Mme de Tencin (with her past left out) and her biographer, Masson, is of opinion that Marivaux's account is more faithful than either Marmontel's or Duclos's. At any rate he is probably giving a correct account of his own impressions. For *esprit* had become so indispensable a feature of the salons that he frequented that it had the appearance of nature. But to this world of *esprit* he contributed a markedly personal note. "One must forgive M. de Marivaux his singular expressions", said his friend Fontenelle, "or renounce his society."

Another characteristic noted by D'Alembert is that he was "sensitive and suspicious (*ombrageux*) in society", and more than one anecdote confirms this. For instance, though Fontenelle's remark quoted above was made in perfect friendliness, Marivaux was evidently annoyed by it. Whereupon Fontenelle turned to him and said, "Do not be so quick, Marivaux, to shew resentment when I am talking about you". Marivaux, in fact, suffered in society from the two qualities which are so conspicuous in his comedies, the faculty of rapid and penetrating observation, and a subtle—at times over-subtle—imagination. A glance in his direction was enough to make him suspect that he was being talked about, and his imagination suggested that the remarks were unfriendly or at any rate critical. But he was always ready to accept an explanation, for, as Fontenelle said, if he was quick to shew resentment, he had an excellent heart. D'Alembert testifies to his "amiable candour, his unaffected modesty, his sympathetic affability".

Even when Marivaux was producing one play a year he could not have been earning much by his pen—in a good year, calculates Larroumet, after consulting the registers of the Comédie Française and the Théâtre Italien, he earned from 1500 to 2000 *livres*—but after 1740 he had for a time nothing to depend on but his profits on occasional productions of his old pieces and the slender remnant of his vanished patrimony. Latterly, however, he had a pension of 3000 *livres* from the king's privy purse, which, without his knowledge, his friends had procured for him through Mme de Pompadour. This must have been after 1745, when her reign began. Moreover in the autumn of his life he had a warm and loyal friend in an old maid named Mlle de Saint-Jean, who invited him to leave his lodgings in the Rue Saint-Honoré, near the church of Saint-Roch, and come and live with her in the Rue de Richelieu, where she had a charming apartment looking at the back on the gardens of the Palais-Royal. This invitation he gladly accepted—their age sheltered them from unfriendly comment—and in 1757 they purchased an annuity (Marivaux contributing 8000 *livres* and Mlle de Saint-Jean 20,000 to the capital sum), which was legally secured to the survivor. In 1763 Marivaux died, leaving his friend as his sole legatee. The legacy consisted of the many poor folk whom Marivaux had assisted during his life, and thus Mlle de Saint-Jean's acceptance of the legacy was a final and touching proof of her loyal friendship.

Of the thirty comedies of Marivaux, including *La Femme Fidèle*, of which only a few scenes are preserved, four or, at the most, five remain in the repertory. But there are at least ten others of great merit, and a knowledge of these is indispensable in order to form a true estimate of his dramatic genius. The theatre at which the great majority—about two-thirds—of his plays were produced was the Théâtre Italien. Its home was the famous Hôtel de Bourgogne in the Rue Mauconseil, where Louis-André Riccoboni, a celebrated Italian actor, had recently established himself with a company from Parma. In 1697 the Italians had been banished from France, their offence, as was generally believed, being a transparent allusion to Mme de Maintenon in a play called *La Fausse Prude*. But in 1716 the Regent had invited Riccoboni to bring his troop to Paris and Riccoboni had accepted the invitation. Their performances were nominally in French, but even those who knew French best spoke it with a strong Italian accent, and there were three or four members of the company who, being unable to speak French at all, used their native dialect, Venetian, or Bergamasque, or whatever it might be. This made their traditional use of vivacious gesture helpful and almost necessary. Another tradition that they kept up was the employment of stock characters. In Riccoboni's troop these consisted of a first male lover (Lélio), a second male lover (Mario), a first leading lady (Flaminia), a second leading lady (Isabelle or Silvia), a Pantaloon, a Doctor, a Scaramouche, a Scapin, an Arlequin, a Colombine, and a Violette (a variety of Colombine). It will be noticed that there is no Pierrot, but to this list, which is that given by Maurice Sand in his *Masques et Bouffons*, we must add Trivelin —a character, introduced into the troupe in order to provide a part for a son of the great Domenico Biancolelli. The rôle of Lélio belonged to Riccoboni himself, who was a fine actor both in tragedy and comedy and a man of considerable literary ability. His wife, Helena Balletti, an equally fine actress, was the Flaminia. Her brother was the Mario, and the famous Silvia (Giovanna Rosa Benozzi), whom he married in 1720, took what hitherto had been known as the Isabelle parts after the famous Isabella Andreini of the *Gelosi* troupe. The part of Arlequin was played by Tommaso Vicentini, known in Paris by his stage-name of Thomassin, who had given a partially new conception to the part. In the hands of his predecessor Domenico Biancolelli, known as Dominique, Arlequin had been a brilliant and resourceful rascal, but Vicentini, who was a first-rate actor in a variety of parts, reverted more or less to an older tradition and turned him into a naïve, ignorant, and essentially honest fellow, whose apparent stupidity concealed considerable shrewdness. Vicentini's wife, Margarita Rusca, was the Violette, but she also took the part of Colombine.

Riccoboni introduced several improvements into the performances of his company. He abolished the horse-play and indecency that had been hitherto characteristic of the Italians: he paid much attention to the scenery, the decoration, the costumes and other accessories; and he adapted his stock characters to the requirements of French comedy. For instance, Arlequin naturally became the valet and Colombine the *soubrette*.

This was the company to which Marivaux entrusted his first comedy. It was, as we have seen, a failure, but the title, as has been pointed out, is significant. *L'Amour et la Vérité* —Love and Truth—these were the two watchwords that Marivaux kept inscribed on his banner. Seven and a half months later (October 20, 1720) the Italians gave him a second chance with *Arlequin poli par l'Amour*. It is a slight little play, but it combines charm with truth of observation, and with the chief parts played by Silvia and Thomassin it is not surprising that it was a success. Half fairy-tale and half pastoral, it is one of the few comedies by Marivaux that give occasion for the often-repeated comparison between him and Watteau. For, if we judge him by his really characteristic pieces, there is all the difference imaginable between the man who lived in the every-day world of society and the man who lived in the world of fancy, between the man whose theme was love with a happy marriage as the goal and the man for whom love was a pilgrimage towards an unknown Cythera, towards a land transfigured by a "light that never was on land or sea". There is, however, this bond of union between the dramatist and the painter, that they were both closely connected with the Italian actors. Marivaux found in them his best interpreters, and Watteau an inspiration for his art. His picture of *Love at the Italian Comedy* in Berlin and the similar picture from Rohoncz Castle in Hungary, that we saw recently at the French Exhibition, bring vividly before us the very Lélio and Flaminia, the Mario and Silvia, the Doctor, the Arlequin, and the Colombine, who acted in Marivaux's comedies.

In his next comedy, *La Surprise de l'Amour*, produced by the Italians after an interval of eighteen months, we are brought back from fairyland to the world around us, and we are introduced to the type of play which Marivaux made peculiarly his own, and which is most closely associated with his name. What that type was may be best explained in his own words as reported by Marmontel:

> J'ai guetté dans le cœur humain toutes les niches différentes où peut se cacher l'amour, lorsqu'il craint de se montrer, et chacune de mes comédies a pour objet de le faire sortir d'une de ces niches.

And again:

> Dans mes pièces c'est tantôt un amour ignoré des deux amants, tantôt un amour qu'ils sentent et qu'ils veulent se cacher l'un à l'autre, tantôt un amour timide, qui n'ose se déclarer; tantôt enfin un amour incertain et comme indécis, un amour à demi-né, pour ainsi dire, dont ils se doutent sans être bien sûrs, et qu'ils épient au dedans d'eux-mêmes avant de lui laisser prendre l'essor. Où est en tout cela cette ressemblance qu'on ne cesse de m'objecter.

Briefly, Marivaux's constant theme is the psychology of growing love, of the peaceful love that is crowned by marriage and durable affection, and not of the passionate love portrayed by Racine, which ends in disaster and death. The title of the new piece is even more descriptive of Marivaux's comedy than that of *L'Amour et la Vérité*, for it might have been given equally well to many of its successors. "That eternal surprise of love, the unique subject of Marivaux's comedies", says Marmontel contemptuously. But Marivaux is quite justified in pointing out the different forms which this surprise assumes. The general idea may be the same, but the applications of it differ.

In *La Surprise de l'Amour* there are only five characters of any importance—Lélio, the Countess, Arlequin (Lélio's valet), Colombine (the Countess's maid) and Jacqueline, Lélio's servant. Both the Countess and Lélio have renounced love, the Countess, who is a widow, because she has a poor opinion of men—her first marriage had evidently been unhappy—Lélio, because he has been jilted. "Vous avez rompu avec les femmes, moi avec les hommes", says the Countess. At their first meeting (I, 7) Lélio is piqued by the Countess's contempt for men as unworthy of a woman's affection, and in the next scene the Baron, an unnecessary character, who only appears once again, suggests that they will fall in love with one another. "Voilà de l'amour qui prélude par le dépit." In the first scene of the second act the Countess begins to think of Lélio, and in the second Lélio declares that if he were capable of loving any woman it would be the Countess. The fifth scene, between Lélio and Arlequin, is perhaps too long, but it is a good example of Marivaux's skill in psychological analysis. Three of Lélio's speeches, though they are twice interrupted by Arlequin with short comments, practically form a single soliloquy. "Vous parlez tout seul", says Arlequin, "vous faites des discours qui ont dix lieues de long." The scene between Lélio and the Countess—the seventh—is certainly too long, and the dialogue is too finely spun. On the other hand, that between the Countess and Colombine (III, 2) is quite excellent. The Countess has come to think that Lélio is in love with her and Colombine assures her that she returns his love. A portrait of the Countess, lost by her and found by Lélio, brings matters to a head. The final scene (III, 6), in which Lélio's declaration, barely put into words, is accepted by the Countess, is at once a model of delicacy and a dramatic triumph. The scenes between Colombine and Arlequin, who, like his master, has sworn never to fall in love again, are all admirable. Arlequin, in accordance with Vicentini's conception of the rôle, is honest, simple and naïve, and his misogamy yields readily to the alluring and accomplished strategy of Colombine. "Je t'aime", says his master, "tu as du bon sens quoique un peu grossier", and his speech, homely and direct, but full of savour, is a racy reflection of his character. So is that of Colombine, whose part was played by Flaminia. Vivacious, enterprising, and almost on terms of equality with her mistress, she is a *grande raisonneuse* with a tendency to indulge in out-of-the-way similes and other forms of *préciosité*. Less satisfactory are Lélio and the Countess, for their characters are left vague, and there seems to be no particular reason for their falling in love, except that each is piqued by the determination of the other not to fall in love. In spite of defects, however, the play shews much psychological insight and a born aptitude for the stage. Its success, no doubt—it ran for sixteen performances, no bad number in those days—was partly due to the admirable acting of Riccoboni, Silvia, Vicentini, and Flaminia.

But Silvia was not altogether satisfied with her interpretation of the Countess and she declared that she would give anything to meet the anonymous author. Accordingly—so the story goes—Marivaux was brought to her dressing-room and introduced as an unknown admirer of her talent. The manuscript of his comedy happened to be lying on her table, and after some conversation he took it up and read to her one of the chief scenes. He was an extremely good reader, and Silvia was filled with admiration. "You are either the devil or the author", she exclaimed. "I am not the devil", replied Marivaux with a smile and a bow. Thus they became firm friends, and in his future comedies Marivaux nearly always had a part for Silvia. She does not seem to have been strictly beautiful. Indeed, according to Casanova, who describes her when she was about fifty, she had not a single really good feature, but there was something about her, he adds, that captivated you directly you saw her. I have not seen the engraving of La Tour's lost pastel, which was painted about the same time, but Larroumet declares that the general expression is cold, though very intelligent. He reproduces her portrait by Carle Vanloo, which represents her as a woman of thirty. It has a certain superficial charm, but it lacks character.

We have seen that in *La Surprise de l'Amour* Marivaux traces the gradual development of love between two persons

who, having loved unwisely, believe that they have done
with love for ever. In *La Double Inconstance*, produced by the
same company eleven months later, he essays the more difficult task of depicting how two persons, who believe that
they are in love, gradually realise their mistake and recognise
the superior power of real love. The scene of the new comedy
is "in the palace of the Prince", but we are not told of what
kingdom he is Prince. We may call it Illyria, if we like, for in
Twelfth Night there is what may almost be called a "double
inconstancy" and it is to the honour of Marivaux that *La
Double Inconstance* with its romantic setting may claim cousin-
ship with Shakespeare's romantic comedies. Silvia is a
rustic sister of Viola and Rosalind and Beatrice. It should
be noted too that this is the one comedy of Marivaux, besides *Arlequin poli par l'Amour*, which justifies the inevitable
comparison with Watteau. Arlequin especially is a Watteau-
like figure, and so truly does he conform to the tradition of
the Italian *commedia dell' arte*, that he carries a baton, with
which he belabours Trivelin, an officer of the court who is
assigned to him as his servant.

Arlequin and Silvia are affianced lovers, and they believe
in their simple hearts that their love is for all time. But the
Prince, in accordance with a law that he must choose one of
his subjects for his bride, has made choice of Silvia and is
keeping her and Arlequin in honourable captivity in the
palace. The problem is how to persuade her—for the law will
not allow him to use force—to transfer her affections from
Arlequin to himself. In this delicate task he has the in-
valuable aid of Flaminia, the daughter of a court official, who
combines with great tact a remarkable insight into both the
male and the female heart. He is also helped by the fact that,
while hunting, he has several times come across Silvia, and
that she, ignorant of his rank, has learnt to regard him with
some degree of favour. In fact, as she naïvely says to him in
a delightful scene with him and Flaminia (ii, 3), his only
drawback is that Arlequin was first in the field and that, if she

had foreseen that the Prince (of whose rank she is still ignorant) would come after Arlequin, she would have waited for him. Later (II, 11) with equal naïvety she acknowledges to Flaminia, who has completely won her confidence, that she loved Arlequin because he was her neighbour, because he amused her, because he followed her about everywhere, because he loved her, because she got accustomed to him. "And so I loved him *faute de mieux*; but I always noticed that he had an inclination for wine and gluttony."

But Silvia is too loyal to give up Arlequin, unless he gives up her. And Arlequin, who, like Silvia, is a simple creature without ambition, is not to be tempted by riches or pomp or even by the prospect of good cheer. " Je suis gourmand, je l'avoue; mais j'ai encore plus d'amour que de gourmandise." Flaminia finds the solution. She is so sympathetic and friendly with Arlequin that he cannot bear the idea of being separated from her. And she is equally unwilling to be parted from him, and so she arrives at the stage, common to so many of Marivaux's hesitating men and women, of saying, " Je ne sais où j'en suis". The *dénouement* is worked out with much charm and delicacy. There is a first-rate scene between the Prince and Arlequin, in which the latter refuses to give up Silvia. The Prince's courtesy and Arlequin's frankness and honesty are admirably depicted, and they part with mutual respect. "Adieu, Arlequin; je t'estime malgré tes refus." Then Flaminia arrives to say that she has been forbidden ever to see Arlequin again and that she has been mistaken in her feelings toward him; it is not friendship but love. This opens Arlequin's eyes. He too recognises that his feeling for her is love and not friendship. But he is innocent, he declares, of any treachery. "Nous nous aimons par mégarde." But Silvia, not having heard of this change in his affections, is uncertain how to act. So she consults her unknown friend, and they agree that if she finds that she loves him she must give up Arlequin. But she will not go further than promise that she will never love the Prince. Then the unknown

Marivaux

confesses that he is the Prince, adding that she is free to accept or refuse his hand and heart. Of course she accepts. So two couples are made happy, and once more love triumphs.

The whole tenor of this charming comedy and many of its scenes are so exquisite that one is tempted sometimes in reading it to regard it as even superior to *Le Jeu de l'Amour et du Hasard* and *Les Fausses Confidences*. But though the whole of the first act is admirable, there are some imperfections in the conduct of the two remaining acts, which shew that Marivaux is not yet quite master of his art. Lisette, Flaminia's sister, promises well on her first appearance, but after the first act she drops out and it is not clear why she was ever introduced. The scenes between Arlequin and a nameless *seigneur* (II, 7 and III, 4) are too long, and indeed the only reason for them seems to be the introduction of some gentle satire on courtiers. "A présent, qu'il ne m'est plus permis de voir le prince, que serais-je à la cour?" says the *seigneur*. "Il faudra que je m'en aille dans mes terres, car j'en suis exilé." This is in the manner of La Bruyère and suggests Bussy-Rabutin and his exile at his country-seat. In fact the *seigneur* is rather Marivaux in person, the Marivaux of *Le Spectateur*, than a character in a comedy.

Ten months after *La Double Inconstance* Marivaux produced another romantic play, *Le Prince Travesti*. The scene is laid at Barcelona, and among the characters are the Princess of Barcelona, the Prince of Leon, and the King of Castile—the two latter under a disguise. But these high-sounding names have no geographical significance, and the kingdom of Barcelona is as purely imaginary as the nameless kingdom of *La Double Inconstance*. Here the resemblance between the two plays ends. The later play is in a more serious vein than its predecessor, but it is enlivened by the character of Arlequin, who, though of the same simple ignorant and fundamentally honest type as the earlier Arlequins, is more broadly comic. It has been called a *comédie héroïque*, a name invented by

Corneille to denote a play which deals with persons of high condition, but in which the hero does not fall into any peril. It is really of the nature of a modern *drame*, something intermediate between comedy and tragedy, or at least a comedy which may at any moment turn to tragedy.

We learn in the second scene—the first scene consists of only a few words—that the Prince of Leon, disguised as Lélio, has rendered great service to Barcelona both in peace and war and is now one of the Princess's ministers. "Young, amiable, brave, generous, and wise", he has won the Princess's heart, and in spite of his being (as she supposes) only a private gentleman she is ready to marry him. The difficulty is that an ambassador has just arrived from the King of Castile to demand her hand for his master. All this is confided by the Princess to her widowed cousin Hortense, who has just arrived at Barcelona after a year's absence, and who in her turn relates how her marriage had been an unhappy one, how in her husband's lifetime an unknown had rescued her from brigands, how, had she not been a married woman, she would have completely lost her heart to him, how she had given him a ring, how her husband had died two months ago, and how the image of the unknown, whom she does not expect ever to see again, had always remained with her. In the fifth scene Lélio explains in a short soliloquy that he is willing to marry the Princess, even to love her, but for his memory of a fair lady whom he had rescued. Then he and Hortense meet. There is a mutual recognition and Lélio declares his love. But Hortense points out that the Princess is an insurmountable obstacle, for she is quick-tempered and imperious and they are her servants.

Thus the way is prepared for a drama very different in character from the type of comedy most affected by Marivaux. The love between Lélio and Hortense is avowed early in the play, and the hindrance to their happiness arises, not from their own questionings and hesitations, but from external causes. The ensuing complications are furnished by the

intrigues of a courtier named Frédéric, a melodramatic villain
and almost the only bad character in all Marivaux's comedies;
the bribery of Lélio's valet, Arlequin, whose naïve betrayal
of Lélio to Frédéric and of Frédéric to Lélio is the occasion
of some good comic scenes; the Princess's jealousy of Hortense; and the King of Castile's proposal, which the Princess
entrusts to Lélio to decide. Unfortunately the disentangle-
ment of a plot is not a business in which Marivaux excels,
and the play as a whole suffers from over-complication. But
the scene between Lélio and Hortense, in which he dis-
closes his real rank, could not be bettered, and there is an
equally admirable scene between Lélio and the supposed
ambassador, each ignorant of the other's identity. The
dénouement is brought about by the Princess's surrender of
Lélio to Hortense—there is a touch of melodrama in this—
while she consoles herself with the hand of the King of
Castile.

The outstanding feature of the play is the character of
Hortense. Honest and intelligent, she combines a lively wit
with an underlying seriousness, and a gay demeanour with a
capacity for silent suffering. With subtle and sympathetic
skill Marivaux has noted the growth of love in her heart,
through the stages of gratitude, admiration, and tender
memory, to love, first concealed and then openly avowed.
He has given us other charming widows who will make
charming wives, but only in Hortense has he portrayed
strong and deep-seated passion.

La Fausse Suivante, which followed in the same year, was,
like its predecessor, a decided success with twelve performances. It provided Silvia with a rôle in which she excelled, that of a woman disguised as a man. In this disguise
she makes love to the Countess in order to arouse the jealousy
of Lélio, with whom the Countess is in love. She also dis-
guises herself as a *soubrette* and in that character takes in not
only the three valets, but also Lélio, so there is plenty of room
for misunderstandings and complications. The play is a good

instance of the *marivaudage* in thought and language of which Marivaux's critics complained. This is especially conspicuous in the scenes between the Chevalier and the Countess and between the Countess and Lélio. The best character is Trivelin, whose speech in the first scene bears so marked a resemblance to Figaro's famous tirade in *Le Mariage de Figaro* that it is difficult to suppose that Beaumarchais had not come across it.

Marivaux's next venture, *L' Ile des Esclaves*, was an experiment on totally different lines. It may be described as a quasi-Aristophanic comedy dealing with social ideas. The scene is laid in an imaginary island, upon which four voyagers from Athens, a general and a lady with their respective slaves, have been shipwrecked. They find that in conformity with the custom of the island they have to change their social rank. The slaves become master and mistress, and the general and the lady slaves. In spite of their being Athenians, the general's slave is called Arlequin and the chief magistrate of the island Trivelin. The latter is the mouthpiece of the author's views on social equality, which are Utopian rather than revolutionary. There is also some satire of a gentle kind on the coquetry and gallantry fashionable in Paris society. After a short experience, beneficial no doubt to both classes, the slaves are quite ready to return to their former stations, so that Marivaux must not be regarded too seriously as a forerunner of Jean-Jacques Rousseau.

Nor need we regard him as a feminist on the strength of a similar comedy, *La Colonie nouvelle ou La Ligue des Femmes* (1729), in which the scene is again laid on an imaginary island. The women, who are already on the island when the play opens, have set up a government in opposition to the men. Silvia is the chief magistrate for the nobility, and Mme Sorbin for the *bourgeoisie*, while Arlequin represents a young man of the people, who is in love with Mme Sorbin's daughter. The play is partly a satire on feminism and partly a sympathetic defence of it. As in *L'Ile des Esclaves* it ends in a reconciliation between the opponents, which is effected by the sudden ap-

pearance of a horde of savages. "Viens, mon mari, je te
pardonne; va te battre, je vais à mon ménage", says Mme
Sorbin. The play was a failure and was withdrawn after the
first performance, but, though it is decidedly inferior to *L'Ile
des Esclaves*, it is not without merit. Marivaux, even in his
social plays, never forgets that he is a dramatist. In 1750 the
Mercure published an abridged version of the play in one act
under the title of *La Colonie*, and this was printed by Édouard
Fournier in his *Théâtre complet* of 1878.

Social satire is also the theme of two other comedies, both
with a more or less mythological setting. In *Le Triomphe de
Plutus* (1728) the chief characters are Apollo and Plutus, who
figure as rival lovers, the mythological element being a veil
for gentle satire on the *nouveaux riches*, especially on the ad-
vantages which they enjoy in the kingdom of love.

> Sans dépenser, c'est en vain qu'on espère
> De s'avancer au pays de Cythère.

In *La Réunion des Amours*, produced at the Théâtre-
Français in 1731, Marivaux contrasts the Platonic and semi-
precious love-making of an earlier age with the *libertinage* of
his own day. His sympathy with the former is not unmixed
with satire, while his satire on the latter is tempered by a
certain amount of sympathy. It should be noted that the two
gods of love, Amour and Cupidon, who champion the old
and new love respectively, were charmingly represented by
Mlle Dangeville and Mlle Gaussin. In the following year
(1732) he returned to the Italians with *Le Triomphe de l'Amour*,
another romantic comedy of a more or less fantastic character. The heroine, played by Silvia, is the Princess of
Sparta, who, with the object of restoring her cousin Agis to
the throne and also of winning his love, assumes the disguise of a man; becomes engaged at the same time to
Hermocrates, a respectable philosopher, who had met her
originally as a woman in a forest, and to his elderly sister;
and then with scant apology throws them both over for her

cousin. The fault of the play is that the Princess's love-making, instead of being treated as pure comedy, is much too serious, which makes it appear unpleasantly heartless.

Of all the comedies that have been hitherto mentioned only one, *La Réunion des Amours*, was produced at the Théâtre-Français, and, in spite of the admirable acting, with only fair success. But the first comedy which he wrote for that theatre was *La Seconde Surprise de l'Amour* (December 31, 1727). Adopting its conventions, he substituted Le Chevalier for Lélio, Lubin for Arlequin, and Lisette for Colombine. The part of the Marquise was played by the celebrated Adrienne Lecouvreur, but she did not satisfy Marivaux so well as his favourite Silvia. At the first performances she was excellent, because she was perfectly natural, but later on, excited by the applause of her audience, she became in his opinion precious and affected. The second *Surprise* starts from the same idea as the first, but the reasons which have led the Chevalier and the Marquise to renounce all idea of love differ so much from those of the hero and heroine of the first *Surprise*, that the two plays do not resemble one another either in their psychology or their action. However, as I propose to analyse the second *Surprise* later as an example of Marivaux's methods, I will say no more about it at present. Two years after it appeared the comedy which is generally regarded as Marivaux's masterpiece, *Le Jeu de l'Amour et du Hasard*. It was produced by the Italians on January 23, 1730, with Silvia in the part which bears her name, her husband in that of Mario, Vicentini as Arlequin, and his wife as Lisette. As Riccoboni was in Italy from 1729 to 1731, the part of Dorante was probably taken by his son, who made his *début* in the Lélio rôles in 1725.

In both *Surprises de l'Amour* the romantic element is decidedly lacking and the love-making, though perfectly sincere, is far from ardent. In the new play, instead of two staid lovers whom adversity and disillusion have taught to take a sober view of happiness and to enter on a fresh adventure

Marivaux

with hesitation and circumspection, we have a young girl with her dreams of perfection and her resolute courage, and a gallant adorer, whose inclination is to follow his heart wherever it leads him. Marivaux, as usual, wastes little time over preliminary approaches. By the end of the fourth scene the whole plot is disclosed. Silvia, who is expecting the arrival of her proposed husband, Dorante, forms a plan, with her father's approval, to change places with her maid, Lisette. Meanwhile a similar change has been made by Dorante and communicated to Silvia's father. Presently Dorante appears disguised as his valet, and there is a great scene between him and Silvia disguised as Lisette (I, 9). They are at once mutually attracted. "Ce garçon n'est pas sot, et je ne plains pas la soubrette qui l'aura."..."Cette fille-ci m'étonne! Il n'y a point de femme au monde à qui sa physionomie ne fît honneur." It had been Silvia's idea that she should question the valet as to his master's character, but he makes love to her so briskly that she has no opportunity. Then the valet, Arlequin, appears in the disguise of Dorante and at once disgusts Silvia with his vulgarity. In two amusing scenes of the second act (II, 3, 5) he makes love to Lisette, whom he believes to be Silvia, even more briskly than his master does to the real Silvia. It has been said with truth that Lisette is too clever not to have detected him at once. But, as Sarcey says, one must accept conventions on the stage, and if the detection had come too soon, there would have been no play. Indeed from these scenes onwards the comedy becomes increasingly subtle and interesting. Some abrupt remarks of Arlequin to Silvia make her furious, and in an admirable scene with Lisette (II, 7) she pours forth her almost tearful indignation at the position into which her rash adventure has led her —her hatred of the man whom she believes to be Dorante and her growing sympathy for the supposed valet. There is another scene between Silvia and Dorante (II, 9), in which the love-making becomes more serious, but, as is natural, more restrained in expression, and then, after the intervention

99   7-2

of her father Orgon and her brother Mario have added to her agitation, there comes the famous scene (II, 13) in which Dorante reveals himself. "C'est moi qui suis Dorante." "Ah! je vois clair dans mon cœur", says Silvia aside, and when Dorante leaves her, "Allons, j'avais grand besoin que ce fût là Dorante",—notes of real passion such as Marivaux rarely permits himself.

But Silvia is not content with "seeing clear into her heart". Dorante must "see clear into *his* heart"; he must be prepared to marry her in spite of her humble condition, in spite of worldly conventions, in spite of his father's possible wrath. Mario comes to her help by pretending that he is in love with her and so arouses Dorante's jealousy. Then in a noble and moving speech Silvia refuses to open her heart to Dorante unless his intentions are really serious. Before "the fire of her words" Dorante gives way. "Il n'est ni sang, ni naissance, ni fortune qui ne disparaisse devant une âme comme la tienne. J'aurais honte que mon orgueil tînt encore contre toi; et mon cœur et ma main t'appartiennent." Meanwhile Arlequin has honourably confessed to Lisette that he is not Dorante, and Lisette has made a similar confession to Arlequin. The result is mutual forgiveness. "M'aimes-tu?" says Lisette. "Pardi oui", replies Arlequin. "En changeant de nom, tu n'as pas changé de visage."

Le Jeu de l'Amour et du Hasard is a play of many merits. In spite of the absence of any external action, the interest from first to last never flags. It is sustained by a dialogue which is always brisk and expressive and which above all gives a continuous sense of movement. The play never stands still, in order that the audience may applaud the author's *esprit* or learn wisdom from his social or philosophical opinions. It progresses steadily towards its appointed goal, and as it progresses the characters develop, not so much, as in many of Marivaux's comedies, by self-analysis, as by the expression of their feelings and the clash of their temperaments. Of all Marivaux's young girls Silvia is the most firmly drawn and

the most captivating. Sarcey insists on her extreme youth—
eighteen at the most—and here he is certainly right. But
when he dwells on her naïvety, her giddiness, her romantic
impulsiveness, he is not so convincing. She is for me a
young woman of considerable character, who has very definite views about matrimony. It has no great attractions for
her—much to her maid's surprise—but if she is to marry, she
must have a husband who is not merely good-looking—"un
bel homme est fat; je l'ai remarqué"—and with a good
figure—"ce sont là des agréments superflus"—but he must
have a good character. He must be amiable and agreeable
and reasonable, not merely in public but in his own home.
And she might have added that he must be in love with her
and she with him. It is with these ideas that the adorable
Silvia conceives her plan of changing places with her maid
and carries it through in the face of difficulties which she had
not foreseen with high courage and unconquerable resolution. Dorante is not quite the equal of Silvia, but he wins
our hearts by his chivalry, his delicacy, and his honesty.
Lisette and Arlequin as the *soubrette* and valet more or less
conform to type. Lisette has the intelligence, promptness
and high spirit of her tribe. Arlequin is equally enterprising,
but he is more naïve and makes no pretence of being precious
or even witty. Orgon and Mario are well-bred kindly gentle-
men with a quiet sense of humour. But all the characters
alike have the great merit of spontaneity, and it was of this
characteristic that Marivaux found such admirable exponents
in the Italian actors.

The same idea of a young girl with a suitor proposed by
her father, whom she has never seen—in neither play is there
a mother—is the starting-point of *Les Serments Indiscrets*, a
comedy produced at the Théâtre-Français in June 1732. It
was badly received. In fact the hissing from the beginning
of the second act was so continuous that the play had to be
abandoned before the end. It ran, however, for eight more
performances. But the critics, with Voltaire at their head,

were severe, and, when the comedy was printed, Marivaux, or almost the only time, defended himself in an interesting preface. To the criticism that the play was too like the first *Surprise de l'Amour* he replied with perfect truth that the situation was quite different. As for the style, he admitted that it was the same in both pieces, as well as in some others, but he added that he was copying, not himself, but Nature. It was his aim to represent the general tone of conversation— meaning no doubt the sort of conversation that he heard in the salons that he frequented.

The play, as I said, starts from precisely the same idea as *Le Jeu de l'Amour et du Hasard*. Lucile, like Silvia, is awaiting the arrival of a young man, whom her father has selected as her future husband. Like Silvia she is in no hurry to get married and like Silvia she strongly objects to marrying a man of whose character she knows nothing. "Je sens un fonds de délicatesse et de goût qui serait toujours choqué dans le mariage"—a sentiment which reveals her as a *précieuse*. It happens that Damis, the proposed husband, is equally averse to matrimony, so that, when he arrives, the pair enter into a compact to refuse to carry out their parents' wishes. Unfortunately for their compact, Damis has lost his heart to Lucile at first sight, and Lucile, if she has not quite lost her heart, is very favourably impressed, and, moreover, is strongly piqued by his readiness to accept the compact. The idea is an excellent one and gives full scope to Marivaux's peculiar talents. But it must be confessed that in this case at any rate Voltaire's criticism is just, and that the road travelled by the hearts of the lovers before they meet is long and devious. For both Lucile and Damis, as appears in the first scene between them, are born arguers and they argue with a subtlety which easily lends itself to the charge of *marivaudage*. The intervention of Phœnice, Lucile's sister, is ingenious, but it unnecessarily complicates the plot, and the scenes between her and Damis are tiresome. On the other hand there is an admirable scene between Lucile and her maid Lisette, which testifies to Marivaux's penetrating knowledge of the female heart. "Notre vanité et notre coquetterie, voilà les plus grandes sources de nos passions.... Pourquoi est-ce que j'aime? Parce qu'on me défiait de plaire, et que j'ai voulu venger mon visage." The part played by Frontin and Lisette in the action of the play is not made very clear. Of all Marivaux's characters they are the most open to the accusation of *marivaudage* in the sense of jargon or *précieux* language —Frontin even more than Lisette. For Frontin prides himself on his *esprit* and is something of a *poseur*. Happily his wit has a dry flavour, which is not unattractive, and he is not without humour.

Marivaux, as we know, was sensitive to criticism, and it may have been the criticism of *Les Serments Indiscrets* which led him to produce in succession from 1732 to 1736 six plays, none of which is a real "surprise of love". We must not, however, press this idea too closely, for the first of these plays was produced with the Italians less than two months after *Les Serments Indiscrets* and must therefore have been written before the production of that play. Its title, *L'École des Mères*, is reminiscent of Molière and as Angélique is described as "une Agnès élevée dans la plus sévère contrainte", it is possible that Marivaux may have meant to improve on his predecessor's portrait of an *ingénue*. It is a comedy of intrigue with a plot of a conventional type. An innocent girl who is to be married that very evening to an elderly suitor at the bidding of a tyrannical mother, a young lover disguised as a valet, a real valet, and a *soubrette*—these are the familiar simple elements out of which Marivaux has made a well-constructed and entertaining little play. Angélique is admirably drawn, and the scene between her and her mother, Mme Argante, in which with filial respect but with tranquil pertinacity she demurs to her proposed husband, could not be bettered. She is equally delightful and equally true to nature in the scene with Damis, the suitor in question, and the four scenes which take place in the dark, when everybody in turn clutches hold of the wrong person, are highly amusing. As Damis turns out to be the father of his rival Éraste, and as, like all Marivaux's fathers, he is disinterested and benevolent, love triumphs once more. The comedy had not been played for half a century when it was revived at the Odéon in 1878. Sarcey witnessed it, he says, with pleasure, but he adds that it is "one of Marivaux's least important pieces", and he finds Angélique less really naïve than Molière's Agnès. "She reasons, analyses, discusses, judges ...she is a philosopher; she examines and studies herself." But if Angélique is less naïve than her predecessor she is just as innocent. The difference surely arises from her bringing up. She has been brought up austerely, but not with the intention of "making her as much of an idiot as possible". At any rate Sarcey was wrong in belittling the play, for it has kept the place in the repertory which it recovered more than fifty years ago.

L'Heureux Stratagème, which followed it in 1733, though equally successful, is neither so well-constructed nor so entertaining. It is briefly the story of two pairs of lovers, who after a species of *chassé croisé* return to their own partners. Dorante is in love with the Countess, the Chevalier, who is a Gascon, with the Marquise. But the Countess embarks on a violent flirtation with the Chevalier, and the Marquise suggests to Dorante that he should pretend to be in love with her in order to restore the Countess to him. This "happy stratagem", it need not be said, has the desired effect, but the manœuvring of the four lovers which it occasions is too complicated and lasts too long. Moreover, though the Countess is a good study of a coquette who is not without heart, and the Marquise of a kind-hearted woman of society with a sense of humour, none of the characters has much individuality. The result is an ingenious game which shews off the skill of the players rather than a true representation of nature.

Marivaux produced two comedies in the following year,

1734, one with the Italians, *La Méprise*, and the other at the Théâtre-Français, *Le Petit-Maître corrigé*. *La Méprise* is a slight affair but not without merit, the scenes between Frontin and Lisette being particularly good. *Le Petit-Maître corrigé*, in three acts, was greeted at the first performance with hisses and the rattling of keys, and was withdrawn after the second. Though the play begins well and has an effective ending, it is unsatisfactory on the whole. The plot is worked out at too great length and with too many complications. But Rosimond, the *petit-maître*, is a good study and the heroine, Hortense, who cures him of his fatuity, is as charming as she is sensible.

La Mère Confidente (May 1735) is founded on the same idea as that of *L'École des Mères*, that of a young and innocent girl with a clandestine lover, whose intentions are perfectly honourable, but who is unable to declare himself. As in the earlier play, there is a well-to-do rival, favoured by the girl's mother. But Mme Argante is very different from the tyrannical mother of the same name in *L'École des Mères*, and from this difference arises the whole treatment of the play. With great tenderness she wins step by step her daughter's confidence, and when at last it appears that the rich suitor is Dorante's uncle and that he renounces his suit in his nephew's favour she pardons the projected elopement to which Angélique has confessed, and receives Dorante, now made rich by his uncle's liberality, as an accepted lover. The play was revived in 1863 for the first time since 1810 and was severely criticised; Sarcey alone warmly defended it. But since then other critics, especially Larroumet, have praised it highly. It is in fact a successful experiment in a kind of comedy which Marivaux had not hitherto attempted, the *comédie sérieuse*. While it does not exclude the comic element, which is here provided by Lubin, it introduces pathos and sensibility and it inculcates a moral lesson. It is a stage on the road to the *comédie larmoyante* and the *drame bourgeoise*. It was not, however, quite a new departure. In 1727 Destouches,

after twelve years' absence from the stage, returned to it with
Le Philosophe marié, an agreeable little piece which he called
a *comédie morale et sérieuse*, and five years later he produced
his masterpiece, *Le Glorieux* (1732), to which he wrote a
preface to the effect that *corriger les mœurs* was the true
function of the stage. He combined, however, comedy with
pathos and moral instruction. In the following year Nivelle
de La Chaussée made his *début* with *La Fausse Antipathie*,
which shews the influence of Marivaux, and from which the
comic element was not wholly excluded. Similar in its mixture
of comedy and pathos is his *Préjugé à la Mode*, which, produced
in the same year as *La Mère Confidente*, had a great success.

But while La Chaussée went on to banish the comic element entirely from his drama, Marivaux returned to his old
vein of high comedy with *Le Legs*, the most popular of his
one-act plays. It met with a cold reception at its first performance in January 1736 at the Théâtre-Français, but recovered at the second, and when revived in 1749, with Préville
in the rôle of the Marquis, took a place in the repertory which
it has never lost. The exposition, which takes the form
of a short conversation between the Chevalier and Hortense,
is particularly skilful. It appears that a relative of Hortense
and a certain Marquis has bequeathed to the latter 600,000
francs on condition that he either marries Hortense or hands
over to her 200,000 francs. But the Marquis is in love with
the Countess, in whose château the scene is laid, and Hortense feels sure that, since he does not care for her and is
already well off, he will prefer to pay the forfeit and marry
the Countess. So she determines to bring him to the point.
But meanwhile he has in a timid fashion declared his love to
the Countess, and, being shy and diffident, has got the impression that she was indignant at his declaration. He therefore accepts Hortense's offer of her hand, though, as she says,
with a bad grace. At this point, it must be confessed, the road
to love's ultimate triumph becomes rather long and devious,
and the incident of the legacy which gives an interest to the

plot at the outset leads to rather tiresome complications. Excellent though the scenes between the shy Marquis and the brusque and sensible Countess are, one cannot help feeling even in the first scene between them that it only needs a word from the Countess to bring about the *dénouement*. It rather looks as if Marivaux himself realised that some explanation was needed. For whereas generally he allows his characters to reveal themselves, the Countess and the Marquis are described rather carefully by others. The Countess, says Hortense, is a "femme brusque, qui aime à primer, à gouverner, à être la maîtresse. Le Marquis est un homme paisible, doux, aisé à conduire". Lépine, the valet, is less flattering as regards the lady:

> Le Marquis, homme tout simple, peu hasardeux dans le discours, n'osera jamais aventurer une déclaration; et des déclarations, la Comtesse les épouvante; femme, qui néglige les compliments, qui vous parle entre l'aigre et le doux, et dont l'entretien a je ne sais quoi de sec, de froid, de purement raisonnable. Le moyen que l'amour puisse être mis en avant avec cette femme!

Lépine is a notable character, a "Gascon froid", who carries off his native self-assurance with a calm imperturbability, which is very entertaining. He does all he can to bring about his master's marriage, partly for his master's sake and partly because he wants to marry Lisette, the Countess's maid, "qui a de l'esprit", and who from self-interest is opposed to the marriage. The play ends with their reconciliation. "Maraud! je crois en effet qu'il faudra que je t'épouse"—"Je l'avais entrepris."

Lisette was doubtless played by Mlle Dangeville. She excelled in the part of *soubrettes*, as one can well believe from her charming portrait by La Tour. That the play was felt to drag towards the end may be inferred from the fact that in the edition of 1758, published in Marivaux's lifetime, the scenes from xii to xvii are cut down to three, nearly the whole of xii and xv being omitted and xvi and xvii being thrown into one. Modern editions, however, follow the text of 1740.

In most of the comedies that have been considered hitherto Marivaux has traced the growth of love from the outset, often indeed in two persons who are entire strangers to one another. In *Les Fausses Confidences*, which followed *Le Legs* a year later (1737) Dorante, though he has never spoken to the beautiful and rich widow, Araminte, is passionately in love with her. But, though her equal in birth, he is as poor as she is rich, and in order to gain access to her, he contrives with the help of his old valet Dubois to enter her service as her intendant. He has in his favour that he is extremely good-looking. "Votre bonne mine", says Dubois, "est un Pérou...il n'y a point de plus grand seigneur que vous à Paris." All this introduces that element of romantic sentiment which was inherent in Marivaux's nature, but which, as we have seen, does not always find expression in his comedies. In many ways this comedy does not keep so closely as his earlier ones to the conventions of the Italian stage. The attractive Marton, who, like Dorante, is of a good *bourgeois* family, is Araminte's friend rather than *suivante*. Dubois is superior to the ordinary type of valet, and there is no love-making between them. M. Remi, an attorney, who is Dorante's uncle, and Mme Argante, Araminte's mother, between whom there is an admirable scene in the third act, are both characters more or less outside the traditional range. In fact the only character that represents the Italian tradition is the delightfully naïve and stupid valet, Arlequin.

Before the end of the first act Dubois tells Araminte that Dorante is madly in love with her, and from this point the gradual awakening of a reciprocal love in her heart is portrayed with marvellous skill and delicacy. She tells Dubois that she is not angry, and she suggests that to see her habitually may cure Dorante of his folly. When he declines in her presence the offer of a rich marriage made to him through his uncle, she says aside: "Il me touche tant, qu'il faut que je m'en aille". There are of course hindrances and misunder-

standings. Dorante has a rival in the Count, who is warmly
supported by Araminte's mother, and Marton, misled by
M. Remi with, it must be confessed, Dorante's tacit con-
nivance, believes that she is the object of Dorante's affections.
There is a pending law-suit between Araminte and the Count,
and there is a mysterious portrait in a box, which Araminte
discovers to be her own portrait, painted by Dorante. And
once more she says, "Je ne me fâcherai point". But the
story of the portrait comes to Mme Argante's ears, and she is
insistent that Dorante shall be dismissed. Then there is a
letter in which Dorante avows his passion and which comes,
by arrangement between Dorante and Dubois, into Marton's
possession. She gives it to the Count to read aloud in
the presence of all the company. Mme Argante is thereupon more disagreeable and more hostile to Dorante than
ever, but her hostility has only the effect of driving Araminte
into a state of irritation with everybody—except Dorante.
When he comes to take leave of her, he asks to have her portrait restored to him. "Vous donner mon portrait! songez-
vous que ce serait avouer que je vous aime?"—"Que vous
m'aimez, madame! Quelle idée! qui pouvait se l'imaginer?"
—"Et voilà pourtant ce qui m'arrive."

"Mlle Plessy", wrote Théophile Gautier in *Le Moniteur
Universel* after a performance in 1855, "a joué ce délicieux
rôle d'Araminte, un des plus heureux qui soient au théâtre,
en y mettant une étincelle de coquetterie." If one may
question the interpretation of so accomplished an actress
as Mme Arnould-Plessy, it seems to me that one of
Araminte's greatest charms is her entire freedom from
coquetry. Add to this her good-nature, her consideration for
others, her placid dignity, and her quiet air of authority, and
the rôle is indeed a delicious one. Even when she is driven
to distraction by the persecution of Dubois on one side and
that of Mme Argante on the other, she quickly recovers her
equanimity and her independence of action. She generously
forgives Dorante for his barely justifiable ruse, and she

follows the joint bidding of her heart and her reason. Once
more love triumphs.

Les Fausses Confidences was followed by three one-act
comedies. The first was *La Joie imprévue* (1738), which, like
La Méprise, is slight but of decided merit. The plot is well
worked out and, like *La Méprise*, is remarkable for the
brilliant dialogue between the valet (Pasquin) and the
soubrette (Lisette), which is witty without being in the least
precious. The other two, *Les Sincères* (1739) and *L'Épreuve*
(1740), are more substantial, and the latter still retains its place
in the repertory. It takes its name from the test to which
Lucidor, a well-to-do *bourgeois de ville* submits Angélique, a
petite bourgeoise living in the country, who with her mother
has looked after him through an illness, in order to assure
himself that she loves him for himself and not for his money.
With this object in view he introduces an ostensible suitor
for her hand in the person of his valet, Frontin, disguised as
a man of fashion. At the same time he insists that a rich
farmer of the neighbourhood, named Blaise, who is in love
with her, should persevere in his attentions. Both Frontin
and Blaise are more comic characters than we usually find in
Marivaux, and the scene between Frontin and Lisette in which
the *soubrette* recognises Frontin, but is almost convinced by
his effrontery that she is mistaken, is an admirable piece of
comedy. Her last words to him, "Je sais garder un secret,
Monsieur, dites-moi si c'est toi", are a delightful expression
of her perplexity. Lucidor's conduct towards Angélique has
been blamed by some critics, notably by Brunetière and Lemaître, as needlessly cruel, for it should have been evident
to him without any test that she really loved him. But this is
taking too serious a view of his conduct. What matters to the
reader is that it provides him with several entertaining scenes,
which give him the idea that they would act even better than
they read.

Les Sincères, which appeared in January 1739, has been
highly praised by Sainte-Beuve, and later by Petit de Julle-

Marivaux

ville. When it was revived at the Odéon in 1891 it had a brilliant success and ran for thirty-three nights. It differs from Marivaux's normal type of comedy in that it is more concerned with the psychology of falling out of love than with that of falling in. It is also interesting on account of its debt to Molière. For it not only owes its governing idea to *Le Misanthrope* but it reproduces the famous scene of the portraits. Unfortunately the Marquise is not a Célimène, and her portraits are prosaic and laboured compared with Célimène's brilliant improvisations. Ergaste too is a very inferior Alceste and the other pair, Dorante and Araminte, are uninteresting. The scenes in which Ergaste and the Marquise, by their unnecessary and tactless sincerity, reveal the unreality of their love, are certainly clever, and so is the scene in which Dorante, by pretending to be sincere, regains the heart of the Marquise. But on the whole I do not rate the play as highly as some of Marivaux's admirers do.

With *L'Épreuve* Marivaux's dramatic career practically ended. After this he produced nothing of importance. In 1744, *La Dispute*, an allegory of inconstant love in a fairy setting, failed at the Théâtre-Français and was withdrawn after a single performance. *Le Préjugé vaincu* (1746) fared rather better, thanks, as we have seen, to Mlle Gaussin and Mlle Dangeville, but it is a slight play with only five characters, and the theme—the hesitation of the daughter of a poor Marquis to marry the rich son of a *bourgeois*—is more interesting from the social than from the dramatic point of view. More significant is the fact that Marivaux's dialogue has lost something of its point and delicacy. With *L'Épreuve* also ended Marivaux's long and honourable connexion with the Italians. After the retirement of Riccoboni and his wife about the year 1732 the old traditional names of the characters began to die out. In fact *Le Jeu de l'Amour et du Hasard* is the last play of Marivaux's in which we have a Silvia, a Mario, and an Arlequin. The last character survived for a time. He appears in *Les Fausses Confidences* (1737), but two years later his great interpreter, Vicentini, died, and Marivaux's comedy knows him no more. In *Les Sincères* (1739) and *L'Épreuve* his place is taken by Frontin and the *soubrette* has become Lisette. To complete the tale of Marivaux's dramatic work, *Les Acteurs de bonne Foi*, original in intention but feeble in execution, was read before the Comédie Française in 1755 but never acted. In the same year, *La Femme Fidèle*, a *comédie sérieuse*, of which the few scenes that have been preserved give one a favourable impression, was acted at the Comte de Clermont's private theatre of Berny. Finally *Félicie*, a moral fairy story for young girls, which met with the same fate as *Les Acteurs de bonne Foi*, was published in *Le Mercure* in 1757.

In 1741, the year after the production of *L'Épreuve*, Nivelle de La Chaussée's *Mélanide*, from which the comic element is entirely banished, was performed with great success, and was followed by the equally successful *L'École des Mères* (1744) and *La Gouvernante* (1747). Thus a new kind of comedy, which was called in derision *comédie larmoyante*, was triumphantly established. Voltaire, who called it *un genre très vicieux et très désagréable*, but who liked to be in the fashion, admitted in his preface to *Nanine* (1749), a dramatised version of *Pamela*, that it had many points in common with sentimental comedy. But Marivaux, though his latest plays were variations from the type of comedy with which he was most at home, never came any nearer to sentimental comedy than he had done in *La Mère Confidente*. He remained to the end of his life wholly original, an imitator of no one.

This great virtue, originality, had been his from the first. In 1720, when he entered the dramatic lists, the comic stage was still dominated by the great figure of Molière. Dancourt, who had retired in 1718, had in some measure substituted the comedy of manners for the comedy of character, but rather because his knowledge of life did not go deep than from any originality in his conception of the drama. Dufresny, indeed, who was more interested in character than in manners, prided himself on his originality in the choice of plots and characters. But he was too indolent and had too little dramatic genius to make any real change. On the other hand, the plays of Destouches, a much younger man, only eight years older than Marivaux, indicate by their titles that he was treading more or less in Molière's footsteps. The great success of two of these, *L'Irrésolu* (1713) and *Le Médisant* (1715), tended to confirm verse as the true medium for comedy, and it was doubtless this success which led Dufresny to employ verse for his last four plays, which appeared from 1715 to 1719.

Then in the year after Dufresny's last play Marivaux, after collaborating in a failure, which was never printed, produced at the Italian theatre in the Rue Mauconseil *Arlequin poli par l'Amour*. Nothing can be more unlike the work of his immediate predecessors than this charming little piece. But it affords no measure of its author's powers. It is little more than an outline to be filled in by the clever and excellent actors of Lélio's troop, especially by Arlequin and Silvia. The stage direction, for instance, in the second scene runs, "Arlequin égaie cette scène de tout ce que son génie peut lui fournir de propre au sujet". Moreover, as Thomassin, the actor of the part, could not speak any French, only a few words are allotted to Arlequin in the first ten scenes, that is to say until his manners have been polished and his intelligence awakened by his love for Silvia. Even after this his longest speech consists of half-a-dozen lines.

But in *La Surprise de l'Amour* Marivaux stands firmly on his own feet. In this play he created an entirely new kind of comedy, which Voltaire, though he denied the allusion to Marivaux, absurdly termed "metaphysical comedy". Modern critics have given it the name of psychological comedy, and with perfect justification, though the term "psychology" was unknown in Marivaux's day. What his aims were has already been pointed out in his own words. It was to track in its hidings and bring to light the love that either ignores itself or is too shy and diffident to make itself known, and then to trace its gradual growth from these modest beginnings to maturity. And this he does in his most characteristic plays (of which *La Surprise de l'Amour* is the pattern) not by means of an ordinary plot with its external obstacles and other complications, but by subtle and progressive analysis of the self-questionings, the hesitations, the advances and retreats of his lovers. In this he is, as has been said, the pupil of Racine, but, while Racine's chief province is love which has grown into a remorseless passion, Marivaux confines himself to its earlier and more equable stages. With Racine love is often a torrent that has overflowed its banks and is charged with disaster; with Marivaux it is an infant stream, rippling pleasantly over obstacles and widening into a placid river. With the one love ends in death, with the other in happiness and matrimony.

But Marivaux often deviates from his type—much oftener indeed than his critics gave him credit for. I can count at least sixteen plays, or more than half of his whole production, which are not concerned with the psychology of growing love. Some are romantic dramas, or, if you like, *comédies héroïques*; some are what may be called classical comedies—comedies, that is say, with a more or less conventional plot; some are social satires with a purely imaginary background; and *La Mère Confidente* and *La Femme Fidèle* are sentimental comedies. It is true that at least half of these are not to be numbered among his successes, but they include *Le Prince Travesti*, *L'École des Mères*, and *L'Ile des Esclaves* as well as the above-mentioned *La Mère Confidente*, all of which, if not quite masterpieces, are of very great merit.

It may seem at first sight inconsistent with originality that Marivaux should so easily accept the conventions of the stage, and not only of the stage in general, but of the particular stage with which he was concerned for the moment. Thus he adopts not only the traditional names of Italian comedy, but the conception of the stock characters, especially that of Arlequin, as interpreted by the Italian actors. He does just the same, when his play is produced by the Comédie Française. Colombine becomes Lisette, Arlequin Frontin or Lubin or Lépine, and Lélio the Chevalier or the Marquis. In the matter of the names of his characters it would have been better if he had conformed less closely to stage conventions. I have known people who have been deterred from reading Molière by the constant recurrence of the same names in his *dramatis personae*. How, they ask, are they to distinguish between the numerous Sganarelles, or between Mariane of *Tartuffe* and Mariane of *L'Avare*, or between Dorimène of *Le Mariage forcé* and Dorimène of *Le Bourgeois gentilhomme*, or between Ariste of *L'École des Maris* and Ariste of *Les Femmes Savantes*, or between the various Cléantes, Léandres, and Valères? But Marivaux presents even greater difficulty. When we speak of Silvia, we no doubt think in the first place of Silvia of *Le Jeu de l'Amour et du Hasard*, but Silvia of *La Double Inconstance* is hardly of less importance and there is also Silvia of *Arlequin poli par l'Amour*. Arlequin is even more confusing, for he occurs in all the earlier plays produced at the Italian theatre. But when we come to the Comédie Française and to the later comedies produced by their rivals, matters are worse, for we have not only all the Mme Argantes and Angéliques and Lisettes and Frontins to disentangle, but numerous Countesses and Marquises and Chevaliers, who have no name at all.

Marivaux observes the unities as strictly as Racine, and is as little incommoded by them. In the great majority of his comedies that represent ordinary social life the scene throughout is a room in a country-house. In *Le Jeu de l'Amour et du Hasard* the scene is definitely stated to be M. Orgon's house in Paris, and in *La Seconde Surprise de l'Amour*, in which no place at all is indicated, we gather from the play that the scene is also a house in Paris. In the two romantic comedies, *La Double Inconstance* and *Le Prince Travesti*, there is more apparent latitude, for in the first the scene is described as "in the Prince's palace", in the second as "at Barcelona". But in each case the action from first to last takes place in a single room. In fact "a single room" would cover all Marivaux's comedies, except those in which the scene is laid in a desert island or in fairyland. The only exception is his first comedy, *Arlequin poli par l'Amour*, in which the scene is alternately in the garden of the Fairy's palace and in open country with "sheep feeding in the distance".

As regards time, it has no more meaning for Marivaux than it has for Racine. It is highly improbable, no doubt, that within twelve hours two young people who have never met before should fall in love, not with the sudden onrush of romantic passion as Romeo and Juliet, but soberly and after careful reflection and self-questioning, or that a widow who is inconsolable for the loss of her husband should give her heart to a man who, when she meets him, is equally inconsolable. It is even more improbable that two lovers who believe that they are all in all to one another should within the same space of time each fall in love with someone else. The answer is that it is not a question of twelve or twenty-four hours. In the kingdom of love time does not count. Whether the reflections and hesitations that Marivaux's lovers experience are an affair of years or hours concerns us as little as it does them. All that matters is that they should "see clear into their hearts".

There is very little external action in Marivaux's plays. Such as there is serves merely as a stimulus to the internal action, or, in other words, to the movement of the mind and the heart. But to arouse and sustain dramatic interest chiefly by means of internal action requires dramatic genius of a high order. This Marivaux possessed, and one sign of it is his feeling for movement.

As soon as he has made clear the position and circumstances out of which the drama is to arise, the action goes gradually forward. Each scene marks a step in advance. Sometimes, indeed, there is an apparent retreat, but that is only because obstacles, almost invariably created by the hesitations of the lovers, and not by external causes, necessitate a devious course. Always, however, as I have said in speaking of *Le Jeu de l'Amour et du Hasard,* there is movement; the piece never stands still. Let us take *La Seconde Surprise de l'Amour* as an illustration of his method.

The first scene is chiefly occupied with the exposition. We learn from a conversation between the Marquise and her maid Lisette that the former is prostrate with grief for the loss of her husband, whom she had loved tenderly for two years before their marriage and who had died a month after it. In spite of her maid's entreaties she takes so little interest in her personal appearance that she refuses to look at herself in the glass. At last Lisette by the exercise of tact and sympathy gains her point, and this small step sets the action of the play in motion. The next scene marks another advance. Having said at the end of the first scene that she will see nobody, the Marquise now tells Lubin, the Chevalier's servant, that she will receive his master. Four short scenes follow, and then the meeting between the Marquise and the Chevalier takes place. It is an admirable scene, in which the exposition is completed by the Chevalier relating how he had lost his Angélique, who in consequence of the persecutions of her father had retired to a convent. A pact of friendship, founded on sympathy, is agreed on by the two bereaved ones. "Depuis six mois", says the Marquise, "je n'ai eu de moment supportable que celui-ci; et la raison de cela, c'est qu'on aime à soupirer avec ceux qui vous entendent", and since the late Marquis had been the Chevalier's friend she offers to take his place. "Vous avez renoncé à l'amour et moi aussi; et votre amitié me tiendra lieu de tout, si vous êtes sensible à la mienne." This is a considerable advance, and when the Chevalier in a short soliloquy exclaims: "Que cette femme-là a de mérite! je ne la connaissais pas encore; quelle solidité d'esprit! quelle bonté de cœur! C'est un caractère à peu près comme celui d'Angélique", we recognise that we are still further on the

road. The arrival on the scene of the Count, a friend of the
Chevalier's, is another step, for it appears that he is an aspirant
for the Marquise's hand, and the prick of jealousy which this
occasions reveals to us that the Chevalier is inspired by something warmer than friendship. But he himself is not aware
of it. He is only disappointed to find—for he jumps to the
conclusion that the Count will be successful—that the Marquise, of whom he thought so highly, is just like other women,
and his one consolation is that he feels how superior
Angélique is to the rest of her sex.

In the second act the gradual change in the feelings of the
Marquise and the Chevalier towards one another is indicated
by some masterly touches, and the two long scenes between
the pair, in the seventh and the ninth, are admirable in their
delicacy and their penetration. When the Marquise learns
from Hortensius, a pedant whom she has installed as her
librarian and reader, that Lisette has told him that the
Marquise is going to marry the Count and that the Chevalier
had rejected Lisette's suggestion that he should marry her
instead, she is highly indignant. "Je ne veux point me
marier", she exclaims, "mais je ne veux pas qu'on me refuse."
In the next scene but one, she still harps upon this. "Mon
veuvage est éternel; en vérité, il n'y a point de femme au
monde plus éloignée du mariage que moi, et j'ai perdu le seul
homme qui pouvait me plaire; mais, malgré tout cela, il y a
de certaines aventures désagréables pour une femme." But
when Lisette says that the Chevalier had refused her "d'un
air inquiet et piqué" she is greatly relieved. "Qu'est-ce que
c'est que d'un air piqué? Quoi? Que voulez-vous dire?
Est-ce qu'il était jaloux? En voici d'une autre espèce." Of
the two admirable scenes to which I have referred the first
may be described as a *dépit amoureux* and the second as a
reconciliation between friends who are on the verge of
becoming lovers—if they are not so already—but who have
not yet "seen clear into their hearts". Hostile critics of Marivaux might find in them examples of *marivaudage*. But it is

marivaudage only in the sense of psychological subtlety. There is not a word of "jargon", as these critics called it, in them from beginning to end.

It may be said that this second act moves rather slowly, but in the third, which is shorter than the other two, the pace quickens. There is a very clever scene between the Count and the Chevalier, in which the Count, having got the Chevalier to declare (in perfect good faith) that he and the Marquise are friends and nothing more, leads him to believe that the Marquise favours his (the Count's) suit and then offers him his sister in marriage. The Chevalier then tells the Marquise that he has accepted the offer and advises her—not very warmly—to take the Count. Whereupon the Count who, by arrangement with the Chevalier, has been concealed in the room, comes forward, makes his declaration, and is bidden by the Marquise to hope. This brings matters to a crisis. The Chevalier realises that he is in love and is not merely a friend, and the Marquise sighs and weeps. Emboldened by Lisette, she determines to dismiss the Count, and when the Chevalier comes to take leave and declares that nothing but a single word will keep him in Paris, she, without saying the actual word, makes her meaning quite clear: " Je rougis, Chevalier; c'est vous répondre"—"Mon amour pour vous durera autant que ma vie"—"Je ne vous le pardonne qu'à cette condition-là ". That is Marivaux's ideal—marriage blessed by a life-long love.

In the above rapid analysis I have barely mentioned three of the characters—Lisette, Lubin, and Hortensius, all of whom play a considerable part in the action. M. Xavier de Courville says that it was no doubt in order to suit the taste of the Théâtre-Français that Marivaux introduced the character of the pedant Hortensius, which is "unique" in his drama. It might be added that the character closely corresponds to the traditional rôle of the doctor or pedant in the *commedia dell'arte*. In *La Seconde Surprise de l'Amour* he supplies the comic element along with Lubin and he makes

pedantic love to Lisette. All three contribute to the movement of the play, though Lisette, in her anxiety to serve her
mistress, and Lubin, in his anxiety to serve his master, introduce complications and hesitations which appear at first to
frustrate the expected *dénouement*. In reality, however, they
help to bring it about, for without the crisis which arises
from the Marquise's acceptance of the Count the Marquise
and the Chevalier might have gone on being friends, and
failed to realise that they were lovers. The skilful fashion
in which Marivaux deals with the effect of these cross-currents
upon their feelings is a proof of the mastery of his art to
which he had now attained.

Gaston Deschamps rightly calls it "a masterpiece of analysis", but, when he goes on to say that the Marquise is "the
most charming of all Marivaux's women", I cannot follow
him. In her liking for men's society—only, of course, as
friends—in her attitude of " Je ne veux point me marier,
mais je ne veux pas qu'on me refuse", in her impulsive
resolution to accept the Count and her despair, when she has
virtually done so, she is a true woman. But she is a womanly
type rather than an individual; she has no marked characteristics to distinguish her from other charming women. The
Chevalier has more individuality. With his physiognomy
"bonne à porter dans un désert", with "the *ennui*, the
languour, the desolation, the despair", painted in his coun-
tenance—such is Lisette's graphic description of him to his
face—he is almost comic. The ease with which he allows the
Count to impose upon him and his blindness to the true
state of his feelings towards the Marquise make him wholly
likable and half ridiculous. It is evident that a very little
exaggeration in the representation of the part would make
him a comic figure, which he is evidently not meant
to be. Of the others, the Count is a mere dummy and
Hortensius is the conventional pedant of comedy. Lubin has
more individuality. His sudden transition from tears to
laughter in the third scene is effective, and we agree with

Lisette that, "Ce bouffon-là est amusant". His grief for his lost Marton—we are not told how he had lost her—is quickly healed by the charms of Lisette:

Ah! pauvre Lubin! J'ai bien du tourment dans le cœur; je ne sais plus à présent si c'est Marton que j'aime ou si c'est Lisette; je crois pourtant que c'est Lisette, à moins que ce ne soit Marton.

Lisette, like most of Marivaux's *soubrettes*, has plenty of *esprit* and is never at a loss for an answer. But she has no characteristic to distinguish her from the other examples of her class.

This general lack of individuality in the characters seems to me to be the reason why *La Seconde Surprise de l'Amour* is not among the most popular of Marivaux's comedies and has not kept its place in the repertory. We must remember, however, that Marivaux himself thought differently. His favourites, we are told, were the two *Surprises de l'Amour*, *La Double Inconstance*, *La Mère Confidente*, *Les Serments Indiscrets*, *Les Sincères*, and *L'Ile des Esclaves*, and in none of these can characterisation be said to be the principal feature. It is a natural inference that Marivaux cared more for psychological analysis than for creation of character.

Not that he could not create character. But his characters are delicately rather than strongly drawn; and possibly the failure of some of them to make a vivid impression on us is due, not to any lack of skill in the artist, but to our inability to detect the finer shades of character. His greatest successes are with women, especially with young girls. Among the latter two Silvias and three Angéliques are prominent. The Silvia of *La Double Inconstance* is a mere country girl, but, set against the background of a romantic court, she has the glamour of a character in a fairy-tale. Angélique of *L'Épreuve* is also a country girl, but of a superior class to Silvia. The other two Angéliques belong to the higher *bourgeoise*, or possibly, for Marivaux is not explicit on this point, to the lower nobility. At any rate they belong to well-to-do families, and have been carefully brought up. They have their own maid, and their manners are perfect. All the Silvias and the Angéliques have one thing in common; they are determined to marry the man they love and not the man favoured by their parent. Silvia of *La Double Inconstance*, indeed, has no parental command to contend against; but she has a more difficult task, for she has to choose between loyalty to her village lover and her own feelings as she gradually discerns them. In their several contests they all shew courage and determination, but their behaviour is nicely discriminated in accordance with their individual characters and circumstances. Angélique of *L'École des Mères* is an *ingénue* of sixteen, who has only spoken twice to her lover, but she faces her mother, when she insists on her marrying a rich elderly man (who turns out to be her lover's father), with a charming mixture of outward respect and inward resistance. Angélique of *La Mère Confidente* is a more pathetic figure. Though she is tenderly attached to her mother, she agrees to elope with her lover, trusting to her instinctive and well-founded belief in his honourable purpose. The third Angélique, the heroine of *L'Épreuve*, has had ample opportunity of knowing her lover, for she has helped to nurse him through an illness. She is so sure of herself—and in her heart also of him—that she comes triumphantly through the somewhat unfair test to which he subjects her. In her resolute spirit, in her wit, and wisdom, she resembles her namesake of *Le Malade imaginaire*. The Silvia of *Le Jeu de l'Amour et du Hasard* is impulsive and outspoken, and as such she reveals herself in her dialogue with her maid Lisette in the opening scene. She does not accept the conventional ideas of her social world. But she is level-headed, and though her plan is a hazardous one, and perhaps not very sensible, the idea at the back of it, that she should make herself acquainted with the character of her proposed husband, is thoroughly reasonable. She is "Reason in person", says Gaston Deschamps, which is just the opposite view to that of Sarcey. The truth, it seems to me, lies between the two views, but it is a testimony to Marivaux's fidelity to life that his characters make a different impression upon different observers. They are in fact drawn with such delicate manipulation of light and shade that the impression varies with the angle at which they are looked at.

It is the same with Araminte of *Les Fausses Confidences*. We have seen that Mme Plessy represented her as something of a coquette. But, following apparently the tradition of Mlle Mars, she also brought out the finer shades of her character which the difficulties of her situation called forth. On the other hand Madeleine Brohan, when she played the part in 1881, made indolent good-nature the key-note of her character. Good-natured she certainly is, but she is much more than this. She is generous and compassionate, she has spirit, energy, firmness, and good sense, and, if she betrays irritability when she is exasperated, she speedily recovers her equanimity. Above all she has an undefinable charm. Of the other young widows by far the most interesting is Hortense of *Le Prince Travesti*, for she has the greatest depth of character. The various Countesses and Marquises have been sufficiently noticed above. What I have said of the Marquise in the second *Surprise* is perhaps true of all. They are delicately rather than strongly individualised. As wives they will make delightful and tactful companions, but they may be just a little capricious. They will love their husbands, but they will accept respectful incense from other men.

A trait common to all these young women, whether married or single, and the one perhaps which most endears them to us, is their honesty—both to themselves and their lovers. They never imagine that they are in love before they really are, but, when once they have "seen clearly into their hearts", they give a straightforward acceptance to their lover's declaration, and even—if they are widows—they gently encourage him, when he hesitates from shyness or diffidence to make an open declaration.

As for these lovers, they are painted with a more rapid and

a more sweeping brush. The two princes of *La Double In-constance* and *Le Prince Travesti* are idealised portraits, rather than careful studies from life. But they arouse our sympathies, the first by the delicacy and magnanimity of his attitude towards Silvia and Arlequin, and the second by his constancy, his rectitude, and his forbearance in the difficult situation in which his disguise has placed him. Dorante's disguise in *Le Jeu de l'Amour et du Hasard* involves him in no less a dilemma, but it is his heart and not his honour that is concerned, and the inward struggle which he goes through is portrayed by Marivaux with absolute fidelity to life. The other lovers are less impressive, but the Marquis of *Le Legs* with his shyness and diffidence, and Lélio of *La Seconde Surprise de l'Amour*, with his modesty and his child-like simplicity, are both good, if not very incisive, sketches.

More than one critic has remarked on the contrast between Marivaux's reasonable and sympathetic fathers and his tyrannical, disagreeable, and sharp-tongued mothers. On the one hand we have Orgon of *Le Jeu de l'Amour et du Hasard*, the less known Orgon of *Les Serments Indiscrets*, and Damis of *L'École des Mères*; on the other, Mme Argante of *Les Fausses Confidences*, and Mme Argante of *L'École des Mères*. But Mme Argante of *La Mère Confidente* is tender and sympathetic and in *Le Petit-Maître corrigé* the mother of Rosimond is as kind and reasonable as the father of Hortense. The contrast then is not as sharp as critics make out; in any case it would be as rash to infer that Marivaux had an indulgent father and a hard mother as it is to regard Molière's father as the model for Harpagon, or Argan, or the Sganarelle of *L'Amour Médecin*. The probable explanation is the simple one that Marivaux adapted the character of the parent to the dramatic requirements of the comedy in question. In any case the fact that he has abandoned more definitely than Molière the traditional rôle of a father as a tyrannical egoist, who is ready to sacrifice his daughter to his own ease and comfort, is another sign of his originality.

He shews originality too in his treatment of his valets and his *soubrettes*, as will be seen by comparing it with that of his predecessors. After *L'École des Maris* Molière made little use of the conventional valet with his rascality and his resourcefulness, the type which in his earliest plays he had represented in Mascarille. The only examples in his mature work are La Flèche (*L'Avare*), Covielle (*Le Bourgeois gentilhomme*), and Scapin. Instead we have a more humorous and more natural type, and in his four greatest comedies there is no valet at all—at least as a speaking character. With his maid-servants he is still less tied to convention. From Dorine, the confidential friend of the family in *Tartuffe*, to Martine, the ungrammatical kitchen-maid of *Les Femmes Savantes*, there are many varieties of character and status, each with her own individuality, but all alike honest, outspoken, and devoted to their employers. With Dancourt and Regnard and Le Sage we return to the old types under different names. But the Frontins and Lisettes who appear so frequently in Dancourt's comedies and who play so important a part in *Turcaret* have a keener eye to their own interests than those gay rascals, Mascarille and Scapin. Their one object, which they always keep before their eyes, is to feather their own nests at the expense of their masters' purse and interests.

Marivaux with his kindly outlook on life had little use for rascals in his drama. His valets and *soubrettes* are with hardly an exception devoted to their master or mistress. They sympathise with their love affairs and are all the more ready to help them to come to an understanding in that they themselves have "seen clearly into their hearts" much more quickly, and are perfectly prepared to follow suit. The valets may be said to fall into two broad classes—the Arlequins and the Frontins. The Arlequin type is largely determined by the conception which Thomassin introduced into that stock character of Italian comedy. He is, as we have seen, naïve and a bit of a blunderer; but with a certain shrewdness underlying his apparent stupidity and not without a blunt and homely wit. In two of the comedies, *La Mère Confidente* and the first *Surprise de l'Amour*, he is called Lubin. Frontin, who makes his first appearance in *Les Serments Indiscrets* (1732) is a very different character. He is not in the least naïve; he is resourceful and self-assured, whether he is promoting his master's suit or making love himself to Lisette. He is witty, and he makes a parade of his wit, especially in *Les Serments Indiscrets*, so that such instances of *marivaudage* in the sense of jargon or affected language as are to be found in Marivaux's comedies are for the most part supplied by Frontin. He is both at his best and at his worst in *L'Heureux Stratagème* (1733), a play which affords an interesting contrast between the two types. While Frontin recalls the brilliant and resourceful valet of classical and Italian comedy, and the Mascarilles and Crispins of later date, Arlequin, the other valet, represents the homely type. With few exceptions Marivaux's valets conform to one or other of the two types, but Lépine, the "Gascon froid" of *Le Legs*, has a more distinctive individuality than the rest, and Dubois, the ex-valet of Dorante in *Les Fausses Confidences*, stands apart, as being in a superior situation to the ordinary valet. Another exception is Trivelin, that forerunner of Figaro, in *La Fausse Suivante*, who is an adventurer, an intriguer, and a cynic.

There is no such difference between the Colombines and the Lisettes as there is between the Arlequins and the Frontins. All alike are alert in speech and action; they advise and abet their mistresses with sympathetic intelligence; they are admirable in their dealings with their valet-lovers, encouraging the backward and putting the too forward in their place. They are generally more than a match for them, except, perhaps, in *Le Legs*, in which the valet with his cool assurance holds his own. "Maraud! je crois en effet qu'il faudra que je t'épouse", says Lisette. "Je l'avais entrepris", replies Lépine. This same Lisette is noteworthy as being more calculating and more concerned for her own interests than the others. Préville, the great comic actor of the second half of the

eighteenth century, gives high praise to the rôle of Marton in
Les Fausses Confidences. As the daughter of a *procureur* by
birth she is superior to the ordinary *soubrette*, and there is no
reason why she should not have believed that Dorante was
in love with her. "Her rôle", says Préville, "does not in the
least resemble that of the ordinary *soubrettes* of comedy. It
requires, besides grace, ease, and amiability, a tone of self-
respect which raises it almost to the level of the *amoureuses* of
high comedy."

Another notable *suivante* is Colombine of the first *Surprise
de l'Amour*. She is fond of displaying her *esprit*—"Mademoiselle Colombine", says her mistress, "vos fades railleries
ne me plaisent pas du tout"—and she indulges in out-of-the-
way similes, which are not without an element of *marivaudage*. But she is especially interesting, because she illustrates
better than any of Marivaux's *soubrettes* a remark of the
brothers de Goncourt in their *La Femme au dix-huitième siècle*,
that the *femme de chambre* of that century was so precious to
her mistress that "she treats her almost as a *femme de com-
pagnie*". They refer to Lisette in *Le Jeu de l'Amour et du
Hasard* as capable of doubling the part of her mistress, but
she is not on the same terms with Silvia that Colombine is
with the Countess.

These confidential relations between mistress and maid
have also considerable dramatic importance. I have pointed
out in the preceding chapter that Racine, following the
general practice of Corneille, with only one exception opens
his tragedies with a scene between one of his principal characters and a confidant, in which, not only is the situation
unfolded, but the personality of the character is revealed.
Molière, who was always making experiments and who never
crystallised a dramatic expedient into an invariable practice,
occasionally adopted a similar procedure. His tragi-comedy
of *Don Garcie* opens in orthodox fashion with a scene between Donna Elvire and her confidante. In his comedies
there are, of course, no confidants, for these were confined

to tragedy, but the opening scene between Arnolphe and his friend Chrysalde in *L'École des Femmes*, and that between Alceste and his friend Philinte in *Le Misanthrope*, admirably answer the double purpose of giving an idea of the plot and of introducing us to the leading character of the play. Arnolphe's arrogance and self-confidence and Alceste's brusqueness, sincerity, and impracticability are vividly portrayed.

Marivaux made valets and *soubrettes* take the place of Racine's confidants and confidantes, and with great advantage, especially as regards the *soubrettes*. For the confidants, whether male or female, are nearly always colourless and submissive, while the terms of closer intimacy on which the Colombines and Lisettes are with their mistresses are much more conducive to the self-revelation of character. *La Seconde Surprise de l'Amour*, *Les Serments Indiscrets*, and *Le Petit-Maître corrigé*, all begin with a dialogue between mistress and maid. In the first of these three plays only half the story is told, but in the other two we are given not only an excellently clear sketch of the situation, but the characters of Lucile in *Les Serments Indiscrets* and of Hortense in *Le Petit-Maître corrigé* are portrayed with a firmness and a distinctness that Molière might have envied. In the brilliant first scene of *Le Jeu de l'Amour et du Hasard* we are again not told the whole story, but Silvia with her common sense, her downrightness, and her wit at once wins our hearts. *Les Fausses Confidences* opens with a very short preliminary scene, but the second scene, between Dorante and his ex-valet Dubois, takes us to the very heart of the situation. "Cette femme-ci a un rang dans le monde...et tu crois que...je l'épouserai, moi qui ne suis rien, moi qui n'ai point de bien", says Dorante. "Point de bien! votre bonne mine est un Pérou", replies Dubois. "Je l'aime avec passion", cries Dorante; "Quand l'amour parle il est le maître; et il parlera", is Dubois's summing up. And this is the whole plot, including the *dénouement*. In *La Double Inconstance* Silvia and Trivelin (a court official) put the situation clearly before us and Silvia, with her *petites résolutions*, her loyalty to Arlequin, and her delightfully expressive speech, wins our hearts as surely as the Silvia of *Le Jeu*.

Finally, we have a first-rate example of a perfect exposition in *Le Legs*, which begins with a scene between Hortense and her lover, the Chevalier. The latter says very little, but we learn from Hortense, first the terms of her cousin's will, and then that the Marquis is in love with the Countess, "qui peut-être ne le hait pas", that she is a "femme brusque", who likes to take the first place, that he is "doux, paisible, aisé à conduire", that his valet Lépine is "un Gascon froid", and that Lisette, the Marquise's maid, has *esprit*. Thus all the six characters are introduced to us in the very first scene.

The above survey of Marivaux's characters seems to justify the statement that they are delicately rather than strongly drawn. But this does not imply that there is any hesitation or fumbling in the drawing. It only means that they have not strongly marked characteristics, that they are ordinary men and women placed in ordinary circumstances, which do not call for heroic action. The only characters who have a touch of heroism are the Prince of Léon and Hortense in *Le Prince Travesti*. The situations in which the two Silvias find themselves invest them with an air of romance, but their essential charm arises from their purity, their invincible honesty, and their high moral courage. Marivaux, in short, carries out to the letter Molière's precept, "Lorsque vous peignez les hommes, il faut peindre d'après nature".

He observes equally well the precept which follows this— "Vous n'avez rien fait si vous n'y faites reconnaître les gens de votre siècle". Moreover, it will be noticed that he subtly marks the distinction of class, the distinction between Araminte, the rich *bourgeoise*, and the aristocratic Countesses and Marquises, and between Silvia (of *Le Jeu*), Lucile, and the two Angéliques of *La Mère Confidente* and *L'École des Mères* on the one hand, and Angélique of *L'Épreuve* on the other.

The element of stage tradition enters rather more into his gallery of valets and *soubrettes*, but, as I have pointed out above, the friendly relations, amounting almost to equality, that he depicts as existing between mistress and maid really did exist in his day. And masters were on hardly less friendly terms with their valets. As for the *esprit* that Marivaux's Frontins and Lisettes display so readily, although this is partly due to tradition, it must be remembered that during the eighteenth century there was a remarkable spread of education among the lower classes. "Pas un petit bourgeois n'eût reçu un laquais, même une cuisinière, qui ne sût lire et écrire", writes the Abbé Du Bos to Bayle in 1696. A cook who could read and write is a decided advance on Molière's Martine of a quarter of a century earlier.

In other respects too Marivaux's comedies, except those that have a mythological or otherwise purely imaginary setting, faithfully reproduce the social *milieu* of his day. But we must not look to them for any material details. When Silvia and Lisette change costumes, we are not allowed the slightest glimpse of what the costumes consisted. The only reference, so far as I can recollect, to eating and drinking is in *La Double Inconstance*, in which Arlequin's love of good cheer is emphasised. The only play in which a specific sum of money is mentioned is *Le Legs*. The scene of the play is generally a country-house, the only exceptions, I think, being *La Seconde Surprise de l'Amour* and *Le Jeu de l'Amour et du Hasard*, and in the former there is no direct indication of scene and it is only from the text of the play that we learn that it is Paris. Thus the study of manners plays absolutely no part in Marivaux's comedy, and we have seen that the study of character, good though it is and quite sufficient for his purpose, is only with him a secondary interest.

His primary interest is the dramatic presentation of the growth of love from a tiny seed to a full-blown flower. "I have searched in the human heart for all the different

corners in which love can hide itself", he says in the passage
that I have quoted above. And in another passage, also
quoted above, he defends himself against the charge that his
comedies were all alike, by pointing out the differences in the
relations of the two lovers. "Sometimes it is a love of which
both are ignorant." This is true of the two *Surprises de
l'Amour* and *La Double Inconstance*. But, as we have seen, there
is a great difference between the first *Surprise*, in which the
two lovers, as they afterwards become, have renounced love
and matrimony owing to their former experiences, and the
second *Surprise*, in which they are still faithful (apparently)
to their lost loves. It is true that the Marquise's adored
husband and the Chevalier's equally adored Angélique are
forgotten rather quickly and that the play has a better right
to be called *La Double Inconstance* than the one which bears
that name. For in the latter play Marivaux evidently wishes
to indicate that the love between Silvia and Arlequin is not
the real thing, but merely the love that springs from pro-
pinquity. To have known one another as boy and girl is not
always the prelude to a happy marriage.

"Sometimes it is a love that they feel, but wish to hide
from one another." This is the theme of *Les Serments Indiscrets*, while "a timid love which does not dare to declare
itself" exactly fits the case of the Marquis in *Le Legs*. Lastly,
the fourth variety, "a love uncertain and undecided, a love
half-born, so to speak, which the lovers suspect without
being quite sure and which they rarely examine within their
hearts before allowing it to come to the light", has its perfect illustration in *Le Jeu de l'Amour et du Hasard*. *Les Fausses
Confidences* does not come under the head of any of these
varieties. On the one hand, Dorante, though he has never
spoken to Araminte, is passionately in love with her. On the
other, Araminte, up to the moment that she first sets eyes on
Dorante, has not the remotest idea of his reason for wishing
to become her man of affairs. Yet note the opening of the
sixth scene of the first act:

ARAMINTE.

Marton, quel est donc cet homme qui vient de me saluer si gracieusement, et qui passe sur la terrasse? Est-ce à vous qu'il en veut?

MARTON.

Non, Madame; c'est à vous-même.

ARAMINTE (*d'un air assez vif*).

Eh bien, qu'on le fasse venir; pourquoi s'en va-t-il?

May not this come under the head of a love, or at least of an attraction, of which the person who feels it is unconscious? For in nearly all these comedies of the discovery of love there is attraction at first sight. There is no sign of it, indeed, in the first *Surprise*, but it is certainly there in the second *Surprise*, still more markedly in *Les Serments Indiscrets*. What of Silvia and the Prince? He had met her while hunting and had been struck by her beauty and simplicity. And she, believing him to be a mere official of the court, had treated him with "beaucoup de douceur". May it not have been on her part "un amour ignoré"? Arlequin, too, is decidedly drawn towards Flaminia. His very first remark to her is, "Allez, Mademoiselle, vous êtes une fille de bien. Je suis votre ami aussi, moi", and in his second meeting with her the friendship makes great progress. Marivaux would, no doubt, not have subscribed to Marlowe's "He never loved who loved not at first sight", but he evidently believes that the spark of true love is often kindled at the first contact between sympathetic souls.

In some of his plays the lovers are already in love when the play opens, and the dramatic interest arises from the obstacles which they have to surmount. These obstacles sometimes arise from the opposition of parents, as in *L'École des Mères* and *La Mère Confidente*, sometimes from a rival of one of the lovers, as in *Le Prince Travesti*, sometimes from one of the lovers themselves, as in *L'Épreuve*, *Le Préjugé vaincu*, and *Le*

Marivaux

Petit-Maître corrigé. Les Sincères, L'Heureux Stratagème, La Fausse Suivante are also plays of which the main interest is the psychology of love, but in all of them—in spite of the favour it has found with competent judges, I venture to include *Les Sincères*—the psychology is too subtle and the situations too complicated to make them really good plays. Although he has succeeded admirably in *L'École des Mères*, which is a comedy of intrigue of the old-fashioned type, Marivaux is not generally at his best in unravelling complications and keeping their threads apart. It is a distinct defect in that otherwise excellent romantic comedy, *Le Prince Travesti*, that the actions of the characters, or at any rate their motives, are not always clear.

It results from this rapid review of those comedies in which Marivaux is dealing with his favourite subject, the vicissitudes and psychology of lovers, that the charge of monotony and repetition that is brought against him falls to the ground. It is quite true that in all these comedies matrimony is the goal. But the roads that lead to it are many and differ greatly in character. Some are more arduous, some are more circuitous, and the starting-point is never the same. The grumblers too forget that, in Marivaux's words, "tout se passe au cœur". We may know from the beginning of the comedy that Lélio will marry Silvia and Arlequin Colombine, but underneath their conventional masks they all have their own personality, and their hearts beat to different tunes.

Further, by no means all Marivaux's comedies are "surprises" or "triumphs of love". Some half-dozen deal with problems of social life; they are half sympathetic and half satirical, and they have an imaginary setting. Some have a background of classical mythology, some of fairyland, while the two best, *L'Ile des Esclaves* and *La Colonie*, adopt that favourite device of social satirists—an imaginary island.

A dramatist who delights in psychological analysis, who can create character and is a master of movement, will almost inevitably excel in dialogue. Marivaux's dialogue is, in fact,

superlatively good. Take, for instance, the scene between
Silvia and the Prince in *La Double Inconstance* (II, 12), that
between Araminte and Dubois in *Les Fausses Confidences*
(I, 14), that between the Countess and Lisette in *Le Legs*
(Sc. 23), that between Frontin and Lisette in *L'Épreuve*
(Sc. 12), or that between Silvia and Dorante in *Le Jeu de
l'Amour et du Hasard* (II, 9). They are very different in character; one is humorous, two are remarkable for their subtlety,
and the other two are both tender and pathetic. But they
all have this in common—and there are many others like
them—that the dialogue reveals, simply and transparently,
the sentiments and character of the speakers, that it is concerned with nothing but the situation in hand, which it expresses perfectly, and that it definitely contributes—the scene
between Frontin and Lisette is perhaps an exception—to the
development of the drama. Finally, it should be noted that
all these scenes are absolutely free from what is called *marivaudage* in any shape or kind.

As for this accusation of *marivaudage* which critics, some
hostile and some friendly, have brought against Marivaux,
I have discussed it elsewhere[1], but it may be well to re-
capitulate my conclusions. A satisfactory definition of it is,
I believe, impossible, for the simple reason that it includes
several counts—firstly the use of what Marivaux's critics
called *jargon*, that is of "precious" or affected language,
secondly the subtle examination by lovers of the condition
of their hearts, and thirdly the abuse of the habit of reflection,
which sometimes leads to repetition of the same reflection in
a different form. This third count need not detain us, for it
chiefly applies to Marivaux as a novelist and an essayist. He
was far too great an artist to interrupt the movement of his
drama by putting reflections of his own in the mouth of his
characters. The only possible exception is in the scene between Arlequin and the *seigneur*, to which I have already referred. The second count is really an attack on Marivaux's

[1] In *The Modern Language Review* for January 1930.

whole method. The psychological analysis of growing love
is the soul of his drama. If you do not care for that you cannot like Marivaux. There are, however, certain plays in
which, as I have already indicated, the analysis seems to me
over-subtle and over-elaborate. One of these, *La Fausse
Suivante*, is admittedly not one of his best works, but the first
Surprise de l'Amour, *Les Serments Indiscrets*, and *Les Sincères*
were not only among his own favourites, but each has been
admired by more than one competent judge in comparatively
recent years. It is after all only a question of degree and
personal taste. Speaking for myself, I think the theatre-going
public are right in preferring those comedies in which the
psychology unfolds itself more by action than by argument.

It remains to consider *marivaudage* as applied to Marivaux's
style. He has defended it both in the preface to *Les Serments
Indiscrets* and in *Le Cabinet du Philosophe*, and the gist of his
defence is that it is the natural expression of subtle and original
ideas. Any unprejudiced reader of his plays will agree that
this is in the main true. But there are, it must be admitted,
exceptional cases, in which, while the thought is simple and
commonplace, the expression is unnatural and affected—in
other words "precious". The few offenders are for the most
part valets—Frontin in *Les Serments Indiscrets*, Arlequin in the
first *Surprise de l'Amour*, Frontin in *L'Épreuve*, and, worst of
all, Frontin in *L'Heureux Stratagème*. Perhaps we should add
Lépine in *Le Legs*. The only *soubrette*, so far as I can remember, who makes a display of her *esprit* in affected language is the Colombine of the first *Surprise*. Now more than
one critic has pointed out that Marivaux in putting this kind
of language in the mouths of his valets and *soubrettes* is true
to nature. A simple-minded peasant, such as Arlequin in *Les
Fausses Confidences*, will, as Fleury says, use in real life
language that is both "low and precious". And the great
majority of Marivaux's valets, who are not simple-minded, use
stilted and affected language to display their *esprit* and because they think it is a sign of social distinction. Thus the

valet of *L'Épreuve*, when he appears in disguise as a suitor for the hand of Angélique, makes his bow to her with "Mademoiselle, l'étonnante immobilité où je vous vois intimide extrêmement mon inclination naissante". Apart from valets and (more exceptionally) *soubrettes*, the only character who can be accused of *marivaudage* in the sense of "precious" or affected language is Lucile, the heroine of *Les Serments Indiscrets*, and as she is represented as something of a *précieuse*, her language is in keeping with her character. In the great majority of the plays it would be difficult to find a single phrase, or even a single word, that can be fairly called jargon. So that when D'Alembert, speaking of Marivaux's style, says, "ce singulier jargon, tout à la fois précieux et familier, recherché et monotone, est sans exception, celui de tous ses personnages, de quelque état qu'ils puissent être", one can only suppose that D'Alembert had not seen or read any of his comedies. Thus his remark serves to shew into what neglect Marivaux had fallen within twelve years of his death.

III

Musset

If it is the mark of a disciple that he should catch the spirit of his master, Brunetière was right in saying that Marivaux was the disciple of Racine. It is true that in his first successful play, *Arlequin poli par l'Amour*, the dominating influence is not Racine, but the Italian comedy. But before he produced his next comedy, *La Surprise de l'Amour*, eighteen months later, he must have become aware of the possibilities of an entirely unworked dramatic field—the progress of love from its birth to its ultimate triumph. So, like Racine, he became the psychologist of love—not as a full-grown and consuming passion but in its shy and hesitating infancy. He must also have learnt from Racine that inward action is as effective a source of dramatic interest as outward action, and that therefore the best method for his purpose was to subject the hearts of his lovers to a delicate scrutiny and to make the conflict which is the soul of drama a purely spiritual one. But his debt to Racine is only a general debt and, as one might expect, seeing that the master wrote tragedies in verse and the disciple comedies in prose, there are no traces of direct borrowing. Nor, so far as I know, is there any reference to Racine either in Marivaux's non-dramatic work or in the scanty records of his conversation. He was whole-heartedly a "modern", and he might well have been reluctant to recognise an obligation to a "classic".

Similarly there is no mention of Marivaux either in Musset's poems or plays or *contes*, or in his correspondence. But the influence is unmistakeable. The most obvious instances are *Il faut qu'une porte soit ouverte ou fermée* and the little comedy of a similar type which made Musset's reputation as a dramatist

—*Un Caprice*. Larroumet, indeed, thinks that the latter play is Musset's version of Marivaux's *L'Heureux Stratagème*, but this I doubt. On the other hand he is probably right in regarding *L'Ane et le Ruisseau* (a late production which was never acted) as suggested by *Le Legs*. M. Lafoscade sees a similarity between *Le Legs* and *Il faut qu'une porte soit ouverte ou fermée*, and the relations of the Countess and the Marquis in Marivaux's comedy are not unlike those of the Marquise and the Count in Musset's proverb. Indeed the dialogue between Musset's pair ends on a note which reminds one forcibly of the last scene but one of *Le Legs*. In the three plays of Musset's above noticed, which are all alike remarkable for their almost complete absence of external action, it is evident that what impressed Musset in Marivaux is his power of creating a genuine dramatic interest by the use of dialogue to disclose the internal working of the heart, and doubtless he paid special attention from that point of view to the first *Surprise de l'Amour* and *Les Serments Indiscrets*, plays which, as we have seen, were special favourites with Marivaux himself, but which more perhaps than any others can be justly taxed with *marivaudage* in the sense of preciosity. Musset is never precious but always perfectly natural. But while he never strains after *esprit*, he has learnt from Marivaux that dialogue which has for its object the development of internal action must be the utterance of quick-witted and apprehending speakers, or in other words that it must be distinguished by *esprit*. "C'est le ton de la conversation en général que j'ai tâché de prendre", says Marivaux in his preface to *Les Serments Indiscrets*, but he adds that "entre gens d'esprit les conversations dans le monde sont plus vives qu'on ne pense", and we saw that when he made this remark he was evidently thinking of the conversation at the dinners and in the salons of Mme de Lambert and Mme de Tencin.

I do not suppose that Alfred de Musset ever read this preface, but when he wrote *Les Caprices de Marianne* (1833) it is permissible to believe that he had learnt something from

Marivaux. The whole tone of the dialogue between Octave
and Cœlio and between Octave and Marianne in the first
scene of the first act and of that between Octave and
Marianne in the first scene of the second act suggests this belief. A better example is the conversation between Van Buck
and his nephew in the opening scene of *Il ne faut jurer de rien*,
which has not the undercurrent of passion to give it interest,
and which, in spite of its length, is never for a moment dull.
An even better example is the last scene of *Bettine* (1851), because it ends with a proposal of marriage and an implied
acceptance quite in the manner of Marivaux.

But there was a stronger influence than Marivaux at work
on Musset. In September 1827 an English company under
the management of William Abbot began to give a series of
representations of Shakespeare and other English dramatists
at Paris and continued them till near the end of July 1828.
Besides the regular members of the company, which included
Miss Smithson the future wife of Berlioz, four leading
English actors, Charles Kemble, Edmond Kean, Macready,
and Terry joined them from time to time, and the Parisians
had the opportunity of seeing Kemble in *Hamlet*, *Othello*, and
Romeo and Juliet, Macready in *Macbeth*, *Hamlet*, and *Othello*,
and Kean in *Richard III*, *Othello*, *King Lear*, and *The Merchant
of Venice*. Kemble's visit was made in September 1827,
Kean's from the middle of May to the middle of June 1828,
while Macready paid two visits, in April and July 1828.
Kean's Shylock roused the audience to enthusiasm, but
they preferred Macready's Othello, though Hazlitt thought
that Othello was Kean's best part. The impression made
upon the leading spirits of the romantic movement was
momentous. Under the influence of the first representations
of *Hamlet*, *Othello*, and *Romeo and Juliet* Victor Hugo began
to write his famous preface to *Cromwell* on September 30,
1827. Dumas, after seeing *Hamlet* for the first time, said, "It
was only then that I realised what the drama could be....
For the first time I had seen real passions on the stage, in-

spiring men and women of real flesh and blood". Neither Hugo nor Dumas at this time knew English, so their enthusiasm must have been largely due to the excellence of Kemble's acting. Alfred de Musset, then a precocious boy of sixteen, could read him in his native tongue. But he was staying with his great-uncle in the country and he wrote to a friend, just a week before Hugo began his preface, "Je donnerais vingt-cinq francs pour avoir une pièce de Shakespeare ici en anglais". But in the following spring his parents went to live at Auteuil, and he may then have had opportunities of seeing one or more of Shakespeare's four great tragedies. This, however, is a pure hypothesis.

In the next few years Musset evidently became very familiar with Shakespeare. In *Les Caprices de Marianne* we have at least three characters whose names are borrowed from him—Claudio, Malvolio, and Hermia—and it is possible that Marianne may be a reminiscence of Mariana in *Measure for Measure*. The name Laerte in *A quoi rêvent les jeunes filles* was probably suggested by *Hamlet*; there are several references to that play in his early poems—in *Le Saule*, in *Mardoche*, and in the dedication to *La Coupe et les Lèvres*. In *Les Secrètes Pensées de Rafael* (1831) he speaks of Shakespeare as lying on his table by the side of Racine and Boileau and he exclaims: "O vieux sir John Falstaff! quel rire eût soulevé ton large et joyeux corps". A poem of 1829 is entitled *Portia*; his unsuccessful play, *La Nuit Vénitienne* (1830), is headed by "Perfide comme l'onde", which is Othello's "false as water", and another quotation from *Othello*, this time in English, heads the poem of *Don Paez*. In *La Quenouille de Barberine* there is a direct reference to *Cymbeline*.

Musset's *début* in the theatre was as unsuccessful as Marivaux's. His first play, produced at the Odéon on December 1, 1830, nine days before his twentieth birthday, and entitled *La Nuit Vénitienne*, "pièce en un acte et trois tableaux", was cruelly hissed and was criticised without mercy by the press. The piece is in truth a very poor one. The second scene, which is much the longest, is throughout its latter half a dialogue between Laurette (the heroine) and the Prince, both of whom are dull and unintelligible. The first scene, indeed, opens well with a dialogue between Laurette and Razetta, written in easy and natural language, but Razetta is left to soliloquise in a strain of the worst possible romantic taste. The one character of any interest is the Marquis, Laurette's guardian, because he is the first of the many imbeciles whom Musset has the art of making supremely ridiculous without altogether alienating our sympathy. They are not exactly puppets, but rather marionnettes, who dance very agreeably, and even with an illusion of life, when their creator pulls the strings.

Musset's sensitive nature was deeply hurt by the contemptuous reception of his play and he determined to write no more for the stage. But the volume, *Un Spectacle dans un Fauteuil*, published in 1832, comprised a *poème dramatique* —"quelque chose approchant comme une tragédie"—entitled *La Coupe et les Lèvres*, and a delicate little extravaganza of the fantastic type—"la scène est où l'on voudra"—entitled *A quoi rêvent les jeunes filles*. Then on April 1, 1833 there appeared, in the *Revue des Deux Mondes*, *André del Sarto*, the first of a series of nine plays which Alfred de Musset wrote for that celebrated review from 1833 to 1837. It is the familiar theme, though not so hackneyed then as it became fifty years later, of the husband, the wife, and the lover, and it is treated from the sickly sentimental point of view which found favour in Romanticist circles, but which accords ill with sixteenth-century Florence. When André discovers that his pupil and greatest friend, Cordiani, is his wife's lover, he explains to him, after reducing him to tears, that he regards his action not as "an odious crime or the trampling underfoot of a holy friendship, but as the severance of the only tie which bound him (André) to life". His sentence is that Cordiani must leave Florence within an hour. But Cordiani is discovered hiding in Lucrezia's room. There is a duel, and Cordiani is wounded. "Tu es blessé, mon ami?" cries André, and then, when left alone, he proceeds to sentimentalise again, "Qu'avais-je affaire de chasser ma femme, d'égorger cet homme? Il n'y a point d'offensé, il n'y a qu'un malheureux". Finally, in the third act, after hearing that his wife has fled with Cordiani, he sends them a message that "the widow of André del Sarto can marry Cordiani", and he takes poison. The curtain falls on the delivery of the message to the fugitives. The lover, Cordiani, is no less representative than André of the Romantic attitude towards love.

De quel droit ne serait-elle pas à moi? J'aime et je suis aimé. Je ne veux rien analyser, rien savoir; il n'y a d'heureux que les enfants qui cueillent un fruit et le portent à leurs lèvres sans penser à autre chose, sinon qu'ils l'aiment et qu'il est à portée de leurs mains.

Cordiani has no characteristics beyond that of being a lover, and Lucrezia is an even slighter sketch. As Gautier said in his favourable criticism of the play when acted, "her rôle is confined to that of being beautiful". On the other hand, André, however much we may smile at his sentimentality, is well-drawn. His passion for his worthless wife, which has led to the sacrifice of his honour—for he has spent on her the money entrusted to him by Francis I for the purchase of pictures—is vividly depicted, though perhaps with an over-abundance of rhetoric, and the sudden downfall of his happiness coupled with his despair for the future of Florentine art makes him a pathetic figure.

There is considerable merit, or at least promise, in the construction and execution of the play. The classical exposition is dispensed with, and the action begins at once with Cordiani's escape from a window and his wounding of André's servant. There is also plenty of movement; indeed, in the third act the movement becomes so rapid that it loses sequence and becomes difficult to follow. The structure, however, would have been better had the author been obliged to conform to the requirements of the stage.

The play was first produced at the Théâtre-Français in 1848, but it was not a success and it was withdrawn after five performances. Two years later it was revived at the Odéon with considerable alterations. The unity of place was established, some minor scenes were omitted, and the *dénouement* was changed. Cordiani dies instead of taking flight with Lucrezia—a change, it may be noted, made in the interests of stage requirements, not in order to provide a more moral ending. This time the play had a longer run and attained to twenty-five performances.

The only other play of Musset's that he calls a *drame* is *Lorenzaccio*, his most ambitious and his most solidly constructed dramatic work. George Sand had written, but had never published, a play on the same subject with the title of *Une Conspiration de 1537*, and a note-book, which she had with her at Venice, contained four roughly sketched scenes. These she made over to Musset, who was taken with the subject, but whose play owes nothing to George Sand, except one or two tirades. He seems to have completed his plan at Venice, but he did not fully develop it till the second quarter of 1834, between his return to Paris in April and the arrival of George Sand with Pagello in August. The play was published, not in the *Revue des Deux Mondes*, for which it was evidently too long, but in the first volume of the second *livraison* of *Un Spectacle dans un Fauteuil* along with the earlier *Les Caprices de Marianne*. His only source is the *Storia Fiorentina* of Benedetto Varchi (1502–1565), who was attached to the party of the Strozzi and consequently opposed to the Medici. Banished by Cosimo I he lived for six years in exile at Venice. In 1543 he was recalled by Cosimo, who gave him a pension to write a history of Florence. Many incidents in *Lorenzaccio* are taken from him—the ball given by Martelli at which Alessandro was present in the dress of a nun, Salviati's insult to Louisa Strozzi, the scene at Monte Oliveto, the attempt to assassinate Salviati, Alessandro's relations with the Marchesa di Cibo, his coat of mail, the rolling of his sword-belt round his scabbard, Lorenzaccio's announcement at various palaces on the Arno of the intended murder of the Duke, the whole scene between Lorenzaccio and Filippo Strozzi at Venice, the proposal by Canigiano to elect Alessandro's natural son as Duke, the silk-merchant's speech at the opening of Act v, Scene v, and Cosimo's speech at the very end of the play, which is literally translated. Finally, "ce visage morne, qui sourit quelquefois, mais qui n'a pas la force de rire", represents Varchi's "non rideva, ma ghignava". The fact that *Lorenzaccio* was written without any idea of stage-production gave Musset complete freedom in the handling of his subject. After every scene there is a change of place, and for the whole thirty-five scenes there are thirteen different localities. This continual change of scene recalls *Antony and Cleopatra*, though *Lorenzaccio* does not range over so wide a field, being confined to Florence and Venice.

Writing definitely for the stage Shakespeare was compelled to be dramatic. Alfred de Musset was under no such compulsion, but he had a natural instinct for drama. His first volume of poetry, *Contes d'Espagne et d'Italie* (1829), contains a one-act comedy, *Les Marrons du Feu*, and *Don Paez* is partly in dramatic form. His next volume, *Un Spectacle dans un Fauteuil, Ire livraison* (1832), contained, as we have seen, two dramas, *La Coupe et les Lèvres*, and *A quoi rêvent les jeunes filles*. But dramatic instinct is not enough in itself, and Musset's great admiration for Shakespeare made it natural that he should turn to this supreme master of drama in order to learn how to construct a play. Certainly the first two scenes of *Lorenzaccio* suggest that he had carefully studied the openings of Shakespeare's four great tragedies and of *Romeo and Juliet*, all of which had been acted in Paris by the English company. Just as in Shakespeare, these two scenes give us the key-note of the whole play, the odious character of the debauched Duke, and the servile condition of Florence under his rule. Lorenzaccio only appears in the first scene, but the cynical libertinism of his one effective speech is profoundly revealing. In the remaining four scenes of the first act these three essential elements of the play, the condition of Florence and the characters of the Duke and his cousin, are further developed. "Regardez-moi ce petit corps maigre," says the Duke, "ce lendemain d'orgie ambulant. Regardez-moi ces yeux plombés, ces mains fluettes et maladives, à peine assez fermés pour soutenir un éventail; ce visage morne, qui sourit quelquefois, mais qui n'a pas la force de rire. C'est là un homme à craindre", and the portrait is completed by Lorenzaccio's mother, Marie Soderini, and his aunt, Catherine Ginori. Marie recalls his boyhood with his "saint amour de la vérité" and "cette admiration pour les grands hommes de son Plutarque", but she adds, "Il n'est même plus beau; comme une fumée malfaisante, la souillure de son cœur est montée au visage". In the third scene we are introduced to the enigmatic Marquise de Cibo, who loves her husband but who in his absence becomes the Duke's mistress, and to her Machiavellian brother-in-law, the Cardinal Cibo. Filippo Strozzi does not appear, but his name is on the lips of the few real patriots. "Tant qu'il y aura un cheveu sur sa tête la liberté de l'Italie n'est pas morte."

Neither the Cibos nor Filippo Strozzi and his children are directly concerned with the main action of the play, but it must be remembered that its subject is not only the Duke's murder but the decadence of Florence. The two scenes between the Marquise and the Cardinal (II, 3 and IV, 4), both very subtle and the second of great dramatic power, and the scene between the Marquise and the Duke vividly portray the corrupt and abject condition of Florence, and the Strozzi scenes (II, 1; II, 5; III, 7; IV, 6) help to deepen the impression of her shame. Moreover, these last are linked to Lorenzaccio's plan for the Duke's murder by the long—perhaps too long— and powerful scene (III, 3) between him and Filippo Strozzi. The one scene in the first four acts which it is difficult to defend from the strictly dramatic point of view is the second of the second act, consisting principally of a dialogue between Lorenzaccio and the young painter, Tebaldeo, but it helps to emphasise the Duke's tyranny, and Tebaldeo with his naïve innocence and his devotion to his art has considerable charm.

In the sixth scene of Act II, which is a very fine one, Lorenzaccio begins his preparations for the murder; he continues them in III, 1 and IV, 3, and so we come to the last scene of the fourth act, in which he accomplishes his purpose. It may be objected that there is too long an interval between IV, 3 and IV, 11, but the seventh scene, though difficult to produce effectively on the stage, in which he announces his intention successively to three possessors of palaces on the Arno, and also to some extent the tenth scene, in which Cardinal Cibo warns the Duke against him, serve to keep our expectation on the alert.

After the fourth act there is a decided drop in the interest. But it must be remembered that in order to fill out the portrait of Lorenzaccio and to complete the picture of enslaved Florence it was necessary to shew the uselessness of the murder. The execution of the fifth act, however, cannot be considered satisfactory. The first scene is good, for it vividly represents the confusion caused by Alessandro's murder, ending in the election of Cosimo as the new Duke. But the other Florentine scenes, except the last, are unnecessary and add nothing to the picture. In the second scene we are transported to Venice, where Lorenzaccio announces the murder of the tyrant to Filippo Strozzi and is hailed by him as the new Brutus. Their conversation is continued in the seventh scene and is followed rather abruptly by the news of Lorenzaccio's assassination. The change of scene from Florence to Venice and again from Venice to Florence is, of course, awkward for stage purposes, but it was necessary from Musset's point of view.

Lorenzaccio is a great advance on *André del Sarto*. Is it rash to suggest that this was partly due to a closer acquaintance with Shakespeare? We have seen that one quality that the

Romanticists so greatly admired in his plays was the impression that they give of vivid life. We have an obvious example in the three scenes at the Boar's-head tavern in *Henry IV*. Falstaff, of course, dominates each scene, but the other characters, the Prince and Poins, Bardolph and Pistol, Mistress Quickly and Doll Tearsheet, have hardly less individuality, and the clash of their conflicting purposes and desires is represented with extraordinary vigour and fidelity. Similar in quality, and with the additional merit that it advances the plot, is the third scene of the second act of *Othello*. There is nothing set or formal here. Iago, Cassio, Montano and others are found drinking together; Iago sings two songs; Cassio gets drunk and falling in with Roderigo beats him; Montano interferes and is wounded by Cassio; Othello appears, asks for an explanation, and dismisses Cassio from his service; Desdemona makes a brief entry; and finally Iago, being left alone with Cassio, hatches his villainous plot. It all seems casual and haphazard; yet the incidents follow one another in a logical sequence, controlled as they are by a master-hand.

There are two scenes in *Lorenzaccio* which have in a high degree this Shakespearian quality of life. These are the second and fifth scenes of the first act, in both of which representatives of different classes of Florentine society, coming together in a perfectly natural and life-like way, give a vivid picture of the condition of Florence previous to the Duke's assassination. Among the characters are a goldsmith and a silk-merchant, the former a republican and the latter a supporter of the Medici. They are really, notes Arvède Barine, shopkeepers of the time of Louis-Philippe, "who have never seen in their lives the Arno or the Ponte-Vecchio". But whether they are true Florentines or not, they help to give life to the scene, as they open their shops in the morning after the ball at the Nasi palace, or display their wares before the church of San Miniato. Other characters in these scenes are two ladies of the court, two cavaliers, a first and a second citizen (just as there are in the opening scene of *Julius Caesar*), Luisa Strozzi, and Salviati, the brutal libertine who insults her, one of her brothers, to whom he brags of the insult, and the Duke himself. Nor is it only the movement and animation displayed in these scenes that remind one of Shakespeare; there is also the power of giving life by means of a few strokes to the unimportant characters.

But it is in the character of Lorenzaccio himself that we most clearly recognise the influence of Shakespeare and particularly of *Hamlet*. There is little resemblance between the two protagonists, but they have this in common that the same task has been imposed on them, on the one by his own decision, on the other by the command of his father's ghost, namely that of killing a relative. Both being introspective—whether by nature or as the result of spiritual loneliness, it matters not—they are given to communing with themselves and to expressing their thoughts (for stage purposes) in soliloquies. But their soliloquies differ in character. While Hamlet is constantly urging himself to action, Lorenzaccio has no hesitations and is chiefly concerned with planning his attack. Again, while Hamlet with his higher intelligence and broader outlook wanders into the region of speculative philosophy, Lorenzaccio, more self-centred, is concerned only with his plan, or with self-justification, or with reminiscences of his past. From his soliloquies (IV, 3, 5, and 9) we learn that he spent his youth in the quiet solitude of his home at Caffaggiolo, loving the meadows and the flowers, reading the sonnets of Petrarch, or watching the pretty daughter of the *concierge* as she dried the clothes and drove away the goats. And his mother, as we saw, remembers "the sacred love of truth that shone on his lips and in his eyes"; and his compassion for the unfortunate and "his admiration for the great men of Plutarch" (I, 6). It was from Plutarch that he got his idea of being the Brutus of Florence and of murdering his cousin Alessandro, "who had done evil to others, but who had shown kindness to him, at least in his way". And so in order to effect his purpose he came to Florence and served his cousin as his spy and his pimp. He had resolved to remain pure at heart, but the mask which he had adopted became his real face, and "vice, like Deianira's robe, was incorporated with the fibres of his body".

There are two passages in these soliloquies which specially recall *Hamlet*. In IV, 3, when Lorenzaccio is wondering why he resolved to kill his cousin, he says, "Le spectre de mon père me conduisait-il, comme Oreste vers un nouvel Égiste?" and in IV, 5 he exclaims, "O Alexandre! je voudrais que tu fisses ta prière avant de venir ce soir dans cette chambre". Is not this suggested by the thought of Hamlet's unwillingness to kill his uncle while he was praying?

Lorenzaccio, as thus portrayed by Musset, is very different from the man whom Varchi represents as given over to every kind of debauchery from his early youth. But there is one trait reported by the Florentine chronicler that is reproduced by the dramatist, "Appetiva stranamenti la gloria", and this comes out in the fine scene between Lorenzaccio and Filippo Strozzi (III, 3), when he explains to the latter why it is that he is bent on committing a murder which he knows will be of no good to his country. It is that he may redeem his character.

> Songes-tu que ce meurtre, c'est tout ce qui reste de ma vertu?... Voilà assez longtemps, vois-tu, que les républicains me couvrent de boue et d'infamie...il faut que le monde sache un peu qui je suis....Qu'ils m'appellent comme ils voudront, Brutus ou Érostate, il ne me plaît pas qu'ils m'oublient.

In his rendering of the character of Filippo Strozzi Musset has departed far more widely from Varchi. According to the latter Strozzi was everything that is bad. In spite of his years he was the companion of the young Florentine nobles in their debaucheries, and so far from being a patriot he helped Alessandro by his advice to establish his tyranny more firmly. His breach with the Duke was due to personal reasons, and only after the poisoning of his daughter did he become his declared enemy. This is very different from Musset's pure-minded patriot, but Musset at least follows Varchi in making him over-prudent, not to say pusillanimous, and a phrase-maker (as his son suggests) rather than a leader of men. The result is a somewhat enigmatic character, who plays indeed a useful part in the drama, especially in bringing out the hope-lessness of the attempt to restore the liberties of Florence, but who is without much individuality.

Duke Alessandro is a much easier character to portray. He is a good example of Musset's power to draw an animated, if rough, sketch with a few broad strokes. He is funda-mentally as bad as Varchi and the other chroniclers represent him—a callous and ruffianly sensualist. But Musset has given him a superficial air of joviality and good-humour which helps to individualise him. Moreover, while he was actually hideous and swarthy with the woolly hair of a negro, Musset makes the Marquise de Cibo say to him, "Tu es brave comme tu es beau". Indeed, without this improvement in his physical appearance, the Marquise's surrender to him would have been quite unintelligible. As it is it is difficult to under-stand her motive. For she is represented as loving her hus-band and as not being really in love with the Duke, while her design of persuading him to restore even a measure of liberty to the Florentines is purely chimerical.

Just, however, as Filippo Strozzi helps to bring out the character of Lorenzaccio, so Maddalena Cibo serves to shew up her brother-in-law Cardinal Cibo in his true light as an unscrupulous and Machiavellian ecclesiastic. He is an Iago with a different mask and a wider outlook, but with the same devilish ingenuity in executing his schemes. He is admirably drawn, and if it is objected that his part is episodic and that he only touches the main action when he warns the Duke against his cousin, the answer is that the play is not a tragedy but a historical drama. Lorenzaccio is not, like Hamlet, the central figure of the piece, towards whom everything con-verges, but he shares our interest with the city of Florence.

Florence, in fact, degraded and down-trodden, plays much the same part as Rome in her majesty does in *Julius Caesar*. Indeed, it is possible that *Julius Caesar* may have helped Musset with some suggestions; Lorenzaccio, who aspires to be the Brutus of his country, is, like Shakespeare's Brutus, given to introspection; in both plays there is the same use of crowds; and in both, as I have already noticed, a first and second citizen figure as representatives of the popular sentiment.

Against a dark world of corruption and intrigue Marie and Catherine Soderini stand out in white innocence. The scene between them in the first act in which Lorenzaccio's mother contrasts his present degradation with her recollections of his boyhood is deeply affecting. The love that these two women still bear him and the love and esteem in which he holds them give him a claim to our pity, if not to our sympathy.

Such is *Lorenzaccio*. In spite of its faults of construction, due partly to its author's indifference to stage requirements, partly to the difficulty of giving an adequate share in the representation to the picture of decadent Florence, it is a great play. The principal character is a remarkable feat of creation, and he is well supported by several others, while various minor characters, though they only make transient appearances, reveal a rare power of creating by a few rapid strokes types that are at once real and imaginative. Moreover there is ever present a dramatic sense, which is never exaggerated into melodrama, and a feeling for life and movement equal to that of Dumas and Hugo, but accompanied by the psychological insight in which they are so conspicuously wanting.

In December 1896 Sarah Bernhardt with courageous enterprise, which was justified by a signal success, produced *Lorenzaccio* at her theatre of the Renaissance. The initiative had come from Armand d'Artois, and it was he who did the work of adaptation, but the success was principally due to Sarah herself, who at the age of 52 undertook the title-rôle and whose wonderful interpretation of this very difficult part united all the critics in a chorus of enthusiastic praise. Nor was the adapter's task an easy one. He had to rearrange the scenes of the play so as to make them succeed one another in an unbroken and orderly sequence, and he had to substitute for the constant changes of place in the original version a single place for each act. Thus he made "a place in Florence" serve for the first act, a room in the Palazzo Soderini for the second, a room in the Palazzo Strozzi for the third (so that this act now included all the scenes in which a Strozzi appears), a room in the ducal palace for the fourth, and Lorenzaccio's bedroom for the fifth. The Cibo theme was much curtailed; the rôle of Cardinal Cibo was diminished in importance, and the Marquis disappeared altogether. If his absence makes the character of the Marquise less enigmatic, it also makes it more commonplace. The play ended with the Duke's death, the curtain falling on Lorenzaccio's apostrophe, "Que la nuit est belle! Que l'air du ciel est pur! Respire, respire, cœur navré de joie!"

The result of these changes was a well-constructed drama, and one suited to the requirements of the stage. Also, wrote one critic, "it brought into the light the essential feature—the character of Lorenzaccio". Essential, no doubt, for "a well-made play", but at the price of sacrificing Musset's intentions. For, as I have pointed out above, he did not intend the play to be a pure drama with Lorenzaccio for its hero, but a historical drama having for its theme not only the Duke's murder but the corruption and decadence of Florence. Anatole France was almost alone in regretting the omission of Musset's fifth act. "The death of this mediocre tyrant", he wrote, "is not a conclusion; the philosophical conclusion of the drama is in the scene which shews the uselessness of the murder."

If *Lorenzaccio* is the most solid and the most ambitious product of Musset's dramatic genius, the one which shews the greatest concentration of effort, his most characteristic pieces are *Les Caprices de Marianne, Fantasio*, and *On ne badine pas avec l'amour*. The first two were written before *Lorenzaccio* and the last probably after it. They were all published in the *Revue des Deux Mondes*; *Les Caprices de Marianne* on May 15, 1833, *Fantasio* on January 1, 1834, and *On ne badine pas avec l'amour* on July 1, 1834. Thus the first was written before the *liaison* with George Sand, which began in August 1833, the second during the *liaison*, but before the journey to Venice, and the third probably, though not certainly, after Musset's return to Paris in April 1834. All three, together with *Lorenzaccio*, were included in the second *livraison* of *Un Spectacle dans un Fauteuil*, published later in the same year. Though all alike are called comedies, the sole theme of the first and last is a love-story which ends in a poignant tragedy. *Fantasio* is a comedy throughout and there is no love-making in it, but like the others it gives us the expression of Musset's views on love. It is often said that he himself is the hero of all three comedies and that in *Les Caprices de Marianne* he appears under the double rôle of Claudio and Cœlio. I think it would be truer to say that in all four characters, Claudio, Cœlio, Fantasio, and Perdican, he has embodied his own experiences and his own meditations rather than that he has identified himself with any of the characters. At any rate he stands sufficiently aloof from them to make them real creations and to differentiate them one from the other.

A common feature is that they contain a fantastic element. In the two latest it is considerable, but it exists also in *Les Caprices de Marianne*. The dialogue, for instance, between Claudio and his servant Tibia is fantastically comic in the irrelevance of some of the remarks, and, although the atmosphere of the play is more or less Italian, the place might be any other Italian city just as well as Naples. So in *On ne badine pas avec l'amour*, though we are evidently in France, there is no attempt to localise the scene, the only place indicated being a château with its immediate surroundings. In *Fantasio* "the scene is at Munich", but Munich is as purely imaginary as Shakespeare's Messina, or Athens, or Bohemia, or Illyria, or the island of *The Tempest*.

Musset's indifference to the usual stage conventions shews itself in the structure of *Les Caprices de Marianne*. He pays, for instance, no regard to the rule that the entry or exit of a character demands a new scene. Thus his first scene consists of what would ordinarily count as four scenes; indeed, twice during this scene the stage is empty. Its place is a public street, which is natural for the meeting between Marianne and Ciuta and for that between Marianne and Octave, but not for the rest of the scene. However, in this Musset is only going back to a classical and Renaissance convention and to the practice of Corneille in *Le Menteur* and of Molière in nearly all his comedies before *Tartuffe*, except *Les Précieuses ridicules*. When Musset revised and rearranged the play for the Théâtre-Français in 1851 he made the street serve throughout.

This may have seemed very old-fashioned to play-goers who had witnessed the production of *Adrienne Lecouvreur* (by Scribe and Legouvé) at the same theatre two years before, but it served quite well for *Les Caprices de Marianne*, with its absence of external action. The plot is extremely simple, but it is original and effective. Cœlio is in love with Marianne, the wife of an elderly judge named Claudio, but she will have nothing to say to him. Thereupon his friend Octave, a young man of drunken and debauched habits, but a thoroughly loyal friend, undertakes to plead his cause, and does so with much eloquence. Marianne at once tells her husband, but Octave is persistent, and Claudio having seen him in conversation with her suspects him of being her lover. His groundless jealousy makes her furious and she is now determined to have a lover or at least a *cavaliere servente*. She tells Octave that anyone who sings under her window that evening will find a door open. Then she has a fresh caprice. It shall not be Cœlio, but anyone else whom Octave chooses, and as she has given him her scarf for the serenader to wear, she evidently imagines that Octave will appear himself. But he is far too loyal to play the traitor and he congratulates Cœlio on certain success. Cœlio accordingly appears at Marianne's window, only to learn from her that her husband has surrounded the house with assassins. He is killed before he can escape, but he welcomes death, for Marianne had taken him for Octave and he believes that his friend has been false. In the final scene Octave and Marianne meet at the cemetery where he is buried. "Cœlio était la bonne partie de moi-même;...Adieu l'amour et l'amitié! ma place est vide sur la terre." "Mais non pas dans mon cœur, Octave. Pourquoi dis-tu: adieu l'amour?" "Je ne vous aime pas, Marianne; c'était Cœlio qui vous aimait!"

This simple tragedy is dramatised with great directness and without any secondary episodes. The first act, in spite of some awkward places in the arrangement of the scenes, is an exposition in the classical tradition. All the characters are introduced and all the necessary facts for the understanding of the plot are set before us. Indeed, in the story which Hermia, Cœlio's mother, relates to him of her husband and a rejected lover who had killed himself the final catastrophe is foreshadowed. This is even accentuated in an addition which Musset made to the scene in 1851. "Il a fini ainsi?" asks Cœlio. "Oui, bien cruellement", says his mother. "Non, ma mère, elle n'est point cruelle la mort qui vient à l'aide de l'amour sans espoir. La seule chose dont je le plaigne, c'est qu'il s'est cru trompé par son ami."

The first scene of the second act is really composed of five scenes, as reckoned by the ordinary practice. Two of these consist of conversations between Octave and Marianne, whom he meets in the street as she is going to vespers and again as she is returning home. She upholds the cause of true love, while he maintains the libertine's view that a woman should give herself to a lover as willingly as a bottle of wine gives itself to a drinker. The woman is ironical and even bitter, and the man is cynical. From the third scene onwards the little drama moves forward with great rapidity. Claudio's unjust suspicion of his wife makes her change her tone and both she and Octave become natural and serious. The fourth scene prepares the catastrophe and in the fifth it takes place. The last scene is an epilogue on the vanity of human life, and whereas in the original version it takes place in the cemetery where Cœlio is buried, and therefore after a certain interval, in the acting version it follows immediately after the fifth scene.

The great merits of the play are its originality, its simplicity, and its tragic intensity. The characters are rapid sketches rather than searching portraits, but they are thoroughly alive, and if the psychology does not go very deep, it is true to nature. The most strongly drawn is Octave, a libertine who has not lost his belief in disinterested love, a drinker whose brain still retains its lucidity, and a man who in spite of his vices attracts us by his frankness and his devotion to his friend. Cœlio is his direct opposite, and yet, as we are told by Paul de Musset, both characters resembled their creator. "Cœlio", says Octave, "était la bonne partie de moi-même." "There were two beings", said Mme Allan-Despréaux, who knew him well, "in Alfred de Musset, one, good, gentle, tender, enthusiastic, the other possessed by a sort of demon." There is nothing of the demon in Octave, but he has the vices to which Musset was in some measure addicted. Cœlio's tragic fate would have made a stronger appeal to our pity, if he had been more fully presented to us. His mother Hermia is a still slighter, though a beautiful, sketch. A reader of the play will naturally conjecture that she is a likeness of the poet's own mother, and that her words,

Quand vous aviez dix ou douze ans, toutes vos peines, tous vos petits chagrins se rattachaient à moi; d'un regard sévère ou indulgent de ces yeux que voilà dépendait la tristesse ou la joie des vôtres, et votre petite tête blonde tenait par un fil bien délié au cœur de votre mère.

are a reminiscence of his own childhood. And the reader will learn from Paul de Musset that his conjecture is right.

Claudio, another secondary character, is a good example of the mixture of pomposity, pedantry, and imbecility that Musset loved to depict. The interchange of repartees between him and Octave in the first scene of the second act is hardly in keeping with his character, and it is tiresome into the bargain; but on the other hand the two short scenes between him and his servant Tibia are inimitable, and in the latter rôle, though he had only twenty lines to speak, Got, the most humorous actor of the Théâtre-Français of his generation, moved the whole house to laughter and scored a great success.

The part of Marianne, which Rachel declined, was played admirably by Madeleine Brohan. She was at that time only eighteen, fresh from the *Conservatoire*, where she had been a brilliant pupil. It was not an easy part to interpret, for Marianne's is a reserved and enigmatic character and her caprices are very sudden. Indeed, her second caprice, the choice of Octave, the cynical libertine, for her lover, is difficult to understand.

It seemed convenient to consider *Lorenzaccio* immediately after *André del Sarto*, first because both are called *drames*, and secondly because this made it possible to consider Musset's three most characteristic plays together. But we must not forget that the publication of *Les Caprices de Marianne* followed only six weeks after that of *André del Sarto*. For there is a remarkable difference in the character and treatment of the two plays—so remarkable as to call for some comment. In both plays we have the husband, the wife, and the lover, but whereas in the earlier play all three behave after the orthodox Romantic fashion, in the later play the only one who conforms at all to the Romantic type is Cœlio. As for Marianne, though she is not in love with her singularly unattractive husband, she is—when the play opens—both in act and in intention a faithful wife. And when she does fall in love, it is not with Cœlio, but with his friend and ambassador, Octave, and Octave remains true to his friend, even after his death. Not only is the situation different in the two plays, but so also—almost necessarily—is the treatment. It is no longer the husband who makes the chief appeal to our sympathies. It is Octave, neither husband nor lover, who stands forth as the principal character, while the others fall into the background. The husband is unpleasant and ridiculous—in speech at least, for in action he is prompt and efficient—the lover confines himself to sighs and serenades, and the wife, unlike Lucrezia, who rhapsodises on the discord between her love and her religion, remains reserved, enigmatic, and, except for a brief outburst, perfectly calm.

What was the reason for this change? Was it not that Musset wished to sever himself completely from the Romantic movement? On the previous Christmas Eve he had read *La Coupe et les Lèvres* and *A quoi rêvent les jeunes filles* to his former friends and comrades, and the reception had been glacial. It was not surprising that, when they were published at the very end of the year 1832 in *Un Spectacle dans un Fauteuil*, the volume, except for a barely appreciative notice by Sainte-Beuve and two other articles, one favourable and the other the reverse, met with a contemptuous silence. The breach between Musset and the Romantic *Cénacle* was complete. He would make this plain in the play that he was now writing (probably in April 1833). It should be as different as possible from Hugo's *Lucrèce Borgia*, which had been produced at the beginning of February, and the grotesque absurdities of which must have been supremely distasteful to his common sense and his innate classicism. It will be remembered that in Dumas's *Antony*, the parent not only of romantic drama but of much modern French drama, the curtain fell on "Elle me résistait; je l'ai assassinée", and that Hugo matched this in *Lucrèce Borgia* with "Tu m'a tuée—Gennaro! je suis ta mère". Was it by way of protest that Musset ended on the calm unromantic statement: "Je ne vous aime pas, Marianne; c'était Cœlio qui vous aimait!"? And was it to seal his separation from the Romanticists that he called *Les Caprices de Marianne*, not a *drame*, but a comedy?

I have noted above that three of the characters, Claudio, Hermia, and Malvolio, owe their names to Shakespeare, and it may be added that Musset's Malvolio, like Shakespeare's, is house-steward to a noble lady. But there is no other trace in this play of Shakespeare's influence, except perhaps in the carelessness about local atmosphere—another departure from the practice of Dumas and Hugo.

Fantasio has never been a great success on the stage. When it was first produced, after its author's death, in 1866 with an exceptionally strong cast—Delaunay as Fantasio, Mlle Favart as Elsbeth, and Coquelin as the Prince of Mantua—it only ran for thirty nights, and by the end of 1925 the whole number of performances had only reached forty-six. It must be admitted that it is not very dramatic, and for that reason Sarcey did not like it. But it is a joy to the reader. The second scene of the first act, which culminates in the famous dialogue between Fantasio and Spark, is one of the finest and most original things that Musset ever wrote, and of all the dissipated youths in whom he has embodied and exaggerated his own experiences Fantasio is the most attractive and comes closest to his creator. Indeed, Paul Foucher in his account of the performance of 1866 declared that Delaunay with his golden curls on his forehead recalled the Alfred de Musset, whom as a youth of eighteen he had introduced to Victor Hugo—Foucher's brother-in-law—thirty-seven years before. "The words to which Delaunay made us listen expressed the poet's soul." And this impression was confirmed by all Musset's friends who heard the play.

Fantasio is a young man who lives for pleasure. He frequently gets drunk, but it would be unfair to call him a drunkard. He goes after women, but he is not a professed libertine. The result of this life of pleasure is that he has ceased to take pleasure in anything. He is bored with everything and everybody. Sitting in the public square at Munich,

he is bored at the sight of his fellow-citizens amusing themselves, bored by his friend and crony, Spark, because he cannot bear seeing the same face day after day, and above all
bored by himself. "Si je pouvais sortir de ma peau pendant
une heure ou deux! Si je pouvais être ce monsieur qui passe."
No wonder his friend says, "Tu me fais l'air d'être revenu de
tout". Spark is a complete contrast to Fantasio. He never
dreams, he is never introspective, he is never bored; the most
ordinary and simple pleasures suffice to give him rapturous
enjoyment. The following passage from their conversation
will give an idea of their respective attitudes:

FANTASIO.

Eh bien donc! où veux-tu que j'aille? Regarde cette vieille ville
enfumée; il n'y a pas de places, de rues, de ruelles où je n'aie rôdé
trente fois; il n'y a pas de pavés où je n'aie traîné ces talons usés,
pas de maisons où je ne sache quelle est la fille ou la vieille femme
dont la tête stupide se dessine éternellement à la fenêtre; je ne
saurais faire un pas sans marcher sur mes pas d'hier; eh bien! mon
cher ami, cette ville n'est rien auprès de ma cervelle. Tous les
recoins m'en sont cent fois plus connus; toutes les rues, tous les
trous de mon imagination sont cent fois plus fatigués; je m'y suis
promené en cent fois plus de sens, dans cette cervelle délabrée,
moi son seul habitant! je m'y suis grisé dans tous les cabarets; je
m'y suis roulé comme un roi absolu dans un carrosse doré; j'y ai
trotté en bon bourgeois sur une mule pacifique, et je n'ose seule-
ment pas maintenant y entrer comme un voleur, une lanterne
sourde à la main.

SPARK.

Je ne comprends rien à ce travail perpétuel sur toi-même; moi,
quand je fume, par exemple, ma pensée se fait fumée de tabac;
quand je bois, elle se fait vin d'Espagne ou bière de Flandre;
quand je baise la main de ma maîtresse, elle entre par le bout de
ses doigts effilés pour se répandre dans tout son être sur des
courants électriques; il me faut le parfum d'une fleur pour me
distraire, et de tout ce que renferme l'universelle nature, le plus
chétif objet suffit pour me changer en abeille et me faire voltiger
çà et là avec un plaisir toujours nouveau.

FANTASIO.

Tranchons le mot, tu es capable de pêcher à la ligne.

SPARK.

Si cela m'amuse, je suis capable de tout.

FANTASIO.

Même de prendre la lune avec les dents?

SPARK.

Cela ne m'amuserait pas.

This contrast between the two friends adds to the effectiveness of the dialogue. They are not, like Rosalind and Touchstone or Millamant and Mirabell, rivals in wit. While Fantasio brims over with it, Spark is brief, simple, and matter-of-fact. Their conversation comes to an end just as a funeral is passing. It is the funeral of the King's fool, Saint-Jean, and one of the bearers impertinently advises Fantasio to apply for the place. He accepts the advice as a means of escape from the bailiffs who are waiting for him at his house, and at once goes to the court tailor to order a costume similar to that worn by the late fool. One wonders whether Musset got this idea from *As You Like It*, where Jaques, who had been "a libertine, as sensual as the brutish sting itself", suddenly says to the Duke, "O, that I were a fool! I am ambitious for a motley coat". Touchstone's dialogue with Corin may also have furnished a hint, for Touchstone is the equal of Fantasio in wit, and Corin is as simple, as matter-of-fact, and as easily pleased as Spark.

With the transformation of Fantasio into the court fool the action of the play, such as it is, begins. The plot is of the slightest. Elsbeth, the daughter of the King of Bavaria, is to marry the Prince of Mantua in order to end a war between the two countries. The Prince, says Elsbeth to her governess, a foolish and sentimental lady, is known to be "horrible and an idiot", in fact, "the most ridiculous creature in the world". But she is ready to sacrifice herself to please her father and save her country from war. Meanwhile the Prince, who is one of those mixtures of pomposity and imbecility that Musset loved to depict, has arrived in Munich. With the romantic idea of being loved for himself he has changed places with his aide-de-camp and by his clumsy attempts to make love to Elsbeth thoroughly justifies the reports of his character.

The greater part of the second and last act consists of conversations between Fantasio and Elsbeth. She had loved Saint-Jean and had regarded him as "un diamant d'esprit". So she receives his successor, when she suddenly comes upon him, with some coldness and proceeds to criticise his attempts at wit—"Pauvre homme! quel métier tu entreprends! Faire de l'esprit à tant par heure!" "Pauvre petite! quel métier vous entreprenez! épouser un sot que vous n'avez jamais vu!"—"Voilà qui est hardi, monsieur, le nouveau venu!" But when Fantasio develops a witty and original comparison between the Princess and a tulip, her interest is aroused, though she still keeps him in his place. At the second meeting she is more friendly, and he returns to the charge with a comparison between princesses and a mechanical canary, which sings when you press a spring. She is still suspicious, for he may be a spy, but she listens to him in spite of herself, because he reminds her of her dear Saint-Jean.

Musset might have got from *As You Like It* a hint as to the amount of licence that should be permitted to a fool in his conversations with his mistress. The conditions of course are different. Touchstone has the familiarity of an old servant, but he is still a dependent; Fantasio on the other hand is a stranger to Elsbeth, but he is only in her service for his own pleasure. He is therefore at once more respectful and more courtly in manner than Touchstone and bolder and more outspoken in matter. Further, while Touchstone as a professional fool exercises his wit at random, Fantasio has a fixed purpose before him—to dissuade Elsbeth from her marriage. As for Elsbeth, she is not witty like Rosalind, or rather she takes too serious a view of her position to bandy witticisms with an unknown fool. She meets his attacks with intelligent questions and criticisms, and her determination remains un-shaken. She has given her word to her father and she will keep it. To avert war she will make a loveless marriage.

From this she is saved by a sudden whim of Fantasio's. Just as the Prince of Mantua, or rather Marinoni disguised as the Prince, is riding into the court of the Palace, his wig is lifted into the air by a hook at the end of a line. The culprit turns out to be Fantasio, who had been drinking in the ser-vants' hall, and he is promptly put in prison. Here we find him in the last scene, which in the acting version became a third act. In a characteristic soliloquy he comments on the capricious working of fate. "The fortune of two countries, the tranquillity of two peoples", has been disturbed, because he had had the idea of disguising himself as a hunchback and had in consequence got drunk and fished with a line for the wig of the King's ally. Then comes a visit from the Princess, accompanied by her governess, followed by the news that the marriage has been broken off. "If war is declared, what a misfortune!" exclaims Elsbeth. "Does your Royal High-ness call that a misfortune?" replies Fantasio. "Would you prefer a husband who goes to war for his wig?"

This last scene, short and slight though it is, is a good example of Musset's power of suggestion. Underlying his airy witticisms there is often a depth of thought, which, be-cause it does not come to the surface, is apt to be lost on the stage. Another of his characteristics is that his leading cha-racters generally make a more favourable impression upon us at the end of the play than at the beginning. His young rakes for instance are often "fanfarons du mal". They exaggerate their vices in a spirit of swagger. This repels us at first, but gradually they reveal an undercurrent of good sense and good feeling, which, added to their innate honesty, both towards themselves and towards others, attracts us to them, and we part from them with regret. They reflect in fact both the worst and the best side of Musset's own character. So it is with Fantasio. Delaunay, indeed, who looked the part to perfection, and whose rendering of it was highly praised, thought him "complicated, fantastic, and bizarre". But beneath the surface there is a real depth of thought and feeling, which a sympathetic reader will detect. Elsbeth, unlike Marianne and Camille, attracts us at once, partly by her affectionate regrets for Saint-Jean, and partly by her unselfish devotion to her father and her country. But she too grows on us. At first cold and reserved towards the new fool, she gradually becomes more friendly, and when he is in prison and unmasked she is full of sympathy and understanding. We leave her, not only with admiration for her serene and smiling courage, but with the feeling that she has the makings of a great as well as a good woman, "J'ai peu connu la vie, et j'ai beaucoup rêvé". But she is not foolishly sentimental like her governess, and if Fantasio ever returns to court with his motley, his hump, and his bells, they will understand one another, but there will be no sentimental feeling between them.

In contrast to the lukewarm reception of *Fantasio*, *On ne badine pas avec l'amour*, which was first put on the stage in 1861, has proved the most popular of all Musset's plays except *Il ne faut jurer de rien* and the two perfect little pieces, *Il faut qu'une porte soit ouverte ou fermée* and *Un Caprice*, which are often given as curtain-raisers. The plot, like that of every comedy by Musset, is at once original and very simple. It captivates us by the intensity of its psychological interest and by the unexpected tragedy of its conclusion. But if in a sense it is the most tragic of Musset's dramas, it also contains the largest and most laughable comic element. This, however, fits in naturally with the serious part of the story, and there is no more discord between the two elements than there is in *Henry IV*. The comic element is represented by four *grotesques*, to use the French term—characters of much the same type as Shallow and Silence, or Dogberry and Verges. They consist of the Baron, Maître Blazius, his son's tutor, Maître Bridaine, the *curé* of the village, and Dame Pluche, the governess of his niece, Camille. We have a full and vivid description of the two first by the Chorus of villagers, for it is one of the original features of this play that there is a Chorus. They are "également gros, également sots", they are both priests, both pedants and ignoramuses, both gluttons and drunkards; and being exactly alike, they cordially hate one another. This is a true account, and their mutual hatred, which largely arises from jealousy, leads to amusing encounters, both with one another and with the Baron: Dame Pluche is another oddity whom the Chorus introduces in the first scene. Elderly, gaunt, and bony, she is devoted to her "chère colombe sans tache", who, however, treats her with scant respect. She has very strict ideas as to propriety, so strict that she rouses the Baron to barely restrained fury. "Vous me donnez envie.... En vérité, si je ne me retenais.... Vous êtes une pécore, Pluche! je ne sais que penser de vous."

Dame Pluche and the two priests are admirable as types, but the Baron is a more individual and a more subtle creation. As appears from his language to Dame Pluche, he cannot bear contradiction or opposition from those about him, but when he is obeyed, he is kindly and condescending. Like the Prince of Mantua he has a strong sense of his own position and importance, but he is fussy rather than pompous. He is meticulous in his love of details and of everything that conduces to order and regularity. When anything goes wrong with his carefully prepared plans, he at once loses his head. "Tout est perdu! perdu sans ressource." "Mes idées s'embrouillent tout à fait." "Passons dans mon cabinet; j'ai éprouvé depuis hier des secousses si violentes, que je ne puis rassembler mes idées." The whole scene between him and Blazius, in which the two last remarks occur, is exceedingly humorous. In spite of his slender intelligence and his other weaknesses, we have a kindly feeling for him, such as we do not have for Claudio or the Prince of Mantua.

It was his cherished plan that his son who has just received his doctor's degree at Paris should marry his niece, who has just completed her education at a convent. They were brought up together as children, but they have not seen one another for ten years, and the Baron has carefully arranged that they shall arrive at his château at the same moment and meet before his eyes. Unfortunately, when they meet, the programme fails. Camille refuses to kiss Perdican, and the next morning tells him that she will not marry him or anybody else, but will return to her convent. Perdican, who a minute before had told Blazius to tell the Baron that he would gladly marry Camille, receives her announcement with an assumption of indifference, which in her heart she evidently resents. Accordingly she appoints a meeting with him by a source in a wood, and we have the long scene (II, 5)—nearly a fifth of the whole play—in which Perdican and Camille discuss with great seriousness the whole question of love. For by far the greater part of the time Camille does all the talking, while Perdican contents himself with very short answers. She cross-examines him as to his love affairs and relates to him the love history of a nun who had been her great friend in the convent. (Would a nun of thirty have confided her intimate experiences to a girl of fourteen?) At last, after her passionate speech, in answer to Perdican's "Tu as dix-huit ans, et tu ne crois pas à l'amour!" which begins "Y croyez-vous, vous qui parlez?", Perdican is moved in his turn to inveigh against nuns who represent the love of men as a lie. Finally with a cynicism worthy of Shakespeare's Timon he proclaims the iniquity of all men and all women. "But there is one thing in the world that is holy and sublime, and that is the union of two of these imperfect and hideous beings."... "J'ai souffert souvent, je me suis trompé quelquefois, mais j'ai aimé. C'est moi qui ai vécu, et non pas un être factice créé par mon orgueil et mon ennui." Here Alfred de Musset is no doubt speaking in his own person, and it must be remembered that the play was written in the early summer of 1834 when he and George Sand, who was living openly with Pagello at Venice, were writing to one another every three or four days in terms of extreme affection, and he was at the same time trying to forget his loss in a life of pleasure and dissipation.

With the words last quoted the second act ends. In the third act, the drama moves rapidly and it is none the less thrilling because the action is entirely of the heart. Perdican, as the result of his conversation with Camille, asks himself whether he loves her or not. Meeting Dame Pluche with a letter which Camille had given her to post he takes it from her and—"est-ce un crime?"—reads it. In it Camille tells her friend at the convent that Perdican is reduced to despair by her refusal to marry him. His pride is deeply wounded, and he determines to revenge himself by making love before Camille's eyes to Rosette, a village maiden and Camille's foster-sister, with whom he has already philandered. So he writes to Camille to ask her to meet him again by the little source, and then takes Rosette to the same place. Camille reaches the rendez-vous just as they are approaching and, hiding behind a tree, hears Perdican not only make love to Rosette but say she must marry him. Camille is furious. "Allez au diable, vous et votre âne!" is her reply to Dame Pluche's announcement that everything is ready for their departure. Then in her turn she prepares an act of vengeance. Having invited Rosette and Perdican to her room, she first assures Rosette that Perdican will never marry her and then in the hearing of Rosette, whom she has hidden behind a curtain, leads Perdican to declare his love for her. They draw the curtain and find that Rosette has fainted. Camille then turns upon Perdican. "I do not love you", she says, "and though you love me, you shall marry Rosette or be regarded as *un lâche*." "Yes, I will marry her", replies Perdican. In the next scene Camille, woman-like, urges the Baron to forbid the marriage, but he "shuts himself up to abandon himself to his grief". Then she appeals to Perdican, but he is obdurate. The last scene is wonderful. At the foot of the altar in an oratory Camille flings herself down in a passion of grief.

Here she is found by Perdican, who bursts forth with "In-sensés que nous sommes! nous nous aimons" and they fall into one another's arms. A cry is heard behind the altar and Camille recognises the voice of her foster-sister. Going into the gallery, she finds Rosette dead. "Elle est morte. Adieu, Perdican!"

The character of Camille is a masterpiece of fine perception and firm construction. Her cold, not to say priggish, greeting of Perdican, her refusal to marry, her subsequent hesitation, her bold catechism of Perdican, her avowal that she had loved him as a child and that in the convent he had constantly been in her thoughts, her conviction that he is in love with her, due partly to her proud consciousness of her own beauty, her struggle between her growing love for him and her intention to dedicate herself to God, her outburst after hearing Perdican's proposal to Rosette, her insistence that he should carry out the marriage, her repentance and attempts to stop it, and finally, when it seems too late, her passionate avowal of her love—all these stages in her development from a cold convent-bred schoolgirl to a passionate woman are portrayed with deep psychological insight and striking dramatic power. On a first reading, the character of Perdican seems to be less firmly drawn, and it may be noted that, when the play was first produced on the stage, the critics were more impressed by Mlle Favart's acting than by Delaunay's. But when we study the character more closely, we become aware of the artistic workmanship with which its finer shades are rendered. Perdican's chief characteristic is his impulsiveness. This makes him inconsistent in what he says and thoughtless in what he does. He says that he believes in nothing: yet immediately afterwards he expresses astonishment at Camille because she does not believe in love, and in the final scene he prays fervently to God. To punish Camille he tells Rosette that he loves her, and then, carried away by his feelings, he says he will marry her. He thinks he knows all about love and women, but Camille's questions

"Do you believe in love?" and "Do you know the female heart?" are thoroughly justified. His knowledge of love comes merely from casual mistresses, whose names he has forgotten. He is blind to Camille's love for him, uncertain for a long time about his love for her, and furious when he realises that she has seen into his heart better than he has himself. He is not a strong character, but he has his good qualities. "Vous n'êtes point un libertin, et je crois que votre cœur a de la probité", says Camille. "Vous avez dû inspirer l'amour, car vous le méritez." Like Octave and Fantasio he prides himself on his truthfulness. "Je ne mens jamais." In this as in other aspects of his character he represents certain features of Musset himself. But in spite of this, he is a real objective creation, and it is only in the last scene of the second act that he speaks more or less with Musset's mouth. In this last scene he repeats with fervour the simple creed that love is the one thing in heaven or earth about which it is not permitted to doubt. In the dedication of *La Coupe et les Lèvres*, written when he was twenty-one, Musset had put this crudely and cynically:

> Doutez de la vertu de la nuit et du jour:
> Doutez de tout au monde, et jamais de l'amour.

> .   .   .   .

> Aimer est le grand point, qu'importe la maîtresse?
> Qu'importe le flacon, pourvu qu'on ait l'ivresse?

Fantasio, it is true, declares that "l'amour n'existe plus", but just before he had expressed to Spark his longing to love somebody, and he does not hesitate to plunge his country into war in order that his Princess may escape a loveless marriage. Again in *Les Caprices de Marianne* Octave tells Marianne that the love with which he has inspired Cœlio is the most cruel of all sufferings, for it is a suffering without hope. "Pourquoi n'aimeriez-vous pas Cœlio? C'est votre amant." "De quel droit ne serait-elle pas à moi? J'aime et je suis aimé", says Cordiani, the lover of André del Sarto's wife. And in the last three stanzas of *La Nuit d'Août*, written in

May 1836, the poet defiantly proclaims his unwavering belief in love:

> J'aime, et je veux pâlir; j'aime et je veux souffrir.
>
> . . . .
>
> Et je veux raconter et répéter sans cesse
> Qu'après avoir juré de vivre sans maîtresse,
> J'ai fait serment de vivre et de mourir d'amour.
>
> . . . .
>
> Après avoir souffert, il faut souffrir encore;
> Il faut aimer sans cesse, après avoir aimé.

Yet in spite of all these expressions of absolute belief in love, the words of Camille to Perdican might be addressed to Musset himself. "Y croyez-vous, vous qui parlez?... Est-ce donc une monnaie que votre amour pour qu'il puisse passer ainsi de main en main jusqu'à la mort?"

We are told by Paul de Musset that when Édouard Thierry, the director of the Comédie Française, determined with his consent to adapt *On ne badine pas avec l'amour* for the stage, he was frightened at the difficulty. For in the original version the place changes with nearly every scene, and no less than twelve different places are indicated for the whole play. But the difficulty was not so great as it appeared at first sight, and one scene was found to suffice for each act—the vestibule of the château for the first, a picturesque landscape for the second, and a small room for the third. Certain suppressions were also made; the rôles of Bridaine, Blazius and Dame Pluche were pruned. Above all cuts were made in the long discussion between Perdican and Camille, and the language was in places considerably toned down to suit delicate ears. Apart from considerations of this kind, it must be confessed that Camille's outspokenness is a little surprising in a girl who had been brought up from her childhood in a convent.

After *On ne badine pas avec l'amour* Alfred de Musset wrote nothing, except one short poem (*Une bonne fortune*), for a year. In August 1834 George Sand returned to Paris, bringing Pagello with her. In October Pagello was sent back to

Venice, and George Sand and Musset again became acknow-
ledged lovers. But they had many violent quarrels, and in
March 1835 there was a final separation, the effect of which
on Musset may be traced in the four immortal *Nuits* and the
Lettre à Lamartine. On August 1, 1835, a month and a half
after *La Nuit de Mai*, he published a new comedy in the
Revue des Deux Mondes, entitled *La Quenouille de Barberine.* The
plot, which is founded on a story of Bandello's (*I^a parte*,
nov. xxi), is briefly as follows. Count Ulric, a Bohemian noble,
and Baron Rosemberg, a Hungarian noble, meet at the court
of Matthias Corvinus, King of Hungary. Some disparaging
remarks by Rosemberg on the virtue of women lead Ulric
to proclaim the many accomplishments of his wife and his
complete belief in her fidelity. Finally he accepts a wager
from Rosemberg that he will visit Ulric's château and successfully attack Barberine's virtue. Thereupon Rosemberg
goes to the château, presents (as agreed upon) a letter of
introduction from Ulric, and is hospitably received by Barberine. He then proceeds to make open love to her, and she,
after pointing out the wickedness and audacity of his proposal, leaves the room with a promise to return. He is full
of hope, but he finds that he is a complete prisoner, and he is
told by Barberine, who appears at a wicket in the wall, that
he will have no food until he earns it by spinning. For that
purpose she has left her distaff and spindle. It is not till cold,
darkness, and hunger have thoroughly subdued his spirit that
he gives in and sets to work. A supper of cucumbers and a
lettuce salad is then put before him, when suddenly the
arrival of the Queen accompanied by Count Ulric is announced. Thus Rosemberg loses his wager, which consisted
of the whole of his property.

Musset has closely followed Bandello in all essential points,
but it is remarkable how out of a simple, though charmingly
told, narrative he has constructed a real drama of conflicting
desires and emotions, and how out of mere names, with only
one or two hints to help him, he has created characters alert

with life and individuality. This is well brought out by Lafoscade. Beatrice of Aragon is portrayed as the ideal Queen, ruling her court by means of sympathy and insight, swift to do justice, but ready to temper justice with mercy. Ulric and Barberine are the ideal husband and wife. Nothing can be more beautiful than the picture of married love which the parting between Ulric and Barberine reveals in the opening scene of the original version. Ulric is little more than a sketch. He is the loving husband who has complete confidence in his wife; he is also modest, brave, and honourable. But Barberine, with her complete lack of self-consciousness, her naïvety, her interest in her domestic occupations, her quick insight into Rosemberg's character, her humorous punishment of his fatuous audacity, is a perfectly delightful and satisfying portrait. As for Rosemberg, "il n'est point méchant", as Barberine writes to her husband. "Avec de bonnes qualités il ne manquait de réflexion." He is extremely young. "Vous qui sortez apparemment de l'école", says the Queen, who like Barberine diagnoses him with a woman's instinctive penetration. In fact he would never have ventured upon his rash enterprise had not his imagination been inflamed by a certain Chevalier Uladislas, whom he meets at the Court, and who, after boasting of his own exploits as a slayer of giants and a lover of princesses, gives him advice how to achieve similar exploits. The scene (1, 2) is a long one and much of it is tedious, but a Polish Jew, named Polacco, who sells a magic mirror to Rosemberg, provides a comic element with his habit of repeating meaningless proverbs. The part was played with great effect by Coquelin *cadet*.

The above is a brief analysis of the play as it runs in the original version. But, after the success on the stage of his other comedies, Musset re-shaped it and offered it to the Comédie Française. This was in 1851, but the first performance of *Barberine*, as it was now called, did not take place till thirty years later (1882). Musset's revised version, how-

Musset

ever, has always been printed in the *Comédies et Proverbes* since
1853, and the original version can only be read in the edition
of 1840 or the *Revue des Deux Mondes*. The play was not a
success on the stage. This was in a great measure due to
Musset's not very skilful revision. In order to comply with
the practice of the Théâtre-Français, he was forced to expand
his two acts into three and to make each act conform to the
unity of place. The beautiful first scene, which should give
the tone to the whole play, was now preceded by two new
ones, and the parting between husband and wife made to
take place on the road before the inn instead of at Count
Ulric's château. The third scene of the first act, which contains the making of the wager, became the second act, and
the second act which originally opened with Barberine
singing, "Beau chevalier qui partez pour la guerre", became
the third. The shifting of the two scenes with Polacco and
his mirror from their original position to the re-arranged
second act was inevitable in view of stage requirements, but
if, as I would suggest, their purpose was to shew that Ulric
and Barberine were constantly in one another's thoughts, a
delicate psychological touch was thus lost. To compensate
the third act for the omission of these scenes Musset introduced an entirely new character, that of Kalékairi, Barberine's young Turkish maid. Her introduction was much
criticised and it may be granted that she is unnecessary, for
Barberine was quite capable of dealing with her gallant
single-handed. But in herself she is an original and attractive
little person.

One small addition to the third act deserves notice. At the
beginning of the fifth scene Rosemberg says that he has read
in a little book given to him by Uladislas the story of a certain
Jachimo, who makes an exactly similar wager with Leonatus
Posthumus, son-in-law of the King of Great Britain (as he
calls it). This is, of course, a reference to *Cymbeline*, which is
founded on a novel by Boccaccio.

La Quenouille de Barberine was followed at short intervals by two more three-act comedies, both of which, partly owing to their success on the stage, are considerably better known than their predecessor. Both appeared in the *Revue des Deux Mondes*; *Le Chandelier* on November 1, 1835, and *Il ne faut jurer de rien* on July 1, 1836. Between the two appeared *La Nuit de Décembre* (written in November) and soon after the second *La Nuit d'Août* (written in May). *La Confession d'un enfant du siècle* was published on August 15. Thus George Sand was still in Musset's thoughts, and the thoughts at times were bitter.

Though *Le Chandelier* is founded on an incident in Musset's own life, it has an air about it of a tale by Boccaccio, the heading of which might run as follows: "Jacqueline, the wife of Maître André a notary, has Clavaroche, an officer of dragoons, for a lover. To throw dust in her husband's eyes she makes Fortunio, a young clerk of her husband's, serve as a screen. She falls in love with him and throws over Clavaroche". Told in Boccaccio's inimitable way, the story need not have been taken too seriously and it would certainly have been entertaining. But Musset, as his habit was, treats it as a drama of real life. It cannot be said that his treatment, as a whole, is quite successful. The characters themselves are well enough. Maître André, Jacqueline, and Clavaroche, who all appear in the first scene, are vigorous sketches of conventional types. Maître André is the elderly, doting, easily gulled husband; Jacqueline is the sensual, deceitful, ill-matched wife, who, without the excuse of Mme Bovary's romantic imagination, passes from one lover to another in pursuance of her caprice; Clavaroche is the vain, self-complacent lady-killer, who is always looking at himself in the glass and who finds a ready captive to his bow in every garrison town. Nor is there any fault to find with the first part of the first scene, in which Jacqueline, with Clavaroche hidden in her wardrobe, by impudently acting the part of injured innocence, triumphantly repels her husband's accusations. But in the second part, after Maître André's departure, there is a long and tiresome speech by Clavaroche, in which he explains the functions and utility of a *chandelier*, or nominal lover, whose business it is to divert attention from the real lover.

The one sympathetic character is Fortunio, "un petit blond...pas mal tourné, avec ses cheveux sur l'oreille et son petit air innocent". Such was Alfred de Musset himself at the age of seventeen, when Achille Devéria made his charming portrait of him in the costume of a page, when he made his first appearance in the circle of Victor Hugo, "Le front male et fier, la joue en fleur et qui gardait encore les roses de l'enfance, la narine enflée du souffle du désir" (Sainte-Beuve), and when he suffered from the experience upon which he founded this comedy. And because he was dramatising his own story, he was able to put into the part all the pathos and the passion that distinguishes it. For Fortunio is his own portrait, inwardly as well as outwardly. Like Fortunio, he was at once a timid and an audacious lover, a Cherubino of deeper feelings; he had too Fortunio's candour, his touch of melancholy, and his poetic accent. These characteristics are well brought out in the scene between him and Jacqueline, when she entangles him in the net of her heartless coquetry. There is nothing remarkable in the two following scenes except the famous *chanson*, "Si vous croyez que je vais dire", which has in it a touch of Heine. The fourth scene is dramatically important, especially the latter part, when Fortunio, hidden in an alcove, learns that Clavaroche is Jacqueline's lover. But except for Fortunio's pathetic and beautiful appeal, "Jacqueline, ayez pitié de moi", the style is not quite up to Musset's high standard. Nor does it improve in the dialogue between Jacqueline and Clavaroche, which occupies most of the first scene of the third act. Fortunio's soliloquy, which opens the next scene, is too long, and for that reason, no doubt, it was omitted in the stage version. But the last part, from "Est-ce bien sûr?" to the end, is as beautiful as it is dramatic.

There follows the great scene of the play, the scene between Fortunio and Jacqueline. Nothing can be finer than
the four speeches of Fortunio which follow Jacqueline's request to him to let her keep his song. Never has the passionate love of a youthful idealist been more delicately expressed;
there is not a word to alter in any of them. But one cannot
help wondering at the sudden change that they produce in
Jacqueline's heart. What does it imply? Is it merely a caprice,
or is she really sincere in the avowal of her love? Would it
not have been more in accordance with her character, if, like
the original Jacqueline, she had callously dismissed her
chandelier when she found that he was too much in earnest? One
is tempted to think that the play should have ended with the
words, "Sais-tu que j'aime, enfant que tu es?" omitting the
last two lines of the scene. The last short scene is, no doubt,
an effective dramatic climax, a pendant to the former dinner-
scene, but it brings us back to sordid fact. Fortunio may
triumph over Clavaroche, but how long will his triumph last?

Le Chandelier was produced on August 10, 1848, at the
Théâtre-Historique, in which Alexandre Dumas was largely
interested. It was one of the theatres known as the Théâtres
du Boulevard and was frequented by a public which delighted
in melodrama. The choice was curious and the moment was
unpropitious, for Paris had not yet recovered from the bloody
fighting of June 23–26, when General Cavaignac decimated
the socialist mob. In these circumstances Musset's comedy
passed almost unnoticed. Its real introduction to the stage
dates from June 29, 1850, when Arsène Houssaye produced
it at the Théâtre-Français, of which he had been appointed
director in the previous November. Delaunay made an ideal
Fortunio and so completely identified himself with the part
that when he took leave of the stage thirty-seven years later
he included in his farewell the third act of the play. Brindeau,
who excelled in Musset's comedies, was Clavaroche, and
Samson was Maître André. Musset had thought Mme Allan-
Despréaux too stout for the rôle of Jacqueline, but she played

it, as she wrote to her friend Mme Samson-Toussaint, Samson's daughter, with "superb success". One would like to know how she interpreted the part. She was an intelligent woman and an admirable actress, but one suspects that she softened the unpleasant features of Jacqueline's character and made the most of her beauty and melting attractiveness. Madeleine Brohan, another actress of great charm and intelligence, probably did the same. It may be noted that the costumes were of the age of Louis XVI. This was quite permissible, for Musset never makes any attempt to introduce local colour and hardly ever dates his plays. *Le Chandelier* might equally well belong to the time of Boccaccio and to Musset's own day, for human nature remains the same. It is possible that the object of assigning it to the age of Louis XVI was to give it a less real air and so to escape the charge of immorality. But the Minister of the Interior, after only a few performances of the play, forbade its continuance, and though he was appeased on that occasion, in 1855, when it was again put on the stage, it was banned as immoral (after forty performances), and not revived till 1872, when Delaunay appeared in his old part and Madeleine Brohan replaced Mme Allan.

Of all Musset's three-act comedies in prose *Il ne faut jurer de rien* is the only one that definitely belongs to the author's own day. Yet the fantastic element in it is as considerable as it is in any of them. Valentin van Buck, the would-be Lovelace, is a *fat* of the first water, but his project of seducing within a week a carefully brought-up girl of good family is perfectly fantastic. Moreover one realises, as the play proceeds, that Valentin's Lovelace airs are very much on the surface and that, when brought face to face with Cécile's naïvety and trusting innocence, he almost at once becomes a humble lover in his heart. The long scene between him and his uncle which opens the play is deservedly famous and contains some of Musset's most brilliant dialogue. It is said to be the reproduction of a conversation which the poet had with himself one morning after a bout of dissipation. The only criticism that seems possible is that Valentin in his witty reply to all his uncle's accusations shews a superhuman memory; here again we have an element of fantasy. In the second scene we are transported from Valentin's bedroom in Paris to the Baroness's château, and we are introduced to two delightful figures of comedy, the Baroness and the Abbé. Neither is grotesque—at least not in the English sense of the term—but both have their comic side, the Baroness with her irrelevances and the Abbé with his little formal scraps of decorous conversation. Cécile only says a few words, but one of her remarks, "Mais, Monsieur, quand on ne veut pas tomber, il faut bien regarder devant soi", expresses at once her common sense and, taken figuratively, the essential rectitude of her character.

The second and third acts are not well constructed, and the reader has some difficulty in following the movements of the actors. For stage purposes there had to be some transposition of the scenes. Individually they are excellent. The first scene, in which Valentin, piqued, as his uncle shrewdly remarks, by Cécile's apparent indifference to him—she only makes a few short and commonplace remarks—begins to be attracted by her, is a fine example of high comedy, and the second, though it begins on a lower and more broadly amusing note, rises to the same height, when the Baroness, after insisting on Cécile's producing the letter from Valentin, at first makes humorous comments on it, and then when she comes to the words about herself—"une tête de girouette"—turns upon Van Buck and orders him and his nephew out of the house. The first scene of the third act between the uncle and nephew is not so good, but the third, which is a continuation of it—the second takes us back to the château—is full of humour and insight into character. Van Buck, under the influence of a good dinner, recalls like Shallow the gay doings of his youth, and Valentin begins to fall in love in real earnest.

Cette petite fille a de l'esprit et même quelque chose de mieux; oui, il y a du cœur dans ces trois lignes; je ne sais quoi de tendre et de hardi, de virginal et de brave en même temps.

The last scene, the love scene under the trees between Valentin and Cécile, with its beautiful setting—the clearing in the wood, the moonlight after the storm, the pearl-drops on the leaves of the birches—is Musset at his tenderest and most charming:

Regarde comme cette nuit est pure! Comme ce vent soulève sur les épaules cette gaze avare qui les entoure! Prête l'oreille: c'est la voix de la nuit, c'est le chant de l'oiseau qui invite au bonheur.

It reminds us of another couple who made love in the moonlight:

The moon shines bright. In such a night as this,
When the sweet wind did swiftly kiss the trees,
And they did make no noise. In such a night

. . . .

Did young Lorenzo swear he loved her well.

If we take Musset's dialogue literally, Valentin had not yet abandoned his black design, but it is impossible to believe that a man who could express himself with such poetic feeling could be really the Lovelace that he thought he was. "Il est trop jeune pour une noirceur pareille", says the good Baroness. She was right. Valentin believed that the universe—the ever-moving worlds which appear as stars—was created by eternal love. "Ils vivent parce qu'ils se cherchent, et les soleils tomberaient en poussière si l'un d'entre eux cessait d'aimer." "Ah! toute la vie est là!" replies Cécile. This was Musset's belief as well as Valentin's.

The play was produced at the Théâtre-Français on June 22, 1848. It was not an auspicious moment. Even while the performance was going on barricades were being erected, and on the following morning the fighting in the streets, which was to last for four days, began. However, when the theatres were re-opened, the piece re-appeared on the boards, and Théophile Gautier, who was an enthusiastic admirer of Musset's dramatic work, reported in his newspaper that to his great delight it was an unqualified success. The rôle of Cécile was created by Amédine Luther, a girl of fourteen, who afterwards married a brother of Rachel's and died young, and Got was highly amusing as the Abbé. The success of the play proved to be permanent, for of all Musset's comedies—not counting the one-act proverbs—it stands first in the number of performances.

In the drama that Musset next contributed to the *Revue des Deux Mondes*—it appeared on June 15, 1837—he made somewhat of a new departure. *Un Caprice* is in one act instead of three, and there are only three characters. Moreover, there is complete unity of place—Mathilde's bedroom—and the division into scenes is perfectly orthodox. The theme is even slighter than in the majority of Musset's comedies. The two purses are merely symbols, the red purse of Mathilde's love for her husband, and the blue purse of her husband's capricious fancy for another woman. The real theme is this caprice, which, aided by the wife's jealousy, the husband's pride, and the inexperience of both, provokes a *scène conjugale*. Neither character is more than a rapid sketch, but each has quite sufficient individuality for the purpose of the play. Mathilde is gentle and timid, but she is deeply in love with her husband and thoroughly loyal to him. Chavigny, the husband, is not attractive, nor is he meant to be. His very first words, "Bonsoir, ma chère; est-ce que je vous dérange?" predispose one against him. His remarks to Mme de Léry in the eighth scene, from "Parlons caprice" onwards, would, if taken seriously, be worthy of Tartuffe, but his involved language, and especially his attempted distinction between "un homme marié" and "un homme", and his subsequent conduct, shew that it was chiefly fatuity that prompted him to make love to his wife's friend. This fatuity, combined with a certain formal correctness in his manners, makes him, as I have said, unattractive, but he is possibly not a bad fellow at heart—"il est méchant, mais il n'est pas mauvais" —and he may profit by Mme de Léry's lesson.

In contrast to the low-toned sketches of this married couple the finished portrait of Mme de Léry stands out in a brilliant light. On the surface she is an agreeable rattle, but beneath her airy *sans gêne* she is a woman of intelligence, good sense, and feeling. She is fundamentally serious, especially where the heart is concerned. She is only twenty-five, but she has had much experience of life, and at an early age she learnt what suffering means. Outwardly, however, she overflows with gaiety, and her novel expressions, such as *re-bon-soir*, and "un *soupçon* de thé et un *nuage* de lait", her witty comparison of governments to inns—"On y entre et on en sort sans savoir pourquoi; c'est une procession de marion-nettes"—her account of how her four "loves of dresses" were ruined at the Custom-house, are all characteristic of her delightful personality. But, as she claims, she can be serious at need, and she is a friend among a thousand. As soon as she enters Mme de Chavigny's room she divines that something is wrong, and she at once detects and ridicules M. de Chavigny's fancy for Mme de Blainville by recognising the precious blue purse as one upon which she had been employed for seven years. "Elle a appartenu en idée à trois personnes de ma connaissance. C'est un trésor que vous avez là, c'est un vrai héritage que vous avez fait." Her winning of Mathilde's confidence, her warm sympathy—"Cette Blainville avec son indigo, je la déteste des pieds à la tête"—and her assurance that she will bring M. de Chavigny to reason, are admirably portrayed. Then after seven lines of soliloquy there follows the great scene of the play, in which Chavigny is lured, through his fatuity, into her carefully laid trap, and suddenly meets with the punishment which is most effective with a man of his temperament—the realisation that he has been made a fool of. "Ni moi non plus, Monsieur de Chavigny." It is a dramatic moment, and it is followed by an admirable speech, in which Mme de Léry, with perfect *bonhomie*, points out to her would-be gallant the folly and ridicule of his conduct. " Je n'oublierai jamais qu'un jeune curé fait les meilleurs sermons" is his grateful and sensible comment, and with this remark the curtain falls.

Mme de Léry is not wholly an imaginary portrait. Alfred de Musset took as his model Mme Maxime Jaubert (Caroline D'Alton-Shee), the wife of a distinguished official, whom he called his *marraine*, because, when her guests were amusing themselves one evening by devising sobriquets for one another, she gave him the name of "Prince Phosphore du cœur volant". She was very tiny and she had an especially tiny foot; though her face was plain it sparkled with intelligence. Alfred de Musset made her acquaintance in 1835 and became one of the *habitués* of her salon, which was one of the most agreeable in Paris. They soon became warm friends. Being seven years his senior she gave him advice as well as sympathy, and he made her the confidante of all his troubles, including his numerous love affairs. The incident of the purse was also founded on fact—on a mysterious purse containing a friendly admonition, which Musset after some gambling losses received at this time. It subsequently transpired that the anonymous donor was a young cousin of Mme Jaubert's, named Aimée D'Alton, who was a great admirer of Musset's poems, at a time when no one read them. The two became friends and, before long, lovers. The *liaison*—for they did not marry—lasted for the two years 1837 and 1838, and according to Paul de Musset, whom the lady married after Alfred's death, they were "two years of unclouded love", without a quarrel or storm, or "coolness of any kind". It is difficult to believe this, knowing Alfred de Musset's temperament. At any rate two years was his extreme limit as a lover.

After 1838, though he was only twenty-seven, he began rapidly to decline in health and happiness and productive power. In 1839 he had fits of great despondency; he pub-

lished nothing but *Croisilles* (the last of his six *nouvelles*) and
two or three short poems. His *marraine* reproached him with
his idleness, which, she said, implied lack of courage. He had
made some attempts, including a five-act tragedy for Rachel
about Frédégonde, the wicked Queen of the Franks, entitled
La Servante du Roi. But he tore up most of what he had
written, and only part of the fourth act survives. In February
1840 he had a very severe attack of pneumonia, the first of
several bad illnesses, and in June he wrote the pathetic little
poem, *Tristesse*.

> J'ai perdu ma force et ma vie,
> Et mes amis et ma gaîté;
> J'ai perdu jusqu'à la fierté,
> Qui faisait croire à mon génie.

In 1841, after a chance meeting with George Sand, he
wrote one of his finest poems, *Souvenir*, and towards the end
of the year he addressed to Buloz, who was only too anxious
to print anything of his in the *Revue des Deux Mondes*, a *causerie*
in verse, *Sur la Paresse*. Less than twenty poems—one of
some interest, entitled *Après une lecture*, another written on
the first anniversary of the death of his school friend, the
Duc d'Orléans, and the rest mostly gay trifles—made up
his poetical output for the years 1842 to 1845. But on
November 1, 1845 he published a new proverb, *Il faut qu'une
porte soit ouverte ou fermée*.

There are only two characters, and as neither of them leaves
the stage for a moment the unities of place and time are not
only completely observed but the action occupies the exact
time that it takes to act the play. Not that there is any action
in the sense of external action; it takes place solely within the
hearts of the actors. The drama begins with the Count paying an afternoon call on the Marquise; it ends with their engagement. To trace the stages by which they arrive at this
result would take too long. They are indicated with such
subtlety and delicacy that it requires close attention and some
divination on the part of the reader to detect them. Evidently

the pair had at least a considerable inclination for one another, and probably the Marquise, who is a widow of thirty, had considered the possibility of a proposal from the Count. He soon makes it clear that he has a warm admiration for her and he hovers on the brink of a declaration. But the Marquise is anxious to know how far he is in earnest, and she deftly launches an attack on men in Paris society for thinking it their duty to make love to women. Then she turns the attack on him. "Vous ne m'aimez pas plus que le grand Turc." This provokes a defence of love from the Count, which expresses Musset's own views. At last, irritated by the Marquise's "indifférence à la mode, cette froideur qui raille et dédaigne, cet air d'expérience qui réduit tout à rien", he plumps on his knees in the orthodox French fashion and declares his love and adoration in fairly passionate language. She becomes at once serious, "Mais, enfin, Monsieur, qu'est-ce que vous me voulez?" He answers with hesitation, and she having heard that gossip connected him with chorus girls—"Vous êtes dans les chœurs" is her way of putting it—declares with indignation that his proposal is revolting. In words of much dignity and real eloquence he makes clear his intentions, "Eh bien! si vous m'aviez dit cela en arrivant nous ne nous serions pas disputés". True, but in that case there would have been no play.

The Marquise has a distinct personality. She is a woman of the world, but she is thoroughly sincere and straightforward, and she is entirely free from coquetry. She hates vapid compliments, meaningless phrases, and all the flimsy stock-in-trade of conventional love-making. She can hold her own in the give and take of *esprit* and epigram, but when she is serious, she is direct and even brusque in speech. The Count as a lover is equally sincere at heart, but he is more complex. Timid and distrustful of himself, he assumes the protective mask of indifference and *ennui*, and when he advances to the attack it is by a cautious and roundabout approach. The Marquise is at once on the defensive, and the defensive

soon becomes an offensive. But when she throws doubt not
only on his professions of love but on the very existence of
love, he defends love in general and himself in particular
with such eloquence and with such evident sincerity that he
gains his cause. Paul de Musset tells us that, when he read
the proverb at Venice, he at once recognised the characters.
The Count was so like his brother that he seemed to see him
seizing his hat at every ring of the bell, leaving the door open,
and unable to decide whether to go or stay. The lady was not
so easy to identify, but the title of Marquise gave him a clue
and he guessed correctly. He also learned from his brother
that the conversation had taken place almost exactly as reported, though of course with a different ending.

I said at almost the beginning of this chapter that *Il faut
qu'une porte soit ouverte ou fermée* and *Un Caprice* were the two
plays of Musset which shewed most strongly the influence of
Marivaux. Like Marivaux he was more interested in character than plot, and like Racine and Marivaux he loved to
probe its inmost recesses. In most of his comedies there is
one great scene, in which two characters act and re-act upon
one another through speech and argument, with the result
that their relations to one another at the end of the scene are
different from what they were at the beginning. Such scenes
are those between Octave and Marianne in *Les Caprices de
Marianne* (II, 4), between Perdican and Camille in *On ne badine
pas avec l'amour* (II, 5), between Fortunio and Jacqueline in *Le
Chandelier* (III, 3), and between Valentin and Cécile in *Il ne
faut jurer de rien* (III, 4). Of these the last comes nearest to
Marivaux, who, as we have seen, habitually used such scenes
to dispel the doubts or break down the defences of hesitating
lovers, but who achieved his purpose by a series of encounters and not by a single and decisive one. In Musset's
Un Caprice the scene between the Marquise and the Count
occupies nearly half the play, but it is not an encounter
between equal antagonists. Rather, Mme de Léry is like a
fisherman coaxing Chavigny to rise to her fly and, as soon as

he has taken it, landing him without a struggle. But the solitary scene of *Il faut qu'une porte soit ouverte ou fermée* would have most rejoiced the heart of Marivaux. The Count is in love with the Marquise and is anxious to marry her, but, being at once modest and reasonably proud, he hesitates to risk a declaration. The Marquise wants two things, one to be assured that his love is genuine and the other to have a straightforward proposal of marriage. In fact the Marquise and the Count are in a more or less similar position to that of the Countess and the Marquis in *Le Legs*, and the quiet composure, with its complete absence of sentiment, with which the Countess accepts his proposal, closely resembles the behaviour of the Countess in the first *Surprise de l'Amour* and the Marquise in the second. It will be noted too that Musset follows Marivaux's example in calling his lovers only by their titles.

When *Il faut qu'une porte soit ouverte ou fermée* appeared in the *Revue des Deux Mondes*, Musset was little known even as a poet except to the readers of that review. Two years later, thanks to *Un Caprice*, his fame as a dramatist almost rivalled that of Scribe. The story of how *Un Caprice* came to be acted at the Théâtre-Français has become a legend. The simple truth appears to be that when Mme Allan-Despréaux, who from 1826 to 1836 had acted with great success in Paris, was acting together with her husband with equal success at St Petersburg, she witnessed the performance of a Russian translation of *Un Caprice*, and, realising the great merit of the little comedy, obtained permission from Buloz, then *administrateur* of the Théâtre-Français, to signalise her return to that theatre by appearing in the part of Mme de Léry. Buloz was only too glad to welcome on the stage a play by an author whom he so greatly admired, and, in spite of some opposition from the *sociétaires*, *Un Caprice* was produced on November 27, 1847. It was a triumphant success, and two days later Théophile Gautier wrote a long and enthusiastic notice of it in *La Presse*. "Depuis Marivaux il ne s'est rien produit

Musset

à la Comédie Française de si fin, de si délicat" and "Mme Allan a joué Mme de Léry en comédienne consommée; on n'a rien exagéré en disant qu'elle rappelait parfois Mlle Mars".

Musset became popular at a bound. *Il faut qu'une porte soit ouverte ou fermée*, with Mme Allan as the Marquise and Brindeau, who had played M. de Chavigny in *Un Caprice*, as the Count, followed in April 1848. Then came, as we have seen, *Il ne faut jurer de rien* and *Le Chandelier* and then, also in 1848, *André del Sarto*, which was not a success, being withdrawn after five performances. At the beginning of 1849 Musset wrote for Augustine Brohan, the queen of *soubrettes*, a comedy in verse entitled *Louison*, of which a *soubrette* is the heroine. But no sooner was the play finished than he was seized with a Platonic caprice for Mlle Anais, another great actress, in spite of her forty-seven years, of *soubrette* parts, and Augustine Brohan made over the rôle to her. The play has a certain charm and interest, but it is evidently written to order, and it only had a *succès d'estime*. The Princess de Belgiojoso, however, on whom Alfred de Musset some years before had written the cruel sonnet, *Sur une morte*, had the magnanimity to write to him and tell him that he had produced a little masterpiece. "Vous pensez et sentez comme Shakespeare, et parlez comme Marivaux", a remark which can hardly be said to apply to *Louison*, but which has, as we have seen, much truth in it as regards Musset's work in general.

His next play, *On ne saurait penser à tout*, a proverb in one act, was also written to order—for a charity performance at very short notice. It was produced at the Théâtre-Français four weeks later (May 30, 1849), but was coldly received and only ran for twelve nights. It is an adaptation of *Le Distrait* of Carmontelle, whose proverbs were very popular in the second half of the eighteenth century and were still acted in Musset's day, especially by amateurs. Musset has boldly appropriated all or part of five scenes almost textually, but his most amusing scene, which is the ninth, is original.

During the years 1848 to 1851 such work as Musset did
was almost entirely for the stage; he either rearranged old
plays or wrote new ones. Of the five or six short poems that
he wrote during this period three are addressed to members
of the Comédie Française. The success of *Un Caprice* had
been especially welcome to him, because in 1848, after the
declaration of the Republic, he had been deprived of his
small sinecure post as librarian of the Department of the
Interior. Yet he sold all his rights as author in *Un Caprice* to
the publisher, Charpentier, for 500 francs. In 1850 he received an offer on a more generous scale from Dr Véron, the
well-known editor of *Le Constitutionnel.* It was that he should
write for Véron's paper a comedy in three or five acts for
1000 francs an act. Musset accepted the proposal and produced *Carmosine* in three acts. Véron was so charmed with
the piece that he wanted to pay 5000 francs, but Musset declined at first to accept more than 3000. Finally they com-
promised at 4000. *Carmosine* is founded on a story of
Boccaccio's (x, 7) of which the summary runs as follows:
"King Peter (of Aragon), having heard that Lisa was sick
with the fervent love that she had for him, went to comfort
her and married her to a young gentleman, and, having
kissed her on the forehead, declared himself to be her
cavalier for ever". This story is told by Boccaccio with all
his direct simplicity, enlivened by his delicate and irresistible
touches of pathos and tenderness, and Musset has kept pretty
closely to his source. But he has introduced two new characters—Perillo, who has loved Carmosine (Lisa) from childhood, in the place of Boccaccio's gentle but poor young man,
found for her by the King, and Ser Vespasiano, one of those
conceited and uncomprehending fools whom Musset loved
to ridicule, but, as Gautier says, a little out of place in *Carmosine.* Also two of Boccaccio's characters are greatly developed—Minuccio the troubadour, and the Queen. The
scene in which the latter by her tactful sympathy administers
consolation to Carmosine (III, 8) is as beautiful as it is

affecting. Equally good is the one (ii, 7) in which Minuccio, who with all his wit and gaiety is no less sympathetic and helpful, tells Carmosine's story to the Court in language as simple and as moving as Boccaccio's. The other characters are more or less sketches; Bernardo, the devoted father, Dame Paque, the foolish ambitious mother, Perillo, the patient and self-sacrificing lover, and Carmosine herself, who, in spite of her romantic and unattainable love, is sweet-tempered, reasonable, and without a trace of affectation. There are some good scenes, especially in the third act, besides the two mentioned above. But on the whole the play is inferior to the best of Musset's comedies, and it is so, I think, for two reasons. In the first place the story, at least as Musset has treated it, has not enough matter for three acts. In consequence he has been obliged to fill out his play, just as he did *Barberine*, with scenes or portions of scenes that can only be called padding. Secondly, though the chief characters are drawn with great charm and with sufficient insight to convince us of their goodness and intelligence, there is no attempt to probe deeper. We know nothing of their internal conflicts, not even of Carmosine's or Perillo's, nothing, in short, of their inner life. Of course this second objection is one which occurs much more readily to a careful reader of the play than to a spectator. But, as a matter of fact, *Carmosine* has never been a success on the stage. It was first produced at the Odéon in 1865, and was revived there in 1918, and there were a few performances of it at the Théâtre-Français in 1926. In spite of its weak points, however, the play has much charm and should be better known than it is. Musset, indeed, regarded it as one of his two best plays, the other being *Lorenzaccio*, and his brother Paul thought it "the deepest and most moving of all his works".

Bettine, Musset's last comedy, was written for Rose Chéri (1824–1861) of the Gymnase theatre, whose acting in *Clarisse Harlowe*, five years before, had so greatly impressed him that he went to see her thirty times running. The piece, which is in one act, was produced on October 29, 1851, but it was coldly received. Nor did it meet with a better fate at the Théâtre-Français, where up to the end of 1925 it had only been played nine times. Paul de Musset, however, is just as enthusiastic over it as over *Carmosine*, and says that he considers it one of his brother's most perfect productions— too perfect to obtain success. This is an exaggerated estimate. *Bettine*, however, is a stronger play than *Carmosine*. It shews greater insight into the human heart and the characters have more depth. Bettine, a distinguished and popular opera-singer, is gay and inconsequent, warm-hearted and generous. The Marquis Stéfani is courtly, sympathetic, and equally generous. But beneath these traits which appear on the surface we detect a real nobility of nature. M. de Steinberg, "ce drôle de monsieur", is less impressive because he is more complex. He is weak and cowardly rather than a born villain; the stages of his descent by a series of mean acts to the culminating desertion of Bettine on their wedding-day are admirably depicted. Nor must the notary with his persistent inquiry for the "futurs conjoints", and Calabre, Steinberg's discreet and clear-sighted servant, be forgotten. The action, which only occupies a few hours, takes place throughout the play in the salon of a villa in Italy. The time is that of the writing of the play, for Stéfani recalls his memories of the great singers of the thirties, Lablache and Rubini, Pasta and Malibran, and of "le vieux Garcia", who died in 1832, as memories of his youth. But in spite of its superficial air of contemporary life, the fantastic element is just as strong as in any of Musset's comedies. The strange wedding, which is apparently about to take place in the presence of the notary as the sole official and the sole witness (except perhaps Calabre), Bettine's unreasoning and unreasonable love for "ce drôle" Steinberg, still more her philosophic acceptance of her old friend Stéfani as his substitute, are all in the highest degree fantastic. Yet, such is Musset's art that under the spell of his dialogue we ignore the improbabilities and are content to follow the inward life of his characters, as he chooses to present them to us.

The success of *Un Caprice* brought fame to Alfred de Musset not only as a dramatist but as a poet. For more than twenty years he was the idol of the younger generation. But, save for the short spurt of dramatic activity, his popularity did not revive his spent creative powers. After 1851 he published absolutely nothing but his *discours de réception* at the Académie Française, to which he was elected in 1852. His lassitude and his melancholy increased; for eighteen months "the hour of his death sounded in his ears"; the release came on May 1, 1857.

In a preface written after the publication of the *Contes d'Espagne et d'Italie* and the first part of the *Spectacle dans un Fauteuil* and afterwards prefixed to the first edition of his *Comédies et Proverbes*, Musset, in answer to certain critics who had accused him of having imitated various poets, French or otherwise, declares that, while plagiarism in literature should be regarded as a crime, to be inspired by a master is not only permissible but praiseworthy. And in the verse dedication to *La Coupe et les Lèvres*, the most Byronic of his poems, he writes the frequently quoted lines:

> On m'dit l'an passé que j'imitais Byron:
> Vous qui me connaissez, vous savez bien que non.
> Je hais comme la mort l'état plagiaire;
> Mon verre n'est pas grand, mais je bois dans mon verre.

Musset was right. As a young man he overflowed with enthusiasm for certain writers, especially for Shakespeare and Byron. But in spite of the Byronic character of the very poem, especially of its hero, in the dedication to which he repudiates the charge of plagiarism, he is never a mere imitator. He comes under the influence of writers whom he admires, but it is only a suggestive influence. He could truly say, "Je bois dans mon verre". And nowhere is he more original than in his dramatic work. It is true that *André del Sarto* evidently comes from the Romantic camp, but it differs considerably from the typical Romantic drama. It shews for one thing far more psychological insight, especially in the character of André. In his next play, as I have pointed out, Musset breaks away altogether from the Romanticists, and henceforth he works entirely on lines of his own—influenced, indeed, by the lessons that he had learnt from great masters, but without a trace of imitation. And if one is asked what these lines are, one might define them as the combination of psychological realism with a fantastic setting.

If " Je bois dans mon verre " is true, so also is "Mon verre n'est pas grand". Musset wrote no poetry and only one drama on the grand scale. His comedies never exceed three acts, and two—perhaps the most perfect—are in one act. The characters are few, and of these only two or three are of the first importance. In his three most characteristic comedies we have Octave and Marianne, Perdican and Camille, Fantasio and Elsbeth. Of these only Perdican and Camille are lovers; but love is the theme of all three plays. Octave and Marianne talk of nothing but love, and the sole purpose of Fantasio's witty pleading is to save Elsbeth from a loveless marriage. The theme of *Barberine* is married love, of *Le Chandelier* illicit love, of *Il ne faut jurer de rien* true love that leads to marriage, of *Carmosine* a romantic but unattainable love transformed into a loyal devotion, of *Bettine* and *Il ne faut jurer de rien* the calm and reasonable love of a man and woman who know the world, of *Un Caprice* the re-capture of a husband's love.

Musset's plots are extremely simple. Some are of his own invention, some are founded on personal experience, and some are taken from books. But if the plot is simple it is often very effective, especially in the two comedies, *Les Caprices de Marianne* and *On ne badine pas avec l'amour*, which have a tragic ending. There are others which, if less striking, have at any rate the merit of originality—those of *Il ne faut jurer de rien*, *Le Chandelier*, and *Un Caprice*, the two latter being drawn from incidents in Musset's own life. The plots too of the two comedies founded on Boccaccio and Bandello respectively are both good, especially *Barberine*. In each case Musset has kept fairly closely to his original, but, while in *Barberine* he has given life to Bandello's characters and has made the last act, at any rate, really dramatic, he has not been so successful with *Carmosine*, charming though it is, chiefly because there is not enough material for three acts. Finally, in two of the comedies, *Bettine* and *Il faut qu'une porte soit ouverte ou fermée*, there can hardly be said to be any plot at all.

When a dramatist takes his plot ready-made either from history or from a story-book, he is bound to make his principal or essential characters conform to the plot. Musset has done this in *Barberine* and *Carmosine*. In the former play neither Barberine, nor Ulric, nor the Queen could in their broad outlines well have been other than he has made them. But he has quite legitimately and with advantage to the structure of the drama substituted Rosemberg for the two nobles of Bandello's story, whom Massinger, working from the same source, has transformed in *The Picture* into ruffians of incredible grossness. So, too, in *Carmosine* the characters of the heroine as a modest and pure maiden and of the royal couple as wise and kindly sympathisers were definitely marked out. It is the same with *Lorenzaccio*. Whatever modifications he might introduce into their characters he had to make the Duke a tyrant and a debauchee and Lorenzaccio his boon companion. But in those plays in which the plot is his own, whether of his own invention or as an incident in his own experience, the characters create the plot, and consequently their development and their reaction to one another become of the first importance.

It has been said that Musset has only one hero, namely himself. It would be fairer to say that, though he generally models his heroes on himself, in the result they are fancy portraits. Moreover there is nothing heroic about them. We have seen that Fortunio is himself as a boy of seventeen, and the Count in *Il faut qu'une porte soit ouverte ou fermée* himself at seven and thirty. Octave, Fantasio, Perdican, and Valentin represent him as he was in the early twenties. They are varieties of the same type. They are all *coureurs de filles*; Octave and Fantasio are given to drink; Valentin is a dandy and a spendthrift. But it may be said of them, as someone has said of Alfred de Musset, that they are "plus fanfarons de débauche que débauchés". They are very youthful, and, being youthful, they exaggerate their vices just as their creator has done in the *Confession d'un enfant du siècle*. But there are distinct differences in their characters. Octave is cynical, Fantasio is *blasé*, Perdican is bitter, but more in love with life than the others and more emotional. He is also more serious and less witty. Valentin, the dandy and would-be Lovelace, has Musset's audacity and charm, and also his reverence for pure and innocent girlhood.

In *A quoi rêvent les jeunes filles* Musset had shewn with what lively and delicate touches he could portray young girls with their vague dreams and their unruffled innocence. But Elsbeth and Cécile have more substance and more actuality than the sylph-like sisters, Ninon and Ninette. They are alike in their charm, their intelligence, and their high-bred simplicity. But there is a difference between them, which M. Doumic has pointed out. Elsbeth is romantic and has her dreams—perhaps, as she herself suggests, because her governess has encouraged her to read novels. Cécile, on the other hand, does not like novels; those that she has read mean nothing to her; they seem to be mere lies and invention. She does not care for descriptions of scenery; she loves reality in nature as well as in life. There is also another difference between them. Each bears the mark of her position in life and her bringing up. Elsbeth, with all her friendliness and sympathy for Fantasio, talks like one who is used to command; she is always the princess. Cécile is the well brought-up daughter of an aristocratic family, dutiful to her mother and gracious to those about her. But she is not altogether submissive, nor is she a prude. Carmosine and Rosette are slighter creations.

They resemble one another in loving out of their sphere. But, while Rosette dies tragically of a broken heart, Carmosine finds happiness by accepting the love that is within her reach. Camille is less gracious and has less charm than Musset's other young girls, but she is the most powerfully drawn of all.

Of the married women Barberine, as M. Doumic observes, is what Cécile will become when she is a wife. She has the same common sense, the same sense of humour, the same innate rectitude and entire freedom from coquetry. The Queen in *Barberine* and the other Queen in *Carmosine* are beautiful types of good women who have learnt from experience how to give advice, sympathy, and practical help to those who are in misfortune or difficulty. They may be regarded as an expression of Musset's gratitude to the women of the world who helped him from time to time. Marianne and Jacqueline are more difficult to understand. Marianne is meant, I think, to be something of an enigma, a woman of "caprices", of which she cannot give a very good explanation even to herself. Jacqueline is enigmatic for a different reason, for the reason—so it seems to me—that the dramatist does not know himself whether she has really fallen in love with Fortunio or whether she merely means to amuse herself with him. In either case it is a "caprice", and, though a spectator of the play may be satisfied, a reader will tremble for Fortunio.

The Marquise in *Il faut qu'une porte soit ouverte ou fermée* and Bettine in the comedy of that name form another couple. Neither is in her first youth; neither is a complete portrait; but both, so far as we are permitted to know them, are thoroughly likable women, largely because of their rectitude and their absence of coquetry. Lastly there is Mme de Léry, but I need not repeat her praises. In the whole history of the drama is there any character within the limits of a one-act comedy that is so brilliant on the surface and so essentially noble?

All the female characters that I have mentioned may be

described as principal ones, that is to say, as essential to the working out of the plot. As in nearly all drama, Musset's female secondary characters are considerably fewer than the male. Of these few the most individual is the Baronne de Mantes, Cécile's mother, with her inconsequent remarks, her aristocratic and slightly autocratic bearing, and her essential goodness. She is altogether delightful. Bettine is more of a type; her generosity and her impulsiveness, especially in her love affairs, are typical of great opera-singers and actresses at all times and in all countries.

Of the older men the most individual and the most attractive are Van Buck, the uncle of Valentin in *Il ne faut jurer de rien,* and Minuccio the troubadour in *Carmosine;* of the others the most carefully drawn is André del Sarto, but the play having been written before its author had freed himself from the influence of Romanticism, he is too much inclined to rhetoric and excessive sentiment. Well studied too are the Count in *Il faut qu'une porte soit ouverte ou fermée* and the Marquis Stéfani, the devotee of grand opera, in *Bettine.* Experienced men of the world, they are not given to the outpouring of their feelings. Yet both have sound hearts and generous impulses, and the Count, when roused, declares his love for the Marquise in terms as unambiguous as she could desire. Clavaroche is a type—a thoroughly unpleasant one— but he is true to type and he has a certain individuality.

I must not forget the "grotesques", as the French call them, for they are a special feature of Musset's comedies. They may be divided into two classes, the "grotesques" proper—Bridaine, Blazius and Dame Pluche, Tibia (Claudio's valet), and the Notary in *Bettine*—and those who combine imbecility with pomposity and pedantry. Such are the Prince of Mantua and his aide-de-camp Marinoni, Claudio, Ser Vespasiano. The Baron in *On ne badine pas avec l'amour* is somewhat different; he is more humorous than the others and we can even feel some affection for him. The Abbé in *Il ne faut jurer de rien* belongs to neither class; he is a good sketch with nothing exaggerated or farcical about him. Got, as we have seen, made a great hit in the part.

It will be seen from this survey of Musset's characters that, so far as his comedies are concerned, there are few which are of a nature to make a great impression on the stage or to tempt the ambition of first-rate actors or actresses. In the front rank are Mme de Léry and Camille, in which Mme Allan-Despréaux and Mlle Favart scored remarkable successes, and the two male parts created by Delaunay—Fantasio and Fortunio. There are not in fact many opportunities in Musset's drama for making great hits. There are few passionate tirades and few dramatic thrills. Great scenes too are rare, hardly more than one in any play. It is not in the glamour of his characters that Musset excels, but in their psychological truth. Like Racine and Marivaux he can penetrate to the recesses of the heart; he can detect its half-formed desires, its hesitations, its sudden changes—in short the whole curve of its wavering course. As a result his characters demand close attention from both spectator and reader, and all the more so because he sometimes records his observations rather by suggestion than by direct statement. As we have seen, neither Marianne nor Perdican—to take a couple of instances—are easy characters to read.

Though Musset does not, as Marivaux practically does, discard soliloquy altogether as a means of revealing character, he makes but sparing use of it. The longest soliloquy by far is Fortunio's in *Le Chandelier* (III, 2). It reveals him as an inexperienced boy, so blinded by love that in face of the strongest evidence he acquits Jacqueline of being worse than a gay and thoughtless coquette. There is also in the same play a soliloquy of some length by Clavaroche, a simple and naïve expression of the vanity of this second-rate but astute ladykiller. In *Les Caprices de Marianne* the heroine's short monologue (II, 3) is rather a natural outburst of anger at her husband's unjust accusations than a true soliloquy. That of Octave (II, 4) is more complex. His assertions that to sup-

plant his friend would be too cheap a rascality for him, that
supper is more important than love, and that all human
actions are determined by chance and caprice serve to round
off his more or less assumed character of a professed cynic.
Fantasio's two fairly long soliloquies (II, 3 and II, 7) express
the same belief in caprice and its influence on human affairs,
and they incidentally portray him as an indifferent and bored
spectator of life rather than as a cynic like Octave. Camille's
outburst at the foot of the altar (III, 8) is an involuntary cry
of anguish, but Perdican is given two true soliloquies. The
first (III, 1) expresses his indecision and subtly indicates that
this is a characteristic failing. The second (III, 2) reveals at
once his readiness to take offence when his vanity is wounded
and his unreflecting impulsiveness. In his long dialogue with
Camille by the source in the wood he had assumed the air of
an experienced man of the world, but the second soliloquy
shews that he is still very young. Rosemberg's three
soliloquies in the third act of *Barberine* are unimportant, but
they confirm Barberine's report of him as *point méchant*. In
Un Caprice Mathilde's soliloquies express her adoring love for
her husband. In none of the other comedies is there any
soliloquy of importance.

Musset's usual method of revealing character is by means
of dialogue, and for that purpose his style is singularly well
adapted. Easy and supple, it lends itself readily to various
uses, and among others to the interchange of conflicting views
in such a way as to bring out the characters of the speakers.
We have first-rate examples in the scenes between Octave
and Marianne, between Perdican and Camille, between Mme
de Léry and Chavigny, and between the Count and the Marquise. The opening dialogue of *Il ne faut jurer de rien* has
already been referred to as a famous example of Musset's ease
and brilliance. It is not only a clear and adequate exposition
of the play, but it gives us considerable insight into the characters of both uncle and nephew.

In the other famous scene of the same play, that between

Valentin, who has now become a devout and adoring lover, and Cécile, we see how naturally and easily Musset's style can assume a poetic tone. No less poetic is the language in the scene between Fortunio and Jacqueline—only here we have tormented passion in the place of blissful tranquillity—and that of Octave in *Les Caprices de Marianne* (I, I):

> Un mal le plus cruel de tous, car c'est un mal sans espérance; le plus terrible, car c'est un mal qui se chérit lui-même et repousse la coupe salutaire jusque dans la main de l'amitié, un mal qui fait pâlir les lèvres sous des poisons plus doux que l'ambroisie, et qui fond en une pluie de larmes le cœur le plus dur, comme la perle de Cléopâtre; un mal que tous les aromates, toute la science humaine ne sauraient soulager, et qui se nourrit du vent qui passe, du parfum d'une rose fanée, du refrain d'une chanson, et qui suce l'éternel aliment de ses souffrances dans tout ce qui l'entoure, comme une abeille son miel dans tous les buissons d'un jardin.

And in the last scene of the same play Musset attains to the height of pathetic eloquence by means of the simplest language:

OCTAVE.

Moi seul au monde je l'ai connu. Cette urne d'albâtre, couverte de ce long voile de deuil, est sa parfaite image. C'est ainsi qu'une douce mélancolie voilait les perfections de cette âme tendre et délicate. Pour moi seul, cette vie silencieuse n'a point été un mystère. Les longues soirées que nous avons passées ensemble sont comme de fraîches oasis dans un désert aride; elles ont versé sur mon cœur les seules gouttes de rosée qui y soient jamais tombées. Cœlio était la bonne partie de moi-même; elle est remontée au ciel avec lui. C'était un homme d'un autre temps; il connaissait les plaisirs, et leur préférait la solitude; il savait combien les illusions sont trompeuses, et il préférait ses illusions à la réalité. Elle eût été heureuse la femme qui l'eût aimée.

MARIANNE.

Ne serait-elle point heureuse, Octave, la femme qui t'aimerait?

OCTAVE.

Je ne sais point aimer; Cœlio seul le savait. La cendre que renferme cette tombe est tout ce que j'ai aimé sur la terre, tout ce que j'aimerai. Lui seul savait verser dans une autre âme toutes les sources de bonheur qui reposaient dans la sienne. Lui seul était capable d'un dévouement sans bornes; lui seul eût consacré sa vie entière à la femme qu'il aimait, aussi facilement qu'il aurait bravé la mort pour elle. Je ne suis qu'un débauché sans cœur; je n'estime point les femmes: l'amour que j'inspire est comme celui que je ressens, l'ivresse passagère d'un songe. Je ne sais pas les secrets qu'il savait. Ma gaieté est comme le masque d'un histrion; mon cœur est plus vieux qu'elle, mes sens blasés n'en veulent plus. Je ne suis qu'un lâche; sa mort n'est point vengée.

Apart from its beauty, this last passage is especially interesting, because it represents the two sides of Alfred de Musset himself. Cœlio is Musset as he was capable of being in his better and happier moments; Octave is Musset's worse self, but with his vices exaggerated, for he was not a heartless debauchee, nor is it true that he "did not esteem women". Octave also appears as generous, loyal, and modest, and this was equally true of his creator. Fantasio, as we have seen, is also drawn from Musset himself. I need not refer again to the wonderful dialogue between him and Spark, except to note that we get from it our first impressions of Fantasio's character.

Revelation of character is only one of the functions of dialogue; it is also a means of developing the plot, and when there is little physical action, this function may become highly important. Musset, in whose comedies physical or external action is of the slightest, is a little capricious in this use of dialogue. In *Les Caprices de Marianne* no advance—at least no apparent advance—is made during the whole of the first act and the first two scenes of the second, except that Claudio's suspicions increase and are diverted from Cœlio to Octave. But from this point onwards the drama moves with great rapidity, and chiefly by means of dialogue, for, except in the fifth scene of the second act, there is very little physical action and Cœlio's assassination takes place off the stage. In *Fantasio* the dialogue throughout contributes little or nothing to the development of such plot as there is, and the *dénoue-*

ment is the result of a pure caprice. It is very different with *On ne badine pas avec l'amour*. From the moment that Perdican and Camille first meet, their conversations determine the whole dramatic movement of the play. Growing love, piqued vanity, jealousy, pride, conflict between love and religion, all find expression; and thus of this play it is pre-eminently true that the plot is created by the characters.

In *Le Chandelier* the story is carried on chiefly by the conversations of the principal characters, but Fortunio's decision to go on loving Jacqueline is expressed in the long soliloquy above referred to, and it is in a short soliloquy (III, 3) that Jacqueline expresses her resolve not to carry out Clavaroche's scheme. In the second and third acts of *Il ne faut jurer de rien* there is more action than usual, and the liveliness that results from this is one of the merits of the play. But the first scene of the second act is an admirable example of Musset's power of advancing his story by means of dialogue. It chiefly consists of a long conversation between Van Buck and his nephew, but they are twice interrupted by Cécile, and though she only utters eight short sentences, these have so marked an effect on Valentin that his uncle is justified in saying, "Tu l'épouseras!" In *Barberine* and *Carmosine*, the two comedies in which Musset took a ready-made story for his plot, he does not employ dialogue to any great extent for its development. In *Barberine*, however, the conversations of the last scene of the first act and of the whole of the second act—I am referring to the version which Musset revised for the stage—lead to the formation of the wager between Ulric and Rosemberg, and in *Carmosine* the scene between the Queen and the heroine (III, 8) is not only one of the most beautiful that Musset ever wrote, but it shews a singularly skilful employment of dialogue to indicate the influence of one character upon another and thus to bring the play a stage further towards its conclusion.

But nowhere is Musset's skill in making speech the mirror of the soul better displayed than in the two one-act comedies,

Un Caprice and *Il faut qu'une porte soit ouverte ou fermée*. The dialogue between the Marquise and the Count is the longest that Musset ever wrote, which is natural, seeing that it forms the whole play, but that between Mme de Léry and M. de Chavigny is more than two-thirds as long. The miracle is that in neither case does the interest ever flag. From first to last we follow with keen intent the jealousy, the bad temper, the amorous desires, of M. de Chavigny, and the skill with which Mme de Léry plays him, and then his sudden rise to the bait and the swift blow with which she crushes him. Less thrilling and less brilliant, but even more remarkable as an example of dramatised psychology, is the encounter between the Marquise and the Count, in which, after many hesitations and misunderstandings, many advances and retreats, an ordinary afternoon call ends in a matrimonial engagement.

If these two scenes have movement in the sense that they carry forward the story to its appointed end, they also have movement in the sense that the actors are far from stationary on the stage. M. de Chavigny is constantly jumping up and walking about; Mme de Léry gets up to tidy her hair before a glass; each pours out tea for the other; a servant comes in with a parcel, which Chavigny opens; Chavigny kneels before Mme de Léry, gets up again, sits down beside her and takes her hand; she asks him for a pack of cards, draws a card which he guesses wrong, makes him give her the blue purse as a forfeit and throws it into the fire. Such are Musset's stage directions, and in reading them one can well imagine how they help to give life and vivacity to the scenes when they are acted.

In *Il faut qu'une porte soit ouverte ou fermée* there is constant movement in the opening of the door by the Count and his shutting of it at the Marquise's bidding. "Fermez donc cette porte." The Count is never still for long; he looks out of the window, he changes his seat, he puts a log of wood on the fire, he gives the Marquise a screen, he brings her a cushion and proceeds to kneel on it before her. She in her turn gets up and goes to the door; she comes back, and the Count cries, "Vous me comblez de joie!" "Mais fermez donc cette malheureuse porte!" replies the Marquise. It is this feeling for movement that makes Sarcey, with his life-long experience of the theatre, say with truth that Musset's comedies are "scenic". This scenic sense was part of that innate love of drama which led him to employ dialogue in his early poems and later to introduce it into pure lyrics like *Les Nuits*.

It was owing to this same dramatic instinct that his plays, written, as they were, without any thought of being acted, were able to be produced on the stage with comparatively little alteration. The changes made in *Le Chandelier* and *Les Caprices de Marianne* were, except for a few omissions in the former play, practically confined to making them conform to the requirements of the Théâtre-Français. *On ne badine pas avec l'amour* with its perpetual change of scene seemed at first to present an insuperable difficulty, but it was found to be a simple business to reduce the dozen different backgrounds to three, and then all went smoothly. *Lorenzaccio* was a tougher job and the stage version, which made the murder of Lorenzaccio the central theme of the play, was a departure from Musset's intention, but it was a triumphant success. Delaunay thought *Fantasio* "peu jouable", and so it has been generally considered, but the cause is not so much faulty construction as a general lack of dramatic interest. The same may be said of Musset's last comedy, *Bettine*, which was only moderately successful when first produced and has been seldom acted since. On this play M. Lyonnet remarks that it is the singular destiny of Musset's drama that, whereas all the plays that were not written for the stage have been brilliantly successful, those written especially for the stage have had only moderate success. But this last remark only applies strictly to *Bettine* and *Louison*, and *Louison*, as we have seen, was imposed upon the author by Augustine Brohan, almost by force. M. Lyonnet was perhaps thinking of *Carmosine*, another comedy which was only moderately successful, but, although it is very likely that Musset had the stage in his mind when he wrote it, as a matter of fact, it was written for the *Revue des Deux Mondes*, not for any theatre. The fault here is that he made a three-act play out of a story, which, without being very considerably re-cast, did not contain enough matter for more than one or two. M. Lyonnet may also have been thinking of *Barberine*, which Musset himself altered with a view to production on the stage, making three acts out of two, and which, when produced, long after Musset's death, in 1882, was severely criticised. On the other hand *Il faut qu'une porte soit ouverte ou fermée*, written expressly for the stage, was, in spite of the revolution of February, hardly less successful than *Un Caprice*, which was not. *Il ne faut jurer de rien*, the piece which followed *Il faut qu'une porte soit ouverte ou fermée* on the stage, had of course to be adapted to stage requirements, and here no doubt, owing to the confused and not very intelligible structure of the second and third acts as Musset first wrote them, a good deal of re-arrangement was necessary. But in this instance it was Musset's constructive ability, and not his dramatic ability, that was at fault, and this was due to inexperience rather than to a natural incapacity.

The four years, 1833 to 1837, during which he wrote his comedies for the *Revue des Deux Mondes* saw the later triumphs of the Romantic drama, of Hugo's *Lucrèce Borgia* (1833), *Marie Tudor* (1833), and *Angelo, Tyran de Padoue* (1835) and of Dumas's *Angèle* (1833) and *Kean* (1836). At the same time Scribe, after his successful career with vaudeville at the Gymnase, was producing with no less success comedy at the Théâtre-Français—*Bertrand et Raton* (1833), *L'Ambitieux* (1834), and *La Camaraderie* (1837). After *Kean* the tide of Romantic drama began to ebb, and Hugo's *Ruy Blas* (1838) was indifferently well received. Scribe's popularity on the other hand continued for another dozen years or more; when he produced *Adrienne Lecouvreur* (1849), written for Rachel with the assistance of Legouvé, and *La Bataille de Dames*

(1851), with Legouvé again as collaborator, he had a new rival in Alfred de Musset. There could be no greater contrast than that between these two men, between the playwright who brought to the manufacture of his perfect plays a phenomenal instinct for the stage perfected by long experience, but who was devoid of all psychology, whose characters were conventional dummies, and whose style was as commonplace as his thought, and the poet, who was alike regardless and ignorant of the technique of the stage, but who could individualise his characters and make them live, whose psychological observation was as just as it was penetrating, and whose style was as dramatic as it was artistic. The contrast is well brought out by Dumas *fils* in his preface (written in 1868) to *Le Père prodigue*. While he does full justice to Scribe's knowledge of the stage and to his marvellous powers as a juggler with lifeless puppets, he points out his lack of conviction, of naïvety, and of philosophical aim, and he declares that all his four hundred pieces would dissolve into air if confronted with one of Musset's little proverbs. For "Scribe worked for the public without putting into his work anything of his heart and soul, while Musset wrote with his heart and soul for the heart and soul of humanity, and sincerity gave him, without his being aware of it, all the technical resources that were the other's sole merit". The term "sincerity" is sometimes questioned as applied to artistic creation, but Dumas's meaning is clear. It means that Musset writes with the candour and conviction that Scribe lacked, and that his characters talk and act in accordance with his conception of them. He neither romanticises them, nor sentimentalises them, nor tones down their more unpleasant features in the supposed interests of morality.

His dialogue is all the more effective because he employs it almost solely for the purpose either of portraying character or of developing his story. He never turns aside to discuss social problems or other topics of the day; he has no theories to air, no gospel to preach. For him the play is the thing.

It is very seldom that sentiments uttered by his characters can be taken as representing his own opinions, though they may be, and no doubt often are, expressions of his varying moods. At least twice, as I have already noticed, he declares that human affairs are governed solely by chance and caprice. But the one doctrine which stands prominently out in his comedies and which certainly represents his own belief, is that the only good thing, the only reality, is love. That is the burden of *Les Caprices de Marianne*, of *Fantasio*, of *On ne badine pas avec l'amour*, of *Il ne faut jurer de rien*. Unfortunately his life contradicted his creed. He never learnt the lesson that without self-restraint and self-renunciation you cannot have true love. His many love affairs were of short duration, and they ended generally through his own fault, either because, like Fantasio, he was quickly bored, or because his companion could endure no longer his moods of uncontrollable temper. He was in short unstable and weak of will. Consequently he lacked the patient perseverance and power of concentration necessary for the production of a really considerable work. Thus with all his great natural gifts—his dramatic instinct, his imaginative hold of his characters, his psychological insight, his transparent sincerity, his easy, vigorous, and always artistic style—he failed to write more than one great drama. But, probably because he recognised his own limitations, he confined himself, after this one more or less successful effort on the great scale, to pieces of more modest aims and dimensions; to three-act and even one-act comedies. All have merits and the majority are, within their limits, masterpieces. In addition to the qualities mentioned above, they have a careless freedom carried to audacity, which reminds one of Shakespeare, an abiding charm, and a convincing originality.

Mon verre n'est pas grand, mais je bois dans mon verre.

For EU product safety concerns, contact us at Calle de José Abascal, 56–1°,
28003 Madrid, Spain or eugpsr@cambridge.org.

www.ingramcontent.com/pod-product-compliance
Ingram Content Group UK Ltd.
Pitfield, Milton Keynes, MK11 3LW, UK
UKHW012347130625
459647UK00009B/600